D1198888

GROWING OLDER

TOURISM AND LEISURE BEHAVIOUR OF OLDER ADULTS

Growing Older

Tourism and Leisure Behaviour of Older Adults

Ian Patterson
School of Tourism and Leisure Management
University of Queensland

CABI is a trading name of CAB International

CABI Head Office	CABI North American Office
Nosworthy	875 Massachusetts Avenue
Wallingford	7th Floor
Oxfordshire OX10 8DE	Cambridge, MA 02139
UK	USA
Tel: +44 (0)1491 832111	Tel: +1 617 395 4056
Fax: +44 (0)1491 833508	Fax: +1 617 354 6875
E-mail: cabi@cabi.org	E-mail: cabi-nao@cabi.org
Website: www.cabi.org	

A catalogue record for this book is available from the British
Library, London, UK.
A catalogue record for this book is available from the Library
of Congress, Washington, DC, USA.

ISBN-10: 1-84593 065 7
ISBN-13: 978 1 84593 065 3

Typeset by SPi, Pondicherry, India.
Printed and bound in the UK by Cromwell Press, Trowbridge.

Contents

About the Author

Associate Professor Ian Patterson is the head of the sport and leisure area within the School of Tourism and Leisure Management at the University of Queensland. He delivers courses in leisure, recreation and sport management and is currently the principal supervisor of six PhD students and associate supervisor of three other PhD students. Between 2001 and 2004, he was research director of the school. He completed his PhD at the University of Oregon in 1991 and has since published over 50 scholarly publications including refereed journal articles, an edited book, book chapters, conference papers and consultancy reports. He is primarily interested in researching healthy older people who are undertaking leisure, tourism and travel. He is also co-editor of the *Annals of Leisure Research* and associate editor of two international journals; *Schole: A Journal of Leisure and Recreation Education* and the *Journal of Park and Recreation Administration.*

Tourism and Leisure Needs of Older Adults

1

The aims of this chapter are to:

- Provide a general introduction to the growing older population throughout the western world.
- Examine the importance of leisure, travel and tourism as emerging markets for older adults.
- Understand and define the concepts of leisure and tourism and examine their similarities and differences.
- Define the different cohort groups that are included in the general category of older adults, particularly the silent generation, new-age elderly, baby boomers and the senior market.
- Explore in greater depth the emerging baby boomer market related to their tourism and leisure behaviour.

Introduction

Robert Browning urged: 'Grow old along with me! The best is yet to be' (Foret and Keller, 1993, p. 2). Our society is growing older. Life expectancy has increased dramatically in the 20th century in most of the developed countries. In the UK, for example, life expectancy at birth has increased by 22 years for men and 23.5 years for women who were born between 1910 and

1992, according to figures obtained from the Office for National Statistics. Life expectancy has also increased in other countries, such as Japan: 79.5; Iceland: 78.8; Sweden: 78.1; Western Europe: 76.7; and North America: 76.2 (Smith and Jenner, 1997, p. 47).

The United Nations has recognized the fact that the older generation is growing at a rapid rate, and estimated that more than 2 billion people will be aged 60 and older by 2050. This will account for 22% (or one out of five) of the world's population, compared with only 10% in 2000, and this demographic shift will be seen across all continents. Ageing is most serious in Europe, Japan and China (United Nations, 2000). For example, MacNeil (1991) stated that, 'as amazing as it seems, over one-third of all Americans were born between 1946 and 1964' (p. 22). Australia's ageing population is also increasing, from around 12% in 1999 to between 24% and 26% by 2051, or one in four people will be aged 65 and older (Australian Bureau of Statistics, 1999).

Because 1999 was declared the International Year of Older Persons, the United Nations sponsored conferences throughout the year to showcase successful designs for 'ageing well'. Concepts such as ageing well, successful ageing and quality of life are complex issues that are often difficult to achieve in a world that is changing so quickly. This is because of the heterogeneity of the older population and the growing recognition by service practitioners that there are multiple pathways to cater for their diverse needs. Solutions need to be provided for older people who require help in overcoming such problems as isolation and loneliness, inadequate health and nutritional services, a perceived lack of respect, and feelings of not being valued by their families and communities (Foret and Keller, 1993).

One of these conferences on ageing and tourism was sponsored by the United Nations and held in February 1999 at Morgan in Spain, and was attended by 140 delegates from Europe, Brazil, Japan and other Asian countries. The aim of the conference was to modernize outdated 20th-century policies, products and practices in preparation for the fast-approaching 21st century. Henry Handszuk, World Tourism Organization coordinator for trade liberalization, safety and health, stated:

> The number of people over 60 in the traditional tourist generating countries of Europe and North America are expected to outnumber 'pre adults' by a third in 2025. The challenge for industry is to properly understand the potential and effective demand of the senior tourism market and to respond by delivering products commensurate with its needs.

(Ing, 1993, p. 4)

Speeches highlighted the dramatic gains made in life expectancy worldwide, and praised increased longevity as one of mankind's greatest achievements of the century, through improvements in health, hygiene and nutrition. Other researchers also have confirmed these findings, concluding that medical advances, better health care and diet, and improved safety awareness have contributed to increased longevity (Veal and Lynch, 2001).

Research was also presented about the travel preferences of older travellers. Most preferred discount travel packages that were well planned and variety-filled vacations, signifying that mature aged travellers were not as interested in slow-paced tours through the countryside as first thought. Speakers emphasized that older travellers wanted variety, clear copy in travel brochures with all the costs included, responsible and reliable information, timely receipt of invoices and ticketing, an efficient and accurate reservations system and, by and large, value for their money. Furthermore, it was stressed that the travel industry must not ignore older travellers as they represented a growing segment and a major challenge, now and in the future (Ing, 1993).

On a global scale, the world is becoming increasingly aware of the significant impact older adults will have on the tourism industry in the decades ahead (Goeldner, 1992). The direct consequence of this ageing pattern is that seniors will be responsible for a bigger share of all holiday spending. For example, in 1999 more than 593 million international travellers were aged 60 and older. This accounted for around one-third of all holiday spending by this segment. By 2050 this figure is projected to be greater than 2 billion trips (World Tourism Organization, 2001). This will also have a notable impact on the type of holidays undertaken, and the destinations that are chosen. For example, it is likely that in the future the volume of beach holidays will fall markedly, while educational or cultural holidays will increase as older people prefer to take holidays where they learn something new and/or embark on different historical and cultural experiences (World Tourism Organization, 2001).

These future population projections imply that becoming older does not necessarily restrict people's desire to travel. Older travellers as a separate market to younger people are increasingly attracting the close attention of researchers and marketeers from the leisure travel industry. Robertson (2001) felt that tourism researchers needed to more clearly differentiate between the impact of travel experiences on older people and that on younger tourists. Robertson (2001) posed the question: 'Is travel [for older people] more than materialistic shopping trips, mass tour buses that isolate travellers from locations they desire to see, or self-indulgent trips that take advantage of Third World Countries?' (p. 100).

Despite this cynical viewpoint, there is little doubt that older people are increasingly placing travel as a higher priority in their retirement years, mainly because they are feeling healthier, wealthier, better educated, more independent and have an abundance of leisure time and a lessening of social and family obligations compared with younger people (Martin and Preston, 1994; Zimmer *et al.*, 1995). In 1992 the American Association of Retired Persons (AARP) commissioned a study that focused on the older adult travel market. This research found that travel was ranked as one of the top leisure activities for the over-50 American population. Furthermore, out of a possible 17 types of trips that older participants were asked to choose from to take in the future, 'travelling abroad' (30%) generated the highest ranking. Cruises and water-based vacations were the second most popular trips (25%), while 20% opted to go to mountains, theme parks and resorts (American Association of Retired Persons, 1992, p. 28).

It has been estimated that in the USA, people who are 65 years and older will dominate the tourism and travel market in the future as they represent the largest group of travellers. This is because they possess a relatively large share of discretionary money that they want to spend on travel, as they are the second richest group in society (Javalgi *et al.*, 1992). They also prefer to take longer holiday trips (Eby and Molnar, 1999), stay away from home for a longer time (Eby and Molnar, 1999; Shoemaker, 2000) and have a greater concern for personal safety while travelling (Kostyniuk *et al.*, 1997; Shope and Eby, 1998) than other age segments of the population. The United States Senior Travel Tips (quoted in Smith and Jenner, 1997) concluded that senior travellers accounted for 80% of all luxury travel, 70% of coach tours, 65% of ocean cruises, 32% of hotel overnights and 28% of foreign travel, while at the same time possessing 50% of the discretionary income of the USA, as well as holding 44% of all adult passports.

Discussion

The populations of most western, and some eastern, societies are growing older. This is because birth rates have decreased and life expectancies are increasing due to medical advances and better health care, as well as greater public health education with regard to diet, exercise and improved safety awareness. As a result, population projections have estimated that there will be huge increases in the numbers of older people in the future; for example, it has been estimated that by 2050, 2 billion people will be aged 60 and older, accounting for 22% (or 1:5) of the world population. Because of their sheer numbers, they will demand greater power and influence on policy and political decisions in the country where they are living.

There has also has been a rapid growth in the numbers of older people who are travelling on a worldwide basis, and it has been estimated that in the future this growth will continue so as to eventually dominate the tourism market. Furthermore, becoming older will not restrict people's desire to travel within their own country or overseas. Research evidence supports the fact that older people, particularly those who have recently retired, are relatively healthier, better educated and more financially secure than previous cohorts of older people. Because they now have more time for leisure and are relatively free of family obligations, they prefer to go on trips for longer periods of time, often travel off season and have a greater concern for personal safety when travelling, compared with younger age groups. Because of the great heterogeneity and diversity of this older population, they require a greater variety of travel options than previously, ranging from soft adventure travel that they may want to organize themselves through the internet to group travel where everything is done for them by the travel agent and they stay in five-star hotels.

Definitions of Leisure and Tourism

Are there common threads that link the concepts of tourism and leisure together? Certainly there are common social and psychological outcomes that occur through participation in what have been regarded as often distinctly categorized behaviours. Similar concepts from an assortment of academic disciplines such as sociology, psychology and geography have been applied to the study of leisure and tourism. The study of human motivation, perceptions, satisfaction, spatial relationships, social exchanges, etc. has been applied to the study of leisure and tourism to better understand the function, form and processes that are involved in each type of behaviour. Theorists have emphasized that the study of leisure and tourism behaviours is not a fragmented social phenomenon, but part of a broader social context that is rapidly changing (Fedler, 1987).

The definitional problems that leisure and tourism have experienced have undoubtedly hindered many attempts to clarify and specify any theoretical relationships that existed between the two concepts. The other concern is that leisure and tourism research has been conducted in separate camps, and for some unknown reason, they have remained relatively isolated from each other.

What is leisure?

Leisure studies had its origins in North America in the mid-19th century, with what was termed the 'Rational Recreation Movement' that sought to improve the quality of life of the newly urbanized working class. Recreation programmes were encouraged by the Christian churches of the time, emphasizing wholesome and socially responsible activities such as outdoor recreation and camping, community sport and supervised children's play. This was achieved through the provision of public parks and open spaces, as well as recreation and sport facilities to counteract idle activity, juvenile delinquency, drinking and gambling. Leisure was also related to the ideals of choice, creativity and freedom that were seen as legitimate activities and essential for a society's survival (Cross, 1990).

One of the earliest writers about the importance of leisure in society was Thorstein Veblen (in Brown, 1998), a sociologist who wrote about leisure around the beginning of the 20th century. He stated that leisure helped to create a wealthy class that did not have to work, and as a result were able to enjoy what he termed the 'conspicuous consumption of leisure', while at the same time exploiting the poor and 'downtrodden' classes that did all the hard manual work. After the Second World War, other leisure scholars such as Josef Pieper (1952) and Sebastian de Grazia (1962) wrote about leisure from a moral and religious perspective, viewing leisure as the basis of culture and stating that it was the only hope for future civilizations because of the emphasis we have placed on work.

Another sociologist, Jofree Dumazdier (1960, 1967) became known as the 'Father of Leisure Studies' through his erudite writings about leisure and its importance in comparison to paid work. He defined leisure as free-time activities that were different from productive work, and concluded that leisure served three main functions: first, relaxation as leisure provides recovery from fatigue; secondly, entertainment as leisure relieves boredom through diversion, or escape through fantasy such as going to the movies, the theatre or reading a book; and, thirdly, leisure helps to liberate people from the drudgery associated with their daily routine of thought and action, by joining recreational, cultural or social groups, and/or by enrolling in a range of educational courses (Dumazdier, 1967).

In the 1970s and 1980s, John Neulinger (1974, 1981), who was a well-known psychologist, developed a major interest in the study of leisure and embarked on a quest to define leisure from a psychological perspective that he termed a 'state of mind'. Neulinger was interested in answering the following question: What are the motives behind people continually seeking out (or approaching) optimally arousing leisure experiences? He concluded that the essence of leisure needed to fulfil certain conditions, which needed to be present before it became a 'pure' leisure experience. Neulinger determined that these conditions were perceived freedom in leisure, intrinsic motivation and internal locus of control; these were the essential ingredients that helped to define the leisure experience.

Contemporary leisure researchers such as Witt, Ellis, Mannell and Kleiber have further operationalized and tested this definition through the application of social psychological research to the field of leisure studies. Such terms as perceived freedom, internal locus of control, optimal arousal, intrinsic motivation, enjoyment and relaxation were also found to be useful concepts that were operationalized in more recent research that helped to define the leisure experience. This research has shared similarities with other psychological research, such as that by another psychologist, Michalyi Csikszentmihalyi (1975, 1990, 1997), who used the term 'flow' to describe those exceptional moments in life and the effortless action that people feel when experiencing leisure, and that athletes often refer to as 'being in the zone'. He defined flow as 'a unified flowing from one movement to the next, in which the person is in control of his/her actions and in which there is no distinction between self and environment, between stimulus and response, or between past, present and future' (Csikszentmihalyi, 1975, p. 36).

As a result of this concentration on social psychological research, leisure researchers have become more interested in studying the overall patterns of leisure behaviour rather than analysing participation in specific leisure activities such as watching television or playing football. In other words, the variety, frequency and quality of the experience has been found to be more important to overall life satisfaction than the actual type of leisure activity that one participates in (Smith and Godbey, 1991).

At the same time, leisure studies researchers have ignored the theoretical basis of the study of tourism. It was not until the 1980s that an increasing number of leisure researchers began to express an interest in researching a variety of tourism topics. This was because they began to realize that tourism and travel were encapsulated within most of the current definitions of leisure, and that tourism and travel were undertaken in people's free time as well as being regarded as a pleasurable, intrinsically motivated and rewarding experience.

Leisure activities and older adults

Leisure research has found that older people spend most of their free time in leisure activities around their home that are mainly sedentary and socially based (Lawton, 1993). For example, solitary activities such as watching television and listening to the radio have been cited as the most popular leisure activities among older age groups, whereas sports and exercise programmes are activities in which participation is least likely to occur (Armstrong and Morgan, 1998). The publication of several academic text books with an emphasis on leisure and ageing has more recently suggested that this is changing, and that retirement is now a time when individuals experience new feelings of freedom to do what they want, when they wish, as well as an opportunity to take risks and try something they were never able to do when they were working (MacNeil and Teague, 1987; Leitner and Leitner, 1996; McGuire *et al.*, 2004).

Cohen (2000) substituted the term 'creativity' for 'leisure' to describe a powerful inner resource that older people yearn for, and that he felt should be regarded as something that should be more than merely 'filling in time'. He gave several examples in which creativity can be achieved through hobbies, a new career, arts and crafts, new relationships, revitalized interests, a challenging new job or involvement in volunteerism. Stebbins (1982, 1992, 1998) coined the term 'serious leisure' to conclude that many older people achieved great satisfaction and fulfilment from being amateurs, hobbyists and volunteers, and that this commitment helped them to keep busy, make new friends and enhance their older years.

Kelly (1992) stated that as people age, they accumulate a core of leisure activities that remains fairly stable during their older years. He noted that these activities were commonly centred around their family and generally took place in and around the home. These included shopping, gardening, walking, watching television, socializing with friends and family and reading

(Kelly and Kelly, 1994). In a further study, Strain *et al.* (2002) collected longitudinal data from 380 respondents in Winnipeg, Manitoba, Canada, in both 1985 and 1993. These researchers were specifically interested in the extent to which older adults continued, or ceased, their participation in specific leisure activities over an 8-year period. They found the following results: 83% continued to shop for pleasure in 1993, 76% continued to dine out at restaurants, 79% continued to walk for fitness, 67% continued to travel, 68% continued to do outdoor yard work, 73% continued to participate in church services activities, 67% continued to play cards, while only 45% continued to attend the theatre, movies and spectator sports in 1993.

Strain *et al.* (2002) concluded that age alone does not sufficiently explain why some older adults ceased participation in some leisure activities. Other factors such as the older persons' self-rated health and their functional ability were also significantly related to changes in leisure activities. Stressful life events or transitions also had an impact on leisure participation to some extent. For example, the loss of a spouse was associated with a reduction in overall participation in leisure activities, and the ceasing of outdoor yard work in particular (Patterson, 1996; Strain *et al.*, 2002). Mok and Hraba (1991) also reported that older people (over 65 years) living in Iowa were more likely to participate in certain types of gambling such as bingo than younger age groups.

Although many leisure activities have been found to be similar among older men and women (Verbrugge *et al.*, 1996), differences were also noted in the following areas: men were more likely to have greater numbers of repair jobs in progress around the house, and to drive the family car more often than women. Women tended to adopt a nurturing or organizational role in dealing with their family, and spent more time in conversations with family and friends (McGuire *et al.*, 2004). Robinson *et al.* (1997) also found that men devoted more time to active, outdoor and sports-related pastimes (Lawton, 1993), while women spent more time doing housework and were more interested in learning hobbies. Moseley *et al.* (2003) concluded that people aged 65 and older who were living in southern Nevada were not more likely to gamble than younger age groups; however, older females were more likely to gamble than younger females.

The variety of leisure activities engaged in by older people while on vacation is also of interest to researchers. This is because participation in leisure activities encourages tourists to engage in conversations that help to facilitate social interaction, which is one of the strongest factors that contribute to leisure satisfaction (Thomas and Butts, 1998). Wei and Millman (2002) used path analysis to ascertain if tourists' psychological well-being was positively affected by the variety of leisure activities which they engaged in while on a vacation trip. Data were collected from a sample of more than 300 senior travellers (of which 60.5% were older than 70 years) who were travelling on several 7-day North American escorted tour itineraries.

The most popular activities that travellers participated in while on tour were city sightseeing (89.3%), visiting historical places (88.1%), restaurant dining (85.7%) and shopping (77.4%). Less popular activities were hunting and fishing (1.2%), water sports and sunbathing (1.2%) and camping and hiking (3.6%). Wei and Milman also found that a positive and significant relationship existed between senior travellers' participation in leisure activities, their overall satisfaction with the travel experience ($p = 0.236$, significance = 0.031) and their level of psychological well-being ($p = 0.358$, significance = 0.01). As a result of their findings, Wei and Milman (2002) concluded that marketing campaigns should be developed to focus on the type and range of leisure activities that were being provided at particular tourist destinations. This would ensure that the senior tourists' satisfaction and psychological well-being were at a high level during their vacation.

Shopping has also been identified as a favourite travel activity and is acknowledged as a primary means of generating tourism revenue as well as contributing to economic development. For example, tourists spend three to four times more money on shopping while travelling than the average shopper (Travel Industry Association of America, 2001). Shopping tourists also express strong preferences for shopping in unique or different kinds of stores where they can buy something special for others, or to hunt for a bargain (Kinley *et al.*, 2003).

Littrell *et al.* (2004) surveyed 146 travellers who were aged 50 and older to investigate their shopping behaviour. These tourists were primarily female (73%) and ranged in age from 52 to 90, with an average age of 65 years. Cluster analysis revealed three groups of senior tourists with significantly different scores on each of the three tourism activity factors: cluster 1 were labelled active outdoor and cultural tourists; cluster 2 were named cultural tourists; and cluster 3 were called moderate tourists. Senior travellers in both clusters 1 and 2 enjoyed visiting museums, attending the theatre and eating at interesting local restaurants. This suggested to the researchers that retail shops should be placed alongside different cultural events such as museum shops and kiosks in theatre lobbies. For senior travellers with an average age of 65 years, shopping was seen as a very important activity that was often integrated with other travel interests. Shopping at malls was especially regarded as important for senior travellers, and in particular, the cleanliness of the mall and service provided were seen to be important for those aged between 50 and 90. A further suggestion from this study was that malls and retailers should display works of art that are indigenous to the particular destination, so as to further enhance the shopping experience (Littrell *et al.*, 2004).

What is tourism?

Tourism researchers have described tourism experience as a religious experience and a quest for authenticity (MacCannell, 1976; Cohen, 1979). Tourism has also been seen as an effective means of escape from routine and stressful environments, and the seeking out of recreational opportunities for certain intrinsic rewards. Research also indicated that people escape from over- and understimulating life situations through vacations in an effort to achieve and maintain an optimal level of arousal (Iso-Ahola, 1983). However, Mannell and Iso-Ahola (1987) concluded that, 'in spite of some intuitively obvious similarities between the two, at present, it is not possible to conclude when and under what conditions tourist experience becomes a leisure experience' (p. 329).

Recent research (Leontido, 1994; Carr, 2002) has found that tourists often behave in a more liberated, and less restrained, manner in contrast to their leisure time behaviour at home. For example, Josiam *et al.* (1996) reported increased alcohol and drug consumption as well as increased levels of sexual activity among a group of American students who travelled overseas. Eisner and Ford (1995) stated that the tourist 'sees oneself as a different kind of person when on holiday, less constrained by normal role demands and interpersonal obligations ... and more sexual activity was reported by those [tourists] who seemed to have felt more "disinhibited" within the holiday setting' (p. 326–327). Leontido (1994) further claimed that individuals are influenced by the tourism atmosphere or, as it has been termed, the existence of a 'tourist culture', which is perceived to be different from their place of origin, and is responsible for less restrained and more hedonistic behaviour.

Several authors have insisted that there is no major distinction between tourism and leisure phenomena, and that tourism shares strong fundamental characteristics and theoretical foundations with the leisure studies field. Swain (1995) agreed that tourism and leisure theories were complimentary, while Shaw and Williams (1994) stated that tourism and leisure were indistinguishable as 'there are a number of points at which tourism and leisure are interrelated, and neither can be adequately understood without reference to the other' (pp. 6–7). Leiper (1995) suggested that '[t]ourism can be defined as the theories and practice of travelling and visiting places for leisure related purposes' (p. 20).

Smith and Godbey (1991) have also suggested that both tourism and leisure share several areas of commonality. First, several authors (Pieper, 1948; Cohen, 1979) have linked leisure and tourism to a spiritual search, with the drive for authenticity in tourism being a similar belief to leisure as an activity that is intuitively worthwhile. Thus, both tourism and leisure can be linked to the existential quest for meaning within an industrialized society. Secondly, both fields have suffered attacks on their academic legitimacy in the university sector as well as from industry for being irrelevant to practical concerns. Thirdly, both sets of scholars in leisure and tourism research have shared common problems in disseminating their research to other fields, as well as to each other.

Because tourism and leisure are clearly seen to have common areas of academic study, a *continuum* approach has been suggested as a better means to study the apparent similarities and differences between the two fields. Ryan (1997) stated that tourism should constitute one end of a broad leisure spectrum, while McKercher (1996) felt that perceived differences between leisure and tourism occur at a series of points along this continuum. Carr (2002) further suggested that leisure behaviour should be placed at one end of the continuum, because it is enjoyed by people within their home environment and influenced by the residual culture. Tourist behaviour needed to be placed at the opposite end of the continuum as it is influenced by the tourist culture. Carr further suggested that in between these two extremes, both tourist and residual cultures influence behaviour to varying degrees. If the residual culture is stimulated by vacation cues, tourists will behave similarly to tourists in their various places of origin. In contrast, if the tourist residual culture is not triggered, tourists will behave differently, potentially conforming to the hedonistic image associated with the pleasure-orientated tourist culture.

Carr (2002) concluded that pleasure-orientated tourism and leisure behaviour were closely related and should not be regarded as separate fields of study. In particular, theories about gendered leisure could be used to better understand the differences and similarities in the tourist behaviour of men compared with women. Furthermore, unitary approaches to marketing appropriate services for both tourism and leisure needed to be developed, and the knowledge about market segmentation that has been developed in tourism research would also be useful when applied within the context of leisure marketing (Hamilton-Smith, 1987).

Discussion

Most authors consider that there are common threads that link the concepts of tourism and leisure. The foundations of both these subject areas have been applied from the academic disciplines of sociology, psychology and geography, and are regarded as part of the broader social context of a society that is constantly changing. However, problems with defining the concepts of tourism and leisure have created separate areas of study with the emergence of two disparate camps that have had very little to do with each other over the years. It has only been in the last 20 years that the academic journals have advocated the importance of philosophical discussion about common linkages between the two areas. This was because there was a growing realization among academics from both areas that there were overlapping common areas of interest, such as that tourism and leisure occur in people's free time and that they both were generally pleasurable, satisfying and intrinsically rewarding for their own sake.

Leisure and tourism studies come from totally different theoretical foundations. The Recreation Movement had its beginnings in the early

20th century, when pressure from the Christian churches and philanthropists such as Joseph Lee encouraged the building of children's playgrounds, and play leaders were employed to keep children off the streets and safely involved in wholesome and socially responsible activities in the slum areas of Boston, Chicago and New York. A number of eminent philosophers, sociologists and psychologists such as Veblen, Piper, Dumazdier, de Grazia, Brightbill and Neulinger emphasized the positive aspects of recreation and leisure, such as a form of relaxation and recovery from the stress and daily drudgery associated with work. Leisure was regarded by these authors as more than free time after work, or an activity, and rather as a 'state of mind' where the emphasis was on freedom of choice, intrinsic motivation, and the enjoyment and satisfaction that were achieved from an optimally arousing experience.

Tourism, on the other hand, means to escape from routine or stressful environments through vacation and travel activities to an idyllic destination for a temporary short-term change of residence. Tourism has its origins in the business and private sector, with emphasis on the economic and social benefits to the host country. Several academics have suggested that a continuum approach should be applied to the definitional conundrum that exists between leisure and tourism. At one end of the continuum is leisure behaviour that is enjoyed by people in their home environments, while at the other end is tourist behaviour that is influenced by a tourist culture. Carr (2002) argued that although they should not be regarded as separate phenomena, one of the major differences that exists between leisure and tourism is in the observable behaviour of people. Tourists often behave differently and in a more liberated and less restrained manner than in their normal home environment. This is because people are influenced by the tourism culture or atmosphere when they are away from their normal home environment and the social roles that constrict them, and have anonymity as well as money to spend.

Definitions of Older Adults

Not so long ago, people aged 65 and older who lived in developed countries were referred to as 'pensioners' or the 'elderly', which were the only terms that were used to describe them. Recently, a review of the tourism and leisure literature has found a puzzling development – there has been a lack of consistency in defining the age cohort and the specific name to describe older people's tourist behaviour at different stages of the life cycle. Names such as 'baby boomers' (Gillon, 2004), 'the senior market' (Shoemaker, 1989), 'the mature market' (Lazar, 1985), 'the grey market', 'young sengies' or young senior generation, and 'woopies' or well-off older people (Lohmann and Danielsson, 2001) have been used interchangeably in the literature to describe the older adult market. In the marketing literature, the term 'muppies' (mature, upscale, post-professionals) has also been applied to the older segment, which is regarded as the fastest growing segment in the USA.

Furthermore, there has been a lack of consistency in using similar age categories, particularly in the tourism and leisure research. The age groups specifically targeted when studying older people have included a range of different ages, from 50–55 to 60–65 years and older depending on the specific study. This indicates that the 'older people' in the definition used by researchers appear to be getting increasingly younger. However, the gerontological literature has been reasonably consistent in defining 'older people' according to their retirement age of 65 years and older. This definition is based on the life course changes such as retirement, and government policies and programmes such as the Social Security Pension and Medicare in the USA that occur at, or near, 65 years of age (Schaninger and Danko, 1993). On the other hand, groups such as the AARP have used the word 'senior' to denote a person who is aged 50 and older, while the tourism industry refers to senior travellers as people aged 55 and older (Smith and Jenner, 1997). Therefore, we can conclude that there is considerable confusion in the literature about what denotes an 'older traveller', and that there has been a noticeable downward shift in their chronological age, which has helped to expand the parameters of what we define as 'old'. Let us now look at the different terms used in the literature that are included within the general definition of 'older adults'.

The silent generation

The *silent generation* (Strauss and Howe, 1991) are people who were born between 1925 and 1943. These people have been described in fairly negative terms as cautious, indifferent, lacking adventure and imagination, and basically just 'silent'. The first half of the generation were born during, or close to, the Great Depression and were therefore frugal and price-conscious, had a social conscience and believed in fair play. The second half were born before, or during, the Second World War, and many fought in the war or joined the Peace Corps. Members of the 'silent generation' were the parents of the 'baby boom' generation, who were born between 1946 and 1964 (Pennington-Gray and Lane, 2001). Many of the silent generation are women and because of historical influences they took on roles as helpers and humanitarians. Many were also pioneers in the civil rights, consumer activism and feminist movements. Unlike baby boomers, they respond favourably to authority figures and value the opinions of experts (Finn, 2000).

The silent generation have been described as a different breed of senior travellers. The majority did not travel much at all, and in fact there was a decrease in domestic travel participation between 1979 and 1989 from 69.5% to 53.7%. In a research study conducted by Pennington-Gray and Lane (2001), the authors found that preferences of members of the silent generation followed a traditional pattern. Their highest preferences were for environmental concerns such as standards of cleanliness, safety, weather and environmental quality of air and water. This is not surprising because females who grew up during the Second World War era tended to dominate this generation, and for them, safety was a major concern. Education was the next most important factor, suggesting that the preference for learning while travelling is an important component of older people's (particularly women's) travel preferences.

New-age elderly

Shiffman and Sherman (1991) used the term *new-age elderly* to describe a different subsegment that does not fit the negative stereotype image of the traditional elderly population. This segment had positive values, attitudes and behaviour that differed from the traditional group. They preferred to travel as much as people in younger age groups, and to engage in adventure tourism activities such as white water rafting. Mathur *et al.* (1998) identified this 'new-age elderly' subsegment using a convenience sample of family members from undergraduate and graduate marketing classes. A total of 257 surveys were returned with an age cut-off at 55 years. The average age of the new-age elderly was 63.3 years, with cognitive age almost 12 years younger than their chronological age.

The researchers found that the value orientations of the new-age elderly were quite different from those of the traditional elderly. New-age elderly were more decisive consumers, individual decision makers, in control of their life, satisfied with their health, their social life and their life generally compared with the traditional elderly. The new-age elderly liked to learn to do new things and enjoyed being themselves more than the traditional elderly.

In regard to travel behaviour, the new-age elderly spent more days on domestic airline vacations compared with the traditional elderly (8.7 vs. 3.7 days, $p < 0.01$). They also spent more days on domestic road trips (9.5 vs. 4.4 days, $p < 0.01$), and on international airline vacations (4.9 vs. 1.1 days, $p < 0.01$). In regard to leisure activities, the new-age elderly showed significantly greater interest in the following activities in comparison with traditional elderly people: outdoor activities, foreign trips, financial markets and news, volunteer work/self-enrichment, learning new things, computers and domestic travel. In regard to the sources of information used for travel, the new-age elderly used travel agents to a significantly greater extent, found travel guide books as valuable sources of information, and used pamphlets, brochures and travel videos to a greater extent in comparison with traditional elderly people.

The researchers found that it is possible to identify a group of elderly people designated as new-age elderly, who were mainly selected on their value orientations. They found this approach superior to chronologic-ally age-based segmentation for leisure travel. The new-age elderly were described as more independent and wanting more control over their travel behaviour. They were less receptive to experiences in which everything was done for them, and their lack of materialism supported their demand for better experiences rather than for cheaper price packages.

Seniors

Seniors are defined as people aged 55 and older, and were one of the most prominent targets for tourism marketeers in the 1990s. Seniors have been described as everything from 'empty nesters' and 'third agers' to 'woop-ies' (well-off older people) and 'zuppies' (zestful, upscale people in their prime) (Shoemaker, 1989). These descriptions of seniors suggest that many people who are aged 55 and older perceive themselves as feeling consid-erably younger than their actual chronological age (Muller and O'Cass, 2001). This concept has been termed 'subjective age' and has been found useful in tourism marketing to help determine senior's attitudes, interests and activities, particularly in regard to leisure, recreation and tourism. Generally, researchers have found that seniors are still physically capable of travelling for pleasure, and have a desire to be physically active, as well as participating in, and still enjoying, youthful activities because these help to keep older people feeling young.

Baby boomers

The term *baby boomers* is frequently used to describe a cohort of young–old people who were born between 1946 and 1964, and are aged between 42 and 60 in 2006 (Gillon, 2004). The term has been criticized in the traditional academic literature as a 'marketing term' that has been mainly used in busi-ness reports, rather than accepted as a defined stage of the life cycle that has a strong theoretical base in the psychological literature. However, the use of this term has gained greater acceptance in wider academic circles.

Baby boomers are a large cohort of people who were born after the Second World War, during a time of high economic growth and prosperity, and the high fertility rates that resulted make it the largest group of any age category in countries throughout the Western world. For example, in Australia, baby boomers comprised approximately 5 million out of a total population of 19 million people in 2000 (Muller and Cleaver, 2000). In the USA, the baby boomer generation has also been described as 'the largest generational group in US history' (MacNeil, 1991, p. 48), with 76 million or 29% of people born after the Second World War at an average birth rate of 4 million babies a year (Radner, 1998). By 2005, this figure is expected to grow to 42% of people who are more than 50 years of age (Zeigler, 2002), and will represent 'the single most powerful economic and political power base within American society' (MacNeil, 1991, p. 48). Their impact has been equated to a tidal wave that is fast approaching a low-lying village (Dychtwald, 1989). In the USA, baby boomers produced the highest travel volume, generating 245 million trips, which was more than any other age group. They also spent on average $479 per trip (excluding transportation to their destination). When travelling, approximately 60% of boomers stayed in hotels, and 25% used air travel as their main mode of transportation (Travel Industry Association of America, 2001).

Baby boomers do not really consider themselves as seniors. Because they are such a large segment of the population, companies are now launching a range of new products to cash in on the boomers' changing body image, as many still consider themselves younger than their chronological age, and do not want to identify or mix with other older people. Del Web Corporation, the largest builder of US retirement communities (including Sun City), has trademarked the term 'Zoomers' to describe those 55-year-olds whom they describe as having snubbed shuffle board courts in favour of climbing walls as their new and novel active ageing activity (McDonald, 2001).

Baby boomers have also been described as the most highly educated and best-travelled group that the resort industry has ever encountered (Kohane, 1998; Smart and Pethokoulis, 2001). This generation is generally financially better off with incomes above the average. In the USA, they make up almost one-third of the total population. More than three-quarters own their homes, and 73% have some form of investment. A recent survey by AARP reported that those in the top quartile of the over-50 generation had a median income of $100,000 and a median net worth of $360,000. They are generally well educated, with nearly 90% of baby boomers having graduated from high school, and more than a quarter having at least a bachelor's degree (Smart and Pethokoulis, 2001). In Australia, baby boomers' income is overrepresented in the highest household income quintile with 63% of married boomers being dual income couples. Furthermore, they have easier access to their private superannuation funds, resulting in greater freedom from mortgage debt, and a larger accumulation of wealth from savings than previous generations (Muller, 1997).

Because of this, baby boomers have higher levels of disposable income available for leisure travelling, and are in the market for 'everything from Winnebagos to cruise ships to timeshare resort properties to golf courses' (Seninger, 2000, p. 3). Others will pursue education into retirement, and enjoy travelling to learn more about other countries. Huber and Skidmore (2003) described Britain's baby boomers as less conforming than younger age groups, ardent consumers and libertarians as they have grown up with women's lib and marijuana. They are also better educated than older age groups, and because of this, will have the skills to enjoy their leisure in retirement.

Although this population is greying, they are increasingly enjoying active lifestyles. The Henley Centre in the UK (1992) provides UK leisure research information, and has argued that 45- to 59-year-olds are increasingly participating in active leisure pursuits such as swimming and walking, going to concerts and theatre visits as well as leading the trend towards eating out more in restaurants. Because many older people are younger in outlook, similar areas of behaviour and attitudes are overlapping between younger and older adults. For example, leisure activities such as going to the movies, participating in do-it-yourself activities, eating out and watching DVDs were blurring across the age groups.

Because many baby boomers are increasingly healthy and affluent, they are travelling more, are more discerning and demanding, and are continually looking for special-interest travel as well as new and innovative experiences. They place a high premium on quality, courteousness and good service, yet they also require value for money (Pritchard and Morgan, 1996).

Conclusion

There has been some confusion in the research literature about the age at which a person starts becoming 'old'. Some studies have used 50 years as their starting point, whereas other researchers have used 55, 60 and 65 years as the defining line that is used to indicate when a person is regarded as being 'older'. Tourism researchers have generally referred to senior travellers as aged 55 and older, whereas older adults have been defined according to the retirement age of 65 and older, which is based on the official age of retirement and eligibility to receive the government pension. In addition, there has been a lack of consistency in defining the specific age cohort group when describing older people's tourist behaviour. The most popular terms that have been used are 'seniors' and 'baby boomers' which have often been used interchangeably in the literature. Other terms such as 'mature', 'grey', 'silent generation' and 'new-age elderly' have also been used with conflicting results.

The older adult market exhibits great diversity in regard to socio-demographic characteristics, lifestyles, interests, attitudes and consumption patterns. However, no matter what the cohort group, they are still demanding a greater share in the travel products and services that have been specifically tailored to meet their individual needs and lifestyles. Because of the great diversity in who have been generally labelled as older adults, an overall marketing strategy is difficult to implement as it may only be found to be attractive for only one category of older consumers, whereas another cohort group may find it less attractive or appealing.

References

American Association of Retired Persons and the Roper Organization (1992) *Mature America in the 1990s*. Maturity Magazine Group, New York.

Armstrong, G.K. and Morgan, K. (1998) Stability and change in levels of habitual physical activity in later life. *Age and Ageing* 27, 17–23.

Australian Bureau of Statistics (1999) *Older People: Australia – A Social Report* (Catalogue No. 4109.0). AGPS, Canberra, Australia.

Brown, D. (1998) *Thorstein Veblen in the Twenty-First Century: a Commoration of the Theory of Leisure Class (1899–1999)*. Edward Elgar, Cheltenham, UK.

Carr, N. (2002) The tourism–leisure behavioural continuum. *Annals of Tourism Research* 29, 972–986.

Cohen, E. (1979) Rethinking the sociology of tourism. *Annals of Tourism Research* 6, 18–35.

Cohen, G.D. (2000) *The Creative Age: Awakening Human Potential in the Second Half of Life*. HarperCollins, New York.

Cross, G. (1990) *A Social History of Leisure Since 1600*. Venture, State College, Pennsylvania.

Csikszentmihalyi, M. (1975) *Beyond Boredom and Anxiety*. Jossey-Bass, San Francisco, California.

Csikszentmihalyi, M. (1990) *Flow: The Psychology of Optimal Experience*. Harper Perrenial, New York.

Csikszentmihalyi, M. (1997) *Finding Flow: The Psychology of Engagement with Everyday Life*. Basic Books, New York.

de Grazia, S. (1962) *Of Time, Work and Leisure*. The Twentieth Fund, New York.

Dumazdier, J. (1960) Current problems in the sociology of leisure. *International Social Sciences Journal* 12, 526.

Dumazdier, J. (1967) *Toward a Society of Leisure*. Free Press, New York.

Dychtwald, K. (1989) *Age Wave*. Jeramy P. Tarcher, Los Angeles.

Eby, D.W. and Molnar, L.J. (1999) *Guidelines for Developing Information Systems for the Driving Tourist.* The University of Michigan Intelligent Transportation System Research Center for Excellence, Ann Arbor, Michigan.

Eisner, J. and Ford, N. (1995) Sexual relations or holiday: a case of situational distribution. *Journal of Social and Personal Relationships* 12, 323–339.

Fedler, A.J. (1987) Are leisure, recreation, and tourism interrelated? *Annals of Tourism Research* 14, 311–313.

Finn, L.(2000) Silent generation women are active, affluent, and often overlooked by marketeers. *Marketing to Women: Addressing Women and Women's Sensibilities* 13, (December), 1.

Foret, C.M. and Keller, J. (1993) A society growing older: its implications for leisure. *Journal of Physical Education, Recreation and Dance* 64, April 30, 47.

Gillon, S.M. (2004) *Boomer Nation: the Largest and Richest Generation Ever, and How it Changed.* Free Press, New York.

Goeldner, C.R. (1992) Trends in North American Tourism. *American Behaviouralist Scientist* 36, 144–154.

Hamilton-Smith, E. (1987) Four kinds of tourism. *Annals of Tourism Research* 14, 322–344.

Henley Centre (1992) Demographic background. *Leisure Futures* 3, 16–20.

Huber, J. and Skidmore, P. (2003) *The New Old: Why the Baby Boomers won't be Pensioned Off.* Demos, London. Available at: www.demos.co.uk

Ing, D. (1993) Potential for senior travel escalates. *Hotel and Motel Management* 208, 4–5.

Iso-Ahola, S. (1983) Towards a social psychology of tourism, *Leisure Studies* 2, 45–56.

Javalgi, R.G., Thomas, E.G. and Rao, S.R. (1992) Consumer behavior in the US travel marketplace: an analysis of senior and non-senior travellers. *Journal of Travel Research* 31, 14–19.

Josiam, B., Smeaton, G., Hobson, P. and Dietrich, U. (1996) Sex, alcohol and drugs on the beach: 'Where the boys are' in the age of AIDS. Paper presented at the 4th WLRA World Congress, Cardiff, Wales.

Kelly, J.R. (1992) Leisure. In: Bogatta, E.F. (ed.) *Encyclopedia of Sociology*, Vol. 3. Macmillan, New York, pp. 1099–1107.

Kelly, J.R. and Kelly, J.R. (1994) Multiple dimensions of meaning in the domains of work, family and leisure. *Journal of Leisure Research* 26, 250–274.

Kinley, T.R., Josiam, B.M. and Kim, Y. (2003) Tourist-destination shopping center: an important performance analysis of attributes. *Journal of Shopping Center Research* 9, 51–72.

Kohane, J. (1998,) Boomers financial power. *Hotelier* 18 (May/June), 18–22.

Kostyniuk L.P., Sreff, F.M. and Eby, D.W. (1997) The older driver and navigation assistance technologies. University of Michigan Transportation Research Institute, Ann Arbor, Michigan.

Lawton, M.P. (1993) Meanings of activity. In: Kelly, J.R. (ed.) *Activity and aging.* Sage, Newbury Park, California, pp. 25–41.

Leiper, N. (1995) *Tourism Management.* TAFE Publications, Collingwood, Victoria.

Leitner, M.J. and Leitner, S.F. (1996). *Leisure in Later Life.* Haworth Press, New York.

Leontido, L. (1994) Gender dimensions of tourism in Greece: employment, substructuring and restructuring. In: Kinnaird, V. and Hall, D. (eds) *Tourism: A Gender Analysis.* John Wiley & Sons, Chichester, UK, pp. 74–104.

Littrell, M.A., Paige, R.C. and Song, K. (2004) Senior travellers: tourism activities and shopping behaviours. *Journal of Vacation Marketing* 10, 348–361.

Lohmann, M. and Danielsson, J. (2001) Predicting travel patterns of senior citizens: how the past may provide a key to the future. *Journal of Vacation Marketing* 7, 357–366.

MacCannell, D. (1976) *The Tourist: A New Theory of the Leisure Class*. Schocken Books, New York.

MacNeil, R.D. (1991) The recreation profession and the age revolution: times they are a 'changin'. *Illinois Parks and Recreation* 22, (September/October), 22–24.

MacNeil, R.D. and Teague, M.L. (1987) *Aging and Leisure: Vitality in Later Life*. Prentice-Hall, Englewood Cliffs, New Jersey.

Mannell, R.C. and Iso-Ahola, S. (1987) Psychological nature of leisure and tourism experience. *Annals of Tourism Research* 14, 314–331.

Martin, L.G. and Preston, S.H. (1994) *Demography of Aging*. National Academy Press, Washington, DC.

Mathur, A., Sherman, E. and Schiffman, L.G. (1998) Opportunities for marketing travel services to new-age elderly. *The Journal of Services Marketing* 12, 265–277.

McDonald, M. (2001) Forever young: marketing to the baby boom generation. *US News and World Report* 130(2 April), 36–38.

McGuire, F.A., Boyd, R.K. and Tedrick, R.E. (2004) *Leisure and Aging: Ulyssean Living in Later Life*, 3rd edn. Sagamore, Champaign, Illinois.

McKercher, B. (1996) Differences between tourism and recreation in parks. *Annals of Tourism Research* 23, 563–575.

Mok, W.P. and Hraba, J. (1991) Age and gambling behaviour: a declining and shifting pattern of participation. *Journal of Gambling Studies* 7, 313–335.

Moschis, G.P. (1996) *Gerontographics: Life Stage Segmentation for Marketing Strategy Development*. Quorum Books, Westport, Connecticut.

Moseley, C.B., Schwer, K. and Thompson, W.S. (2003) Elderly casino gambling behaviour: marketing implications. *Journal of Hospitality and Leisure Marketing* 10, 87–99.

Muller, T.E. (1997) The benevolent society: value and lifestyle changes among middle aged baby boomers. In: Kahle, L.E. and Chiagouris, L. (eds) *Values, Lifestyle and Psychographics*. Laurence Erlbaum Associates, Marwah, New Jersey, pp. 299–316.

Muller, T. and Cleaver, M. (2000) Targeting the CANZUS baby boomer explorer and adventure segments. *Journal of Vacation Marketing* 6, 154–169.

Muller, T.E. and O'Cass, A. (2001) Targeting the young at heart: seeing senior vacationers the way they see themselves. *Journal of Vacation Marketing* 7, 285–301.

Neulinger, J. (1974) *The Psychology of Leisure*. Charles C. Thomas, Springfield, Illinois.

Neulinger, J. (1981) *To Leisure: An Introduction*. Allyn & Bacon, Boston, Massachusetts.

OEDC (1998) The basic demography: sources and methods used in Annex 1 of Maintaining prosperity in an Ageing Society, OEDC.

Patterson, I.R. (1996) Participation in leisure activities by older adults after a stressful life event: the loss of a spouse. *International Journal of Aging and Human Development* 42, 123–142.

Pennington-Gray, L. and Lane, C.W. (2001) Profiling the silent generation. *Journal of Hospitality and Leisure Marketing* 9, 73–95.

Pieper, J. (1948) *Leisure: The Basis of Culture*. Pantheon, New York.

Radner, D.B. (1998) The retirement prospects of the baby boom generation. *Social Security Bulletin* 61, 3–19.

Robertson, D.N. (2001) The impact of travel on older adults: an exploratory investigation. *Tourism* 49, 99–108.

Robinson, J.P., Werner, J. and Godbey, G. (1997) Freeing up the golden years. *American Demographics* 20–24.

Ryan, C. (1997) *The Tourist Experience.* Cassell, London.

Schaninger, C.M. and Danko, W.D. (1993) A conceptual and empirical comparison of alternative household life cycle models. *Journal of Consumer Research* 19, 580–594.

Senniger, S. (2000) Winnebagos, funeral homes and cruise ships: the graying of baby boomers in the new millennium. *Montana Business Quarterly* Spring 38, pp. 2–9.

Shaw, G. and Williams, A. (1994) *Critical Issues in Tourism: A Geographical Perspective.* Blackwell, Oxford, UK.

Shiffman, L.G. and Sherman, E. (1991) Value orientations of new-age elderly: the coming of an ageless market. *Journal of Business Resarch* 22 April, 187–194.

Shoemaker, S. (1989) Segmentation of the senior pleasure travel market. *Journal of Travel Research* Winter 27, 14–21.

Shoemaker, S. (2000) Segmenting the mature market: 10 years later. *Journal of Travel Research* 39, 11–26.

Shope, J.T. and Eby, D.W. (1998) *Improvement of Older Driver Safety Through Self-Evaluation: Focus Group Results.* University of Michigan Transportation Research Institute, Ann Arbor, Michigan.

Smart, T. and Pethokoulis, J.M. (2001) Not acting their age: baby boomers doing retirement their own way. *US News and World Report* 130(4 June), 55–58.

Smith, S.L. and Godbey, G.C. (1991) Leisure recreation and tourism. *Annals of Tourism Research* 18, 85–100.

Smith, C. and Jenner, P. (1997) The seniors travel market. *Travel and Tourism Analyst* 5, 43–62.

Stebbins, R.A. (1982) Serious leisure: a conceptual statement. *The Pacific Sociological Review* 25, 251–272.

Stebbins, R.A. (1992) *Amateurs, Professionals, and Serious Leisure.* McGill-Queen's University Press, Montreal.

Stebbins, R.A. (1998) *After Work: The Search for an Optimal Leisure Lifestyle.* Detselig Enterprises, Calgary, Alberta.

Strain, L.A., Grabusic, C.C., Searle, M.S. and Dunn, N.J. (2002) Continuing and ceasing leisure activities in later life: a longitudinal study. *The Gerontologist* 42, 217–223.

Strauss, W. and Howe, N. (1991) *Generations: The History of America's Future, 1584–2069.* Quill, New York.

Swain, M. (1995) Gender in tourism. *Annals of Tourism Research* 22, 247–266.

Thomas, D. and Butts, F. (1998) Assessing leisure motivators and satisfaction of international Elderhostel participants. *Journal of Travel and Tourism Marketing* 7, 31–38.

Travel Industry Association of America (2001) *Economic Research: Economic Impact of Travel and Tourism.* Available at: http://www.tia.org/Travel/ecoimpact.asp

United Nations, Division for Social Policy and Development, Department of Economic and Social Affairs (2000) *The Sex and Age Distribution of the World*

Populations, 1998 revision. Available at: http://www.un.org/esa/population/publications/ageing/Graph.pdf

Veal, A. and Lynch, R. (2001) Australian leisure. Longmans/Butterworth, French's Forest, New South Wales.

Verbrugge, L.M., Gruber-Baldini, A.L. and Fozard, J.L. (1996) Age differences and age changes in activities: Baltimore Longitudinal Study of Aging. *Journals of Gerontology. Series B, Psychological Sciences and Social Sciences* 51, S30–S41.

Wei, S. and Millman, A. (2002) The impact of participation in activities while on vacation on seniors' psychological well-being: a path model analysis. *Journal of Hospitality and Tourism Research* 26, 175–185.

World Tourism Organization (2001) *Tourism 2020 Vision: Global Forecasts and Profiles of Market Segments* 7. World Tourism Organization, Madrid, Spain.

Ziegler, J.J. (2002) What's a boomer? *Parks and Recreation* 37(10), 58–61.

Zimmer, Z., Brayley, R.E. and Searle, M. (1995) Whether to go and where to go: identification of important influences on senior's decisions to travel. *Journal of Travel Research* 33, 3–10.

Motivations and Constraints to Tourism and Leisure for Older Adults

2

The aims of this chapter are to:

- Define motivation and discuss how it has been applied to the study of tourism and travel for older adults.
- Discover the main reasons that encourage or discourage older adults from travelling and decide whether they differ from younger generations.
- Examine the importance of travel and healthy ageing, and explain the psychographics of different older market segments for leisure and travel.
- Explore the main constraints to travel and show how each of these constraints might be overcome.

What is Motivation?

Motivation has been defined in the psychological literature as 'an inner state that energizes, channels, and sustains human behaviour to achieve goals' (Pizam *et al.*, 1979, p. 195). In other words, motives are internal to the individual, helping to guide or direct behaviour so that personal goals are achieved, and in so doing to bring satisfaction and enjoyment to the individual.

What Motivates People to Travel and to Experience Leisure?

The motivations for leisure travel have received considerable attention in the literature over the last two decades (Kim *et al.*, 1996). Tourist motivations have been regarded as important in helping to explain tourist behaviour (Iso-Ahola, 1989). To Iso-Ahola, tourism motivations were seen as a process of escaping personal and/or interpersonal environments, and seeking out personal and/or interpersonal intrinsic rewards. Iso-Ahola based his theories on the work of Deci (1975), who was the first theorist to acknowledge that there was a distinction between intrinsic (internal drives) and extrinsic motivation (external or environmental drives). He defined intrinsic motivation as 'the inherent tendency to seek out novelty and challenges, to extend and exercise one's capabilities, to explore and to learn' (Ryan and Deci, 2000, p. 69). Thus, to Iso-Ahola (1983) tourist behaviour was the 'interplay of forces – avoidance of routine or stressful environments and seeking recreation places for certain psychological rewards' (p. 55).

The motivation to travel is seen as a set of needs and attitudes that predispose a potential tourist to act in a specific goal-directed way (Pizam *et al.*, 1979). Since the early 1980s, a large number of conceptual and empirical studies have attempted to identify the most significant travel motives, to develop a range of conceptual travel motivational models and to apply existing theories to the study of tourist motivations.

Studying the Motivations of Older People to Travel

Gerontologists have proposed that as people reach a mature stage in their life, many become preoccupied with a search for self-fulfilling activities and experiences. Older people have the desire to squeeze in as many new activities as possible into their lives, and have the need to explore the world around them for as long as they experience good health and physical ability (Muller, 1997).

A review of Table 2.1 found that the most frequently mentioned motivations sought by older adults when they travel were education and learning, rest and relaxation, physical exercise and fitness and visiting friends and relatives. A closer examination revealed that there has been a change in the motivations sought by older adults in the pre-1990 studies when comparing them with studies in the late 1990s. This recent shift has been towards greater participation in active pursuits with a strong focus on health and fitness.

Table 2.1. A comparison of the motivations and benefits sought by senior travellers in the 1980s.

Author	Motivation/benefit sought
Guinn (1980)	Rest and relaxation, time with family and friends, physical exercise, learning experience and self-fulfilment
Tongren (1980)	Differentiated between pre- and post-retirement plans and expectations for travel, finding differences in ocean, air and mobile home travel
Anderson and Langmeyer (1982)	Rest and relaxation, visit relatives, travel to historical sites and group package tours were popular
Romsa and Blenman (1989)	Time with friends and relatives, health and physical fitness

Several of the earlier studies of senior travellers have used age as the basis for their segmentations. Guinn's research has focused on the travel behaviour of newly retired tourists, whom he described as a group that was moving away from work and achievement of goals, towards more leisure-based goals. He saw this as a natural progression in the ageing process, as older people left their paid work behind and learnt to adapt to a leisure lifestyle. Guinn (1980) studied nine main motivations that he considered to be the most important for leisure participation. He then narrowed them down to five motivations and correlated them with selected leisure activities to identify if there were any significant relationships. The motivations in order of importance were rest and relaxation, association with friends and family, physical exercise, learning experiences and self-fulfilment. Significant relationships were obtained with age, occupation, income and perceived health status.

Tongren (1980) studied the travel plans of people in both the pre-retirement and post-retirement stages to determine if any changes in travel planning occurred between the two stages. The data collection was part of a larger study conducted by researchers at George Mason University on the buying habits of retired consumers for large ticket goods and services. Tongren found that more than half of the respondents thought they would take three or four trips a year before retirement; however, only one out of every five took that many trips after retirement. There were also changes in the type of trip: e.g. although 34 people indicated that they expected to take an ocean cruise during the pre-retirement phase, only 15 actually went on a cruise post-retirement. The same was found to be the case with mobile home travel, with 27 respondents indicating that they would choose this mode of travel before retirement; however, only 14 actually undertook a mobile home trip after retirement. The most popular means of transport was by motor car, with 96 respondents (31.5%) expecting to travel this way; however, 113 (36.8%) actually did after retirement.

Tongren concluded that people older than 65 years went through two distinct phases in preparation for their travel behaviour:

1. Planning or idea-generation phase generally occurs a few years before retirement when dreams start to become more focused, and ideas are formulated about post-retirement travel but are placed on hold until the actual retirement stage commences.

2. Actual retirement phase begins in the first year after retirement when the real search began. Data indicated that if older people found travel to be uncomfortable, such as having to undertake long tiring walks at airports or they experienced baggage problems, their dreams never became actual purchases. Furthermore, rail or bus travel was almost a last resort for this market, while mobile home travellers were more likely to have owned their own vehicle before retirement, rather than deliberately buying a mobile home after retirement.

Anderson and Langmeyer (1982) studied the similarities and differences between travellers who were under 50 and those who were older than 50. A questionnaire on travel behaviour was developed and pre-tested at the University of South Carolina, then mailed to a random sample of 1000 households in the counties of Montgomery, Greene, Miami and Preble. Of the 1000 questionnaires, 826 were returned and deemed usable, 333 (40%) were from older adults aged 50 and older, while 493 (60%) were from younger adults aged between 20 and 49. The following motivations for travel were found to be different between the younger and older travellers:

- Under-50 travellers were more likely to take a pleasure trip for rest and relaxation or to visit relatives. They were also more likely to travel for outdoor recreation purposes and to visit man-made amusement facilities. The most likely time to travel was during the summer vacation months, July to September, with the most likely length of trip being between 4 and 9 nights. They were most likely to travel by automobile and only one in five people was likely to use a travel agent. Younger travellers took significantly less expensive trips than the over-50 group. The main leisure activities were more active and sports-orientated such as golf, tennis and skiing.

- Over-50 travellers were more likely to take a pleasure trip for rest and relaxation or to visit relatives, as well as to travel to visit historical sites. The months that they were more likely to travel were between August and November because many had retired from work and were not tied down to the summer vacation months. Leisure travel was seen to be most popular with this group, with only one in four people using a travel agent. The most popular method of travel was by automobile, but clearly airline travel was more popular for this group than the under-50s who generally had the extra expense of children's travel. The over-50s were more likely to travel as a group and were more prepared to do what others wanted to do.

Romsa and Blenman (1989) used a large sample of 3512 German tourists aged 14 and older who had been on a vacation when the Institute for Tourism at the Free University of Berlin collected these data in 1979. The random sample was stratified by regions, gender and age cohort groups. The researchers found that taking a vacation as a leisure experience declined with a person's age. They also found that older travellers placed a higher priority on wanting to see their friends and relatives than on their own health.

The seasons of the year also played a role in regard to the time at which vacations were taken. Senior German tourists were more likely to take longer vacations, some for up to 5 months between May and September, rather than the traditional annual vacation time of 3 months from June to August. Seniors preferred to take domestic vacations within Germany, as familiarity of the vacation destination seemed to be important for older people: 25% of vacationers from the 70 years and older age group had taken the same destination six or more times in the past (Romsa and Blenman, 1989).

Discussion

Studies that were conducted in the 1980s found that age was the most important variable that was used to segment older and younger people, with 50 years of age being the marker. Most people who are 50 years and older were found to be relatively healthy, and because many had recently retired, they had more time to travel. The major difference between the two age groups (under 50 compared to over 50) was that travellers in the under-50 age group engaged in greater amounts of active, sports-orientated activities while on holiday, while people older than 50 preferred pleasure trips for rest and relaxation, to visit friends and relatives, or to tour historical and cultural sites. The authors concluded that the profiles of the two groups were quite different in a number of important dimensions, indicating that age can be used effectively as a segmenting variable. However, recent studies of older adults have shown an increasing trend towards more active leisure pursuits with an emphasis on health and fitness. Because of this trend, people in the 50 years and older age group are becoming an economically lucrative market, and there is a growing realization that the older market has been untapped and neglected by the travel industry in the past.

Market Segmentation

Market segmentation is the process of segmenting consumers on the basis of their similarities or characteristics in regard to their wants, needs and

attitudes towards a particular marketing stimulus (Ahmad, 2003). Dibb
et al. (2001) defined segmentation as 'a process of grouping customers in
markets with some heterogeneity into smaller, more homogeneous segments . . . with similar requirements and buying characteristics' (p. 206).
Marketeers have mainly used the traditional approach of comparing demographic, socio-economic and psychographical variables.

Segmenting the mature market has become increasingly important in
helping to understand people's travel behaviour. Traditionally, the older
population was seen as a predominantly homogeneous group; however,
over the last 10 years there has been a growing body of research that has
shown that this is changing, and that the mature market is now quite heterogeneous (Penalta and Uysal, 1992). However, chronological age is still
one of the most widely used measures for market segmentation, probably
because it is more commonly understood, easily measured and the information is readily available. For many tourism operators, it is easier to segment their travel products according to a person's chronological age, or
stage of the family life cycle, than by any other measure. As a result, travel
agents use brochures filled with travel packages and messages aimed at
segmenting the market into such categories as singles, couples, families
and seniors (Pritchard and Morgan, 1996).

Push and pull factors

A prominent approach to the study of travel motivations has been the use
of 'push' and 'pull' factors that have been generally accepted as making
a significant contribution to tourism research (Dann, 1977, 1981). Dann
described the two stages in the travel decision-making process as push and
pull factors:

- Push factors are the internal socio-psychological motivators that predispose or push an individual to travel. In other words, they are the
  motives that establish the desire for taking a pleasure or vacation trip.
- Pull factors, on the other hand, are external motives that pull an individual towards a particular destination once the decision to travel
  has been made. Dann (1981) further suggested that anomie and ego
  enhancement are the basic underlying reasons to travel.

Crompton (1979) agreed with Dann's basic idea about the importance of
push and pull motives, and undertook an additional step when he identified
the motives that influence pleasure vacationers in their selection of specific
destinations. Nine motives were empirically identified and classified into
two categories. Seven of the motives, termed socio-psychological or *push
factors*, were to escape from a perceived mundane environment, exploration and evaluation of self, relaxation, prestige, regression, enhancement
of kinship relationships and facilitation of social interaction. The last two

motives, termed cultural motives or *pull factors*, were novelty and education. Pull factors have helped researchers to better understand why an individual chooses a particular destination.

Push and pull factors and travel for older people

Although push and pull factors have been used extensively in tourism research to differentiate between groups, their use in understanding older people's travel behaviour has not received the same amount of attention by researchers. One of the few studies that has used older people as the sample population was a study by You and O'Leary (1999), who used push and pull travel motivation factors to segment older travellers in the UK into three distinct groupings:

- Passive visitors (19%): the most dominating push motivation for this group was to visit friends and relatives, while the most important pull forces were good public transportation, good standards of hygiene and cleanliness, personal safety and opportunities to meet and socialize with people.
- Enthusiastic go-getters (40%): the most important push motivations for this group were being together as a family, novelty seeking, knowledge enhancement and escape from the demands of home. The most important pull factors included various destination attributes such as good transportation, good standards of hygiene and cleanliness, personal safety and nice weather.
- Culture hounds (41%): the most important push motivations for this segment were associated with cultural and heritage-related activities. Similarly, the most important pull motives were arts and cultural activities and historical or archaeological places.

Another study by Norman *et al.* (2001) also used push and pull travel factors to compare the travel motivations of two older groups of people:

- veteran-mature market members (aged 65 and older); and
- neo-mature market members (aged between 50 and 64).

They collected data using a questionnaire that measured the vacation travel motivations of a sample of 827 older people in the USA living in Illinois, Michigan, Minnesota and Wisconsin. In particular, the researchers were interested in comparing the importance of 35 different travel benefits (or push factors) and 85 vacation attributes (or pull factors) between the two groups of older travellers.

This study found that when they considered the push and pull factors separately, two distinct and discrete market segments of older people emerged. Neo-mature market respondents who were not retired indicated that the factors of escape and action were more important than for the veteran-mature market respondents who were not retired. In regard to pull factors, the neo-mature market respondents indicated that the factors of tourism infrastruc-ture, people and outdoor recreation opportunities were more important than for veteran-mature market respondents who were not retired.

Overall their study found that *younger older people* were more likely than veteran-mature travellers to seek holidays that displayed the following characteristics: escape, education, action, relaxation, natural surroundings, upscale facilities and outdoor recreation. However, the authors concluded that the variables of retirement and income altered the link between age and motivation to travel, warning researchers that they needed to be cautious about using 'age' as the only predictor variable in future studies (Norman *et al.*, 2001).

Discussion

What motivates people to travel has fascinated tourism researchers for the last two decades – it has been described as an intrinsic drive to escape a mundane lifestyle, to travel to an exotic location and/or to seek out novel and challenging experiences. This is a fantasy that most people have experienced sometime during their lives. The use of push and pull factors has been developed as a common approach to describe what influences people's choice of a particular destination and to help segment the market. Older people in particular experience such push factors as the urge to escape from the demands of home and to be more active in their leisure activities. Older travellers also show a strong preference for visiting relatives and friends, socializing with other peo-ple, visiting cultural and heritage attractions, and learning more about different cultures. The most important pull factors are the need for good transportation, high standards of hygiene and cleanliness, and the importance of personal safety.

Market segmentation using psychographic variables

Another technique called psychographic segmentation has also been used to segment different markets. A psychographic profile has been defined as the classification of people according to their particular lifestyles. 'Those attitudes and beliefs that frame the way people think about themselves and their world' (Zotti, 1985, p. 27). Psychographic data include such things as attitudes, inter-ests and opinions that are not directly related to specific product characteris-tics, and are more related to a global notion of the product (Antonides and Van Raaiji, 1998). Psychographic variables have been found to be useful in deter-mining their impact on the travel mode choice, as well as positively influencing marketing and promotion strategies.

Table 2.2.   A comparison of the motivations and benefits sought by senior travellers in the 1990s and 2000.

Author	Motivation/benefit sought
Shoemaker (1989)	With family members, spiritual and intellectual stimulation, meet and socialize, rest and relax, physical activities
Vincent and De Los Santos (1990)	With family and friends, good weather, friendly hosts
Lieux *et al.* (1994)	Cultural activities, physical activities in warm weather, visit family
Shoemaker (2000)	Spiritual and intellectual enrichment, rest and relax, casino gambling, socialize, escape everyday routine
Backman *et al.* (1999)	Education and nature, camping, socializing, relaxing, information
Kim *et al.* (2003)	Health and well-being, new friends, companionship, leisure activities
Sellick (2004)	Learning, social contact, relaxing, nostalgic reminisance

Several of the earlier studies (e.g. Woodside and Potts, 1976; Abbey, 1979) found that specific psychographic data were more effective than socio-demographics in predicting external travel search behaviour. Morgan and Levy (1993) distinguished between different travel segments based upon people's attitudes, motivations and needs. Morgan *et al.* (1993) used terms such as 'highway wanderers' to refer to seniors who preferred to drive their own cars; 'pampered relaxers' tended to enjoy ocean cruises; 'global explorers' sought out new experiences; 'independent adventurers' included several family generations on their trips; and 'anxious travellers' who focused more on safety and costs.

Further studies have divided older people into numerous submarkets or clusters based on their psychographic data as they relate to particular travel characteristics such as spending money, retirement status, activity preferences, motivations and other psychographic variables. A summary of the main studies and other findings in regard to travel motivations is included in Table 2.2.

Shoemaker (1989) was one of the first researchers to conduct market segmentation studies using cluster analysis to segment senior residents in Pennsylvania, USA. Three main groups of senior travellers emerged based on the main reasons for undertaking pleasure travel (see Table 2.3). These findings showed that the senior market is able to be segmented based on the main reasons given for pleasure travel.

Vincent and De Los Santos (1990) replicated and validated Shoemaker's study using a sample of senior winter Texans. In their research methodology, they conducted a stratified random sample design of RV/mobile home parks in the Rio Grande Valley that yielded a total of 100 parks that were considered

Table 2.3. Motivations of seniors for participation in leisure travel. (From Shoemaker, 1989.)

Family travellers	Enjoyed taking short trips with family members and preferred to return to the same destination rather than visit a new one
Active resters	Took holidays for spiritual and intellectual enrichment and to meet people and socialize, to rest and relax, escape everyday routine, engage in physical activities and to visit historical sites
The older set	Preferred to take all-inclusive package tours and to visit resort settings

suitable for surveying in this area. The researchers administered 1757 questionnaires to winter Texans in these 100 parks, yielding 1222 (70% response rate) usable returns. They also telephoned a sample 459 (23%) of all the rental units, hotels, condominiums and motels in the Rio Grande Valley to ask a further set of questions.

The researchers found that the main reasons given for visiting the Rio Grande Valley were related to the good weather, the reception by the local population and opportunities to spend time with family and friends. Vincent and De Los Santos (1990) found that two of their groups strongly resembled the same segments that Shoemaker (1989) had termed 'active resters' and 'the older set'. Winter Texans who stayed in parks matched more closely the profile of active resters, whereas the small number who owned or rented apartments, homes or condos shared similar characteristics to the older set. They preferred to plan their trips, take long vacations and pursue numerous tourist activities such as visits to Mexico, the beach, the zoo and wildlife refuges.

In a follow-up to his first study, Shoemaker (2000) used a different sample of 234 respondents (11.8% response rate) who were aged 55 and older living in Pennsylvania, USA, in 1996. He used the same questionnaire as he did in the 1986 study; however, he mailed 2000 surveys to different Pennsylvanian residents at random postal zip codes. He then compared the results from this study with the earlier study that he conducted in 1986, to ascertain how much the market had changed over a 10-year period. While this study did not track the same people over a 10-year period, it replicated the study methodology undertaken in 1986.

Shoemaker found that 85.4% of his sample took at least one pleasure trip per year in 1996 compared with 80.9% in the 1986 study. The most important reason for overnight vacation travel was to visit new places, whereas in 1986 it was to be able to experience new things. However, overall the response patterns were similar between both studies, suggesting that the reasons for travel had remained fairly stable over the last 10 years. Activities that were engaged in for pleasure were only collected in the 1996 study. These included visiting local attractions, and historical sites were mentioned by

Table 2.4. A further study of the motivations for participation in leisure travel by seniors. (From Shoemaker, 2000.)

Group name	Percentage of group	Characteristics of the market segment
Escape and learn	41.8	A total of 51.2% worked full- or part-time, with a median age of 65 years. This segment had more people in the highest-income category, which helped to explain why they liked to visit new places and experience new things. Members in this cluster sought spiritual and intellectual enrichment, rest and relax, escape the everyday routine, visit historical sites and engage in physical activities.
The retirees	19.3	This group was mainly retired or unemployed with a median age of 66 years. Members of this cluster preferred to return to a particular destination rather than to visit a new one. They also liked casino gambling.
Active storytellers	34.8	The median age was 62 years, which was the youngest of the three groups. More members of this group had been retired less than 1 year. They wanted to escape everyday routine and to experience new things. They also wanted to meet people and to socialize with members of the opposite sex. They liked doing physical activities and attending festivals. They sought intellectual enrichment and liked to visit museums and historical sights.

more than 50% of respondents, while only slightly more than 25% engaged in casino gambling. At the lower end, less than 20% slept more than normal, and engaged in physical activities. Although the data were similar in both samples, Shoemaker (2000) developed a slightly different profile for each of the three segments than in his previous study (see Table 2.4).

Lieux *et al.* (1994) provided further validation to both Shoemaker's and Vincent and De Los Santos' studies. In their study they used a larger sample of 914 older people (31% response rate) of the US population who were aged 55 and older. On average, the survey respondents were aged 62, with 47% having travelled three times a year; 98% were white, 71% were women, among whom less than 9% classified themselves as homemakers. They segmented their sample on the basis of their tourism motivations, and found three different clusters that had distinct characteristics, needs and wants, which were similar to the three clusters identified by Shoemaker (1989). The three groups were:

- Novelty seekers travelled to visit new places and experience new things. They were generally younger seniors who were likely to be retired and have a good income. Novelty seekers contained fewer people in the upper income range than the active enthusiasts, and were more likely to stay in cheaper types of accommodation. They were interested in cultural and event-type activities but not in physical activities.

- Active enthusiasts were interested in physical and warm weather activities and took trips for a longer duration. They were young seniors who enjoyed a good income.
- Reluctant travellers took trips for a shorter duration, were older and had lower incomes than the other clusters. People in this segment were the hardest to motivate and less likely to use hotels of any type. They had little interest in intellectual pursuits, and were mainly interested in travelling to visit their immediate family. The lower incomes also made them less likely to spend significant amounts of money compared with the other two clusters.

The researchers concluded that marketeers in the tourism industry would find 'active enthusiasts' the most attractive segment. This group contained most people who were in the upper income brackets, and who stayed for a longer period per trip than the other two segments. They were also more likely to stay in upscale and luxury properties. These people were active and particularly interested in escaping the cold weather and seeking warm weather activities.

Backman *et al.* (1999) studied the nature-based tourism market in southeast USA. They used psychographic research to identify five segments, which they called: education/nature, camping/tenting, socialization, relaxation and information. Their study also found differences between different age groups, specifically younger seniors (between 55 and 64 years) who were less interested in the education/nature and information aspects, and more interested in the camping/tenting and relaxation experiences.

Although these previous studies were conducted in the USA, their findings have been confirmed in other countries as well. An Australian study by Kim *et al.* (2003) investigated the travel attributes of 200 senior travellers who lived in Western Australia aged 50 and older. An independent marketing consultant developed a questionnaire of senior travel attributes that were considered important by industry specialists. This questionnaire was mailed to 2400 randomly selected customers who were 50 years and older, of which 720 questionnaires were returned (30% response rate). They found four main segments of senior tourists who were categorized as indicated in Table 2.5.

The main motivations that encouraged older people living in Western Australia to travel were for health and well-being, making new friends, companionship and participating in leisure activities. The main concerns were expressed as falling ill, unavailability of doctors, theft, a lack of personal security and peace of mind, safety concerns, and poor hygiene and sanitation.

Sellick (2004) segmented and profiled the senior travel market using a 48-item battery that measured travel motives, perceived travel risk and cognitive age as well as a number of demographic variables. A random stratified sample was selected based on age and state of resi-

Table 2.5. Motivations for older Australians to travel. (From Kim *et al.*, 2003.)

Name of group	Travel characteristics
Active learner	Mainly female, travelled with family and friends, most were widowed, highly motivated by personal growth and learning, embraced new experiences and took part in activities
Relaxed family body	Mainly female with lower incomes, main travel motivations were rest and relaxation and visiting family and friends
Careful participant	Mainly males with higher incomes, travelling mainly with partner/spouse who were highly motivated by observing new experiences and activities that involved health and well-being
Elementary vacationer	Mainly males with higher incomes who travelled with partner/spouse and were highly motivated by embracing and observing new experiences

dence. The sampling frame was made up of Australian residents aged 50 and older who were members of the National Seniors Association. In all, 2223 questionnaires were mailed to members of the NSA and 986 (45%) were returned and found to be reusable. The findings identified ten travel motive factors of which four major travel motive segments emerged from the analysis and were titled:

1. Discovery and self-enhancement ($n = 244$, 26%). This group was excited about learning. They were not as motivated to travel to build self-esteem, relax, visit family or to find spirituality and solace. The motives of discovery through learning and of social contact with others were seen to be more important. Members of this group had higher educational attainment and household incomes than the other three groups.
2. Enthusiastic connectors ($n = 192$, 20%). This group travelled for all the travel motives indicating their overall enthusiasm for travel. They reported the highest scores for the importance of the four travel motives – self-esteem building, indulgent relaxation, generational kinship, spirit and solace seeking. They also rated the perceived travel risk factors more highly than the other three groups. This cluster was therefore a complicated mix as it had the highest scores for both travel motives and the perceived travel risk.
3. Reluctant travellers ($n = 242$, 25%). They were not very motivated to travel. Surprisingly this group was least concerned about the perceived risks of travel. This may indicate that their reluctance to travel was not due to any perception of risks involved but was more due to a lack of travel motives. They were not openly motivated to travel by any of the motive factors, yet they displayed no real concerns about any travel risks.
4. Nostalgic travellers ($n = 274$, 29%). This group was overwhelmingly dominated by the travel motive of nostalgic reminiscence. They rated the four travel motives higher than both Group 1 and Group 3.

These four travel motive segments that were identified in the study acknowledge that there is heterogeneity within the senior travel market. Senior travellers were attracted to pleasure travel for different reasons or groups of reasons. Therefore, it is important that researchers clearly target their specific tourism needs so that they can be more adequately discussed in the future.

Market segmentation using VALS typing

Values and lifestyles (VALS) is a well-known consumer segmentation tool. Blazey (1991) segmented the senior travel market by a traditional socio-demographic variable, age, and by a proprietary segmentation technique called the values and lifestyle battery of questions, commonly known as VALS typing. VALS was conceived as a means of standardizing profiling techniques, and as a 'comprehensive conceptual framework describing people's values and lifestyles in such a way that it would help to explain why people act as they do, both as consumers and as social beings' (Mitchell, 1983, p. 4). Respondents responded to attitudinal and demographic questions, and their responses were scored according to a weighted algorithm, thereby identifying their predominant VALS type. The eight VALS lifestyle types are survivor, sustainer, belonger, emulator, achiever, I-Am-Me, experiential and socially conscious. Lifestyles and values of older adults (LAVOA) is the older consumers' equivalent of VALS which includes six psychographic segments: explorers, adapters, pragmatists, attainers, martyrs and preservers (Sellick, 2004).

Blazey (1991) sampled a total of 1350 people from a nationwide survey research panel, who were between 50 and 85 years. The sample was sent the two-part 16-item questionnaire in March 1988. A response rate of 88% was recorded, with 1184 usable questionnaires returned. VALS typing revealed that the 'belongers' were the largest group that travelled (58.7%), 'achievers' were the second largest group (28%), 'survivors' and 'socially conscious' types were only small segments of 5.3% and 5.2% of the sample, respectively. The remaining four VALS types accounted for less than 3% of the sample and these 34 respondents were excluded from further analysis.

Achievers and socially conscious types were classified as travellers at greater than anticipated rates. Achievers took three or more trips at higher rates than anticipated. Trips by survivors and belongers were more likely to be for family reasons, while achievers and socially conscious travellers indicated that it was for business only. All groups travelled by automobile at the expected rates, although belongers were underrepresented in travel by air and overrepresented when travelling by bus or recreational vehicle. Trips taken by survivors included stays with friends and relatives, while belongers used campground facilities at almost the same rate as visiting friends and relatives. Achievers mainly stayed in hotels, motels and resorts.

When studying the 703 respondents who travelled one or more times in 1987, Blazey found significant relationships between age and their reasons for travel, the number of nights away from home, the types of lodging used and the number of people in the travel party. Blazey found that the oldest age group who were 65 years and older travelled at a significantly greater rate to visit friends and relatives than other groups. Approximately 60% of all travellers spent 4–7 nights away from home, with 55% of the oldest travellers (aged 65 and older) taking trips that exceeded 3 weeks in duration.

Market segmentation using gerontographics

The concept of gerontographics was developed by Moschis (1996) and is similar to psychographics or lifestyle segmentation but specifically focuses on the needs, attitudes, lifestyles and behaviour of older adults. Four gerontographic segments were identified in Moschis's research:

1. 'Healthy indulgers' were settled within their careers, had high financial capabilities, enjoyed life and had not experienced stressful life events such as retirement and widowhood.
2. 'Healthy hermits' had suffered life events that have altered their self-concept and encouraged their enforced withdrawal from society.
3. 'Ailing outgoers' maintained a positive self-image despite their ailments, and aimed to get the most out of their life.
4. 'Frail reclusers' had accepted old age and behaved in a manner they believed reflected their final stage of life (Moschis, 1996).

Moschis felt that the 'healthy indulgers' segment was a prime market for the airline and cruise ship industries, while the 'ailing outgoers' segment might provide a better market for hotel and motel chains.

Cleaver *et al.* (1999) used a similar approach to the gerontographics classification to market segmentation that was advocated by Moschis (1996). Their research added to the gerontographic model by investigating the underlying reasons for holiday travel among seniors, and to cluster groups of senior tourists with common motives so that they would become the basis for tourism product development for the senior market. They used a convenience sample of 356 senior citizens who were between 56 and 93 years. Interviews were conducted in groups of 20–30 people in community halls and senior citizens clubs around south-east Queensland, Australia, in June 1998. The results found that there were four large senior travel motive segments that they called the 'nostalgics', the 'friendlies', the 'learners' and the 'escapists' that, when combined, represented around 83% of the total senior travel market (see Table 2.6).

Table 2.6. Motivations for travel using gerontographic segmentation. (From Cleaver *et al.*, 1999.)

Group name	Characteristics
Nostalgics	Travel for the sake of renewing memories, achieving family togetherness, and make pilgrimages to places to renew pleasant aspects of their past. Their primary value is to have warm relationships with others by visiting friends and relatives, as well as fun and enjoyment and a sense of accomplishment.
Friendlies	Travel to meet new people and make new friends, and to be together with people who share their common interests and values. Social travellers preferring holiday packages to have fun and enjoyment with others and are very security-conscious.
Learners	Travel to collect new experiences, to discover the world around them, learn new things to satisfy their hunger for knowledge and adventure. Most popular values are fun and enjoyment in life and self-respect.
Escapists	Travel to get away from the demands of daily life and responsibilities, and to experience rest and relaxation. The most common values were also fun and enjoyment in life and self-respect. Prefer to travel with just one other person.

Discussion

Segmentation by psychographic variables that are related to lifestyle aspects (such as VALS typing) has become more popular in recent studies of older people. This is because they can better predict travel search behaviour and as such develop more precise marketing and promotional strategies. Shoemaker's classical studies (1989, 2000) have shown us that you can differentiate between different segments of older travellers based on psychographic variables that remain fairly stable over time. Shoemaker found three main groups of older travellers that he categorized as: family – retirees who prefer to return to the same destinations each year; active resters – escape and learn, and like to visit new places and experience new things; and older set – active storytellers who like to escape routine and to meet and socialize with new people. Shoemaker noted, however, that there has been a trend away from package tours to older people independently organizing their own trips that were more active, and involved intellectual learning and visiting historical sites.

Further research has found that active older travellers with high incomes tended to stay away from home for longer periods of time. Because of this, they are seen as more attractive to marketeers in the tourism industry, as older people in the higher income brackets like to buy or rent luxury properties so as to escape the colder weather, and prefer being active in healthy leisure activities. Relaxation activities and escaping home life seem to be more attractive for the younger older person who is still working in paid employment. Finally, these studies suggest that there is great hetero-geneity within the older travel market, and that older people travel for a multitude of reasons – to experience new places, to learn, to visit family and friends, to meet new people, to participate in active and adventurous leisure activities, to rest and relax and for nostalgic reasons.

Qualitative Research

Ryan (1995) interviewed a convenience sample of 59 respondents older than 50 years. He posed the same questions to all respondents about why they went on a holiday? what they thought of Majorca in Spain? and, where appropriate, what changes they had noticed over the last 5 years? The inter-views were conducted in two locations in Magalluf in February 1993. Of the sample, 36% stayed for 7 nights, 56% for 14 nights and the remainder for up to 1 month. The main reason for visiting Majorca was expressed as the need to escape the British winter, and the older the respondents were, the more likely they were to value the opportunity to visit interesting places, and to do things not normally done. A major theme that emerged was the strong identification with the island and what it had to offer resulting in a high number of repeat visitations, indicating that there was a high level of satisfaction with their holiday. Ryan (1995, pp. 214–215) strongly supported the importance of 'conversations' with the tourist that he stressed needed to be open and wide-ranging so as to be a valid means of data collection. Tourists must be given the opportunity to speak out about their experi-ences in their own words, so as to satisfy the ongoing need for increased subjectivity through this type of tourism research.

Botterill and Crompton (1996) focused on the unique qualitative experiences of two travellers who visited Britain, using Kelly's 'Personal Construct Theory' (1955) as the theoretical underpinning of the study to better understand their recollections of the tourist experience. Data were gathered from five structured interviews with each respondent spaced over an 8-month period. They noted that regardless of the traveller, each recon-structed their trip within their own unique framework of meanings. The authors recommended that a new type of tour guide be trained – to use the trip as a platform that enables travellers to arrive at their own conclusions, to take advantage of lessons learned while on the trip and be prepared to return home with a greater perspective on their lives. They stated that when people travelled, there were usually accompanying issues involved such as separation and attachment, identification, intimacy and rejection.

Robertson (2001) addressed the impact of the travel experience on the older traveller to discover if these experiences were personally transformative.

The author sought individuals through his own personal network who were frequent travellers and were aged 50 and older. Out of a pool of 50 who indicated that travel had been a significant experience for them, 8 respondents were finally chosen. Four major themes emerged from the data:

1. A new perspective on what they had at home. Their experiences in a range of different countries with different architecture, food, money, language and people resulted in a new dimension of knowledge, as well as a greater appreciation of life in their own country.
2. A changed sense of self. One respondent stated that she felt liberated and more self-confident, while another stated that he felt strengthened as a result of visiting authentic holy sites.
3. Disrupted assumptions were caused by these new experiences. Many of their initial assumptions had changed because of the travel experience. For example, one respondent could no longer assume that the world was an unfriendly or hostile place.
4. A deeper sense of understanding of the problems associated with a particular country. Travel provided a deeper sense of knowledge about the country that was visited. For example, one couple had a deeper sense of the economic problems associated with a particular country by staying with a host family during their visit.

Of special importance was the role of the tour guide whom it was determined could make or break a trip. The attitude of the tour guide was important, especially if he or she incorporated personal reflection during the tour, was unhurried and allowed time for discussion and questions. This resulted in learning taking place that had special significance, and the transformative experience was changed (Robertson, 2001).

Discussion

Qualitative research is an approach that has largely been ignored by tourism researchers in the past. However, this method of data collection needs to be further developed and applied to the study of older people's leisure and tourism experiences. This is because the qualitative interview enables the researcher to gain a better and more in-depth recollection and understanding of the actual trip experience from a different perspective than through quantitative research. Robertson's study has shown in particular that older travellers face various disorienting dilemmas (e.g. language, money, travel directions) and, although not a life crisis situation, result in the loss of self-confidence and learning when these challenges are not solved. Most travellers further identified that learning was the main focus of their trip: learning about the different destinations as well as themselves, and for several respondents, their lives were transformed in subtle yet important ways.

Barriers to Older People's Travel and Leisure Behaviour

Several of the early studies (McGuire, 1984; Blazey, 1986) concluded that there are many factors that prevent seniors from participating in tourism and leisure activities. These studies have also shown that seniors are not all alike and travel for a multitude of different reasons. However, in most cases, seniors have different needs and preferences than younger people. Therefore, they suggested that it was important for the industry to recognize that there are certain barriers that prevent seniors from travelling, and that they need to be prepared to help to overcome them if they want to tap into this market.

In the 1980s, some of the previous studies that looked at older non-travellers concluded that the most frequently cited barriers were lack of time, insufficient financial resources, poor health, being too old or frail and family responsibilities. McGuire (1984) identified five major constraints in a more detailed examination of why older travellers do not travel as much as younger travellers:

- external resources – lack of information, too much planning, insufficient money, lack of appropriate clothing and luggage, and lack of transportation;
- time factors – no time to travel, the need to work, tourism interrupting normal routine and being too busy doing other things;
- approval – family and friends would not approve, feel guilty about going on trips and afraid to make a mistake by going to a disappointing place;
- social – spouse dislikes travel, no companion and no interest in going away; and
- physical well-being – no energy, poor health, afraid to take certain modes of transportation and too old or disabled to travel.

Blazey (1986) surveyed barriers to travel in a study for the Washington Parks and Recreation Department in Vancouver, Washington. He developed a 24-item self-administered questionnaire that was sent to a random sample of senior citizens. The typical respondent was found to be a retired, white, female, who was equally likely to be married or widowed. They were most likely to be between 65 and 74 years, had some college education and were experiencing average, or better than average, health.

Four constraint factors were found to create barriers to the participation of more than 20% of those who had never previously participated in travel programmes. These constraints were lack of money, poor health, lack of a travelling companion and a reluctance to drive at night. Two of the constraints affected more than 25% of participants: the cost of the trip and a reluctance to drive at night.

- Lack of money was found to be the number one constraint, as many trips are too expensive. Trip organizers decided as a result of this feedback to plan additional 1-day trips that were quite inexpensive.

- Health-related issues were also regarded as a major constraint, and trip organizers needed to reassure older people that their minor health or disability problems were not a barrier to participation.
- Lack of a travelling companion was also voiced as a problem for a large number of older people. Current participants were encouraged to invite a non-travelling friend to join them on short trips or to attend one of the trip information evenings.
- Travelling to the Recreation Centre at night was also seen as a problem, with a solution being that trips should be scheduled for departure and return during the daylight hours. Organizing a car pool was also seen as another solution to this problem.

In regard to the types of travel activities offered, it was recommended that trips to unusual places, historical sites and scenic locations be provided on a regular basis. Trips to a residential camp, or river rafting, were seen as very specialized activities, but should still be offered to those older people who were active and healthy and enjoyed outdoor experiences, although they needed to be fully self-supporting activities.

Romsa and Blenman (1989) found that choice of vacation was often dependent upon such constraints as a lack of transportation opportunities. Old age often affects the person's ability to operate a motor vehicle for long distances and to navigate through unfamiliar places. As a result, for the 70 years and older group, train and bus transportation has become more important. In addition, older holiday travel was preferred within Germany, while travel to more distant, warmer climates was still perceived to be difficult due to financial, physical or stress-related barriers.

Hong et al. (1999) examined the likelihood of taking a trip by US senior tourists and found that the factors of race, education, marital status and economic factors determined whether or not the older person wanted to travel. Income, in particular, was the only variable that was significant for both the likelihood of going away and tourism expenditure while on the trip.

Fleischer and Pizam (2002) accessed data from a large national survey of tourism activities of the Israeli population who were 55 years and older. They surveyed 400 Israeli adults through telephone interviews and asked them a series of questions in Hebrew related to vacation patterns and preferences. The respondents were equally split between males and females, with the majority aged between 55 and 65 years, married (76.8%), having income levels below average (58.6%) and assessed themselves as being healthy (90.7%). Only 51% (202 people) took a vacation in the preceding year with a mean length of 7.3 days.

The researchers concluded that the decision to take a vacation was mainly dependent upon an individual's self-assessed health condition and his or her present level of income. They also found that once older people decided to take a vacation, constraints varied according to the specific age group. As a result, time and income constraints will increase until the age of 65; however, with retirement, the time constraint becomes obsolete, income is at its peak, health is generally good and, thus, the number of vacation days will be at its maximum. However, as people grow older and move into retirement, income constraints become more important, decreasing the number of days spent on vacation. In the very old age categories, health constraints prevent more and more people from taking vacations.

The results of this study confirmed the findings of McGuire's (1984) study, and concluded that insufficient money, lack of time, poor health and/or disability are constraints to senior tourism. The researchers concluded that between 60 and 70 years is the most important age span for the tourism industry to focus its marketing, as this cohort generally experiences good health, their income is high and vacation times are at their longest. Income and health were found to be the only constraints that affected seniors' propensity to undertake a vacation. Declining income and deteriorating health are the main causes for a decrease in the number of vacation days (Fleischer and Pizam, 2002).

Shoemaker (2000) studied the barriers to overnight holiday pleasure travel with a sample of 234 respondents aged 55 and older who lived in Pennsylvania, USA (Table 2.7), and compared them with his 1986 study. He found that more than one-third of his sample of non-traveller respondents stated that substantial barriers to travel included 'financial considerations' (48.3%), 'their health' (43.3%), 'lack of someone to travel with' (41.7%) and 'physical disability' (37.9%). Other barriers included a fear of the hassles associated with travel, and leaving their home unattended.

Table 2.7. Barriers to overnight holiday pleasure travel: non-travellers vs. travellers. (From Shoemaker, 2000, p. 18.)

Barrier	Travellers (%)	Non-travellers (%)
Dietary considerations	7.0	11.0
Fear of not having a good time	2.3	2.7
Fear of hassles (making reservations; no one to help, etc.)	5.1	20.0
Age	5.1	21.4
Fear of leaving home unattended	6.1	28.6
Physical disability	7.9	37.9
Lack of someone to travel with	17.2	41.7
Health	14.9	43.3
Lack of information about where to go	11.6	7.4
Deciding where to go	8.8	11.5
Finding the time	27.2	18.5
Commitments and responsibilities at home or work	32.3	28.6
Financial considerations	32.7	48.3

Perceived safety as a barrier to travel for older adults

One of the constantly reported barriers to travel for older people is safety and a sense of security. With terrorism attacks being common occurrences today, travelling to places where older travellers feel safe and secure is an important consideration. Travel agents and package tour promoters need to convey a sense of safety and security in their promotions and advertisements aimed at the older market. However, it is important to note that many older people want to travel to places that are safe but not boring. They still desire a sense of adventure (Penalta and Uysal, 1992).

Lindqvist and Bjork (2000) investigated the importance of perceived safety as a barrier to tour decision making which tends to increase as the tourist becomes older. There are two common types of threats to a tourist's safety: environmental factors such as fire, earthquake, crime and violence, and unhealthy food and water. In addition to the external threats, data also indicated that there are threats that are a result of the ageing process, such as declining health status. The researchers used qualitative research methods to conduct personal interviews with respondents aged 55 and older who were living in Finland. The average age of respondents was 66 years, with women making up 57.6% of the sample and men 42.4%. Most of the respondents were married (66.8%), retired (67.1%) and 77.5% of the sample stated that they travelled every year.

Apart from the lack of time available, less money, a lack of interest and deteriorating health were the main barriers to travel. The importance of safety was also discussed and all respondents indicated that safety was an important concern. In particular, travel propensity declined dramatically as the older person's health status declined, and senior tourists considered it increasingly important that trained medical personnel be available on the trip and that there be good accessibility to health care facilities.

Discussion

A number of barriers have been listed as preventing older people from travelling, declining income levels and deteriorating health being among the most researched. Therefore, the tourism industry needs to concentrate their marketing efforts on the age range of 60–70 years, when older people's health is generally good and income levels are at their peak. Lack of time does not really become an important issue once the older person has retired. Recently, safety and a sense of security from terrorism attacks has become an important consideration for older people, especially if they have declining health status. Most reports have found that it is important to have access to good health care facilities at the destinations that are visited. The main constraints for senior travel can be classified as:

1. Traveller's personal problems such as lack of time, cost, health, age and family responsibility considerations;

2. Travel product providers' responsibilities such as cost considerations and the provision or lack of information; and

3. Government travel policy responsibilities that include external resources, security concerns and environmental barriers (Huang and Tsai, 2003).

Travel is mainly conditioned by the individual's health that often decelerates downwards at a more advanced age, impacting on the older person's ability to travel. At any stage of the older life cycle, individuals have to pass a certain threshold that is a combination of income, time and health, as well as conditioned by their personal preferences in order to undertake a leisure-related trip.

Conclusion

Motivations to travel have been described as a specific drive to seek out novel and challenging experiences while at the same time avoiding routine or stressful environments. Generally, older people want to experience self-fulfilling leisure activities so long as they have good health and the physical ability to enjoy them. In particular, studies indicate that older people are particularly motivated to travel for the following reasons: education and learning, physical exercise and health, visiting friends and relatives and for rest and relaxation.

Recent research has used psychographic segmentation and VALS typing to classify older people into specific submarkets or clusters according to the type of lifestyle that they want to experience when they are travelling. Catchy titles such as active learners, active storytellers, family travellers, novelty seekers and elementary vacationers have pervaded the research literature to describe different groupings of older travellers and their specific travel and leisure behaviour. However, at this stage there has been a lack of good qualitative research studies to describe the impact of the travel experience on the older tourist.

A number of studies have shown that there are many factors that restrict or prevent older people from participating in tourism and leisure activities such as poor health, inadequate financial resources, too old or frail, lack of a travelling companion and transport problems. Lack of time is not really a major problem after retirement; however, income constraints may become more important to retirees as they no longer have a weekly salary. Recently, the importance of perceived safety has become important for older travellers, especially with the fear of terrorist attacks. However, environmental factors such as fire, earthquake, crime, violence, as well as unhealthy food and water, are also major concerns that restrict older people's travel to Asia and Middle Eastern countries. In such turbulent times, older tourists generally favour countries that are regarded as safe and allow access to high-level health care facilities.

References

Abbey, J.R. (1979) Does lifestyle profiling work? *Journal of Travel Research* 18, 8–14.

Ahmad, R. (2003) Benefit segmentation: a potentially useful technique of segmenting and targeting older consumers. *International Journal of Market Research* 45, 373–390.

Anderson, B. and Langmeyer, L. (1982) The under-50 and over-50 travellers: a profile of similarities and differences. *Journal of Travel Research* 20, 20–24.

Antonides, G. and Van Raaiji, W.F. (1998) *Consumer Behaviour: A European Perspective.* John Wiley & Sons, New York.

Backman, K.F., Backman, S.J. and Silverberg, K.E. (1999) An investigation into the psychographics of senior nature-based travellers. *Tourism Recreation Research* 24, 13–22.

Blazey, M.A. (1986) Research breathes new life into senior travel program. *Parks and Recreation* October, 55–56.

Blazey, M.A. (1991) Socio demographic and psychographic variables in the senior travel market. *Visions in Leisure and Business* 9, 37–46.

Botterill, T.D. and Crompton, J.L. (1996) Two case studies exploring the nature of the tourist experience. *Journal of Leisure Research* 28, 57–83.

Cleaver, M., Muller, T.E., Ruys, H. and Wei, S. (1999) Tourism product development for the senior market, based on travel motive research. *Tourism Recreation Research* 24, 5–11.

Crompton, J.L. (1979) Motivations for pleasure vacation. *Annals of Tourism Research* 6, 408–424.

Dann, G. (1977) Anomie, ego-enhancement and toursim. *Annals of Tourism Research* 4, 184–194.

Dann, G.M. (1981) Tourist motivation: an appraisal. *Annals of Tourism Research* 8, 187–219.

Deci, E.L. (1975) *Intrinsic Motivation.* Plenum, New York.

Dibb, S., Simkin, L., Pride, N. and O'Farrell, O.C. (2001) *Marketing Concepts and Strategies.* Macmillan, New York.

Fleischer, A. and Pizam, A. (2002) Tourism constraints among Israeli seniors. *Annals of Tourism Research* 29, 106–123.

Guinn, R. (1980) Elderly recreational vehicle tourists: motivations for leisure. *Journal of Travel Research* 19, 9–12.

Hong, G.S., Kim, Y. and Lee, J. (1999) Travel expenditure pattern of elderly households in the US. *Tourism Recreation Research* 24, 43–52.

Huang, L. and Tsai, H-T. (2003) The study of senior traveller behaviour in Taiwan. *Tourism Management* 24, 561–574.

Iso-Ahola, S. (1983) Towards a social psychology of tourism. *Leisure Studies* 2, 45–56.

Iso-Ahola, S. (1989) Motivation for leisure. In: Jackson, E.L. and Burton, T.L. (eds) *Understanding Leisure and Recreation: Mapping the Past, Charting the Future.* Venture, State College, Pennsylvania, pp. 247–279.

Kelly, G.A. (1995) *The Psychology of Personal Constructs.* Norton, New York.

Kim, Y., Weaver, P. and McCleary, K. (1996) A structural equation model: the relationship between travel motivation and information sources in the senior travel market. *Journal of Vacation Marketing* 3, 55–64.

Kim, J., Wei, S. and Ruys, H. (2003) Segmenting the market of West Australian senior tourists using an artificial neural network. *Tourism Management* 24, 25–34.

Lieux, E.M., Weaver, P.A. and McCleary, P.A. (1994) Lodging preferences of the senior tourism market. *Annals of Tourism Research* 21, 712–728.

Lindqvist, L.-J. and Bjork, P.B. (2000) Perceived safety as an important quality dimension among senior tourists. *Tourism Economics* 6, 151–158.

McGuire, F.A. (1984) A factor analytic study of leisure constraints in advanced adulthood. *Leisure Sciences* 6, 313–326.

Mitchell, A. (1983) *The Nine American Lifestyles.* Macmillan, New York.

Morgan, C. and Levy, D. (1993) *Segmenting the Mature Market.* Probus, Chicago, Illinois.

Moschis, G.P. (1996) *Gerontographics: Life Stage Segmentation for Marketing Strategy Development.* Quorum Books, Westport, Connecticut.

Muller, T. (1997) The benevolent society: value and lifestyle changes among middle-aged baby boomers. In: Kahle, L.R. and Chigouris, L. (eds) *Values, Lifestyles and Psychographics.* Lawrence Erlbaum Associates, Mahwah, New Jersey, pp. 299–316.

Norman, W.C., Daniels, M.J., McGuire, F. and Norman, C.A. (2001) Whither the mature market: an empirical examination of the travel motivations of neo-mature and veteran mature markets. *Journal of Hospitality and Leisure Marketing* 8, 113–130.

Penalta, L.A. and Uysal, M. (1992) Aging and the future travel market. *Parks and Recreation* 27, 96–99.

Pizam, A., Neumann, Y. and Reichel, A. (1979) Tourist satisfaction: uses and misuses. *Annals of Tourism Research* 6, 195–197.

Pritchard, A. and Morgan, N.J. (1996) Marketing practice and opportunities in the tour operators' senior travel market: beyond bowling and ballroom dancing. *Journal of Vacation Marketing* 3, 153–163.

Robertson, D.N. (2001) The impact of travel on older adults: an exploratory investigation. *Tourism* (Zagreb) 49, 99–108.

Romsa, G. and Blenman, M. (1989) Vacation patterns of the elderly German. *Annals of Tourism Research* 16, 178–188.

Ryan, C. (1995) Learning about tourists from conversation: the over-55s in Majorca. *Tourism Management* 16, 207–215.

Ryan, R.M. and Deci, E.L. (2000) Self-determination theory and the facilitation of intrinsic motivation, social development and well-being. *American Psychologist* 55, 68–78.

Sellick, M.C. (2004) Discovery, connection, nostalgia: key travel motives within the senior market. *Journal of Travel and Tourism Marketing* 17, 55–71.

Shoemaker, S. (1989) Segmentation of the senior pleasure travel market. *Journal of Travel Research* 27, 14–21.

Shoemaker, S. (2000) Segmenting the mature market: 10 years later. *Journal of Travel Research* 39, 11–26.

Tongren, H.N. (1980) Travel plans of the over 65 market pre- and post-retirement. *Journal of Travel Research* 19, 7–11.

Vincent, V.C. and De Los Santos, G. (1990) Winter Texans: two segments of the senior travel market. *Journal of Travel Research* 29, 9–12.

Woodside, A.G. and Potts, R.E. (1976) Effects of consumer lifestyles, demographics and travel activities on domestic and foregin travel behavior. *Journal of Travel Research* 14, 13–15.

You, X. and O'Leary, J.T. (1999) Destination behaviour of older UK travellers. *Tourism Recreation Research* 24, 23–34.

Ziotti, E. (1985) Thinking psychographically. *Public Relations Journal* 4, 27–30.

Socio-demographic Variables Associated with Tourism, Leisure and Ageing

The aims of this chapter are to:

- Ascertain if 'age' is important in leisure and tourism research.
- Discuss the differences between chronological age and subjective age.
- Examine socio-demographic variables such as gender, income and education to determine their effect on the older tourist.
- Examine other factors such as heterogeneity, seasonality and ethnicity to determine their effect on the older tourist.

Is Age Important?

There appears to be no universal acceptance about how to define an 'older person'. Chronological age is the main measure that has been used to determine whether a person is ageing. Previously, tourism marketeers tended to treat the senior market as one large homogeneous segment of the holiday travel population. This originated from the fact that the older market was often misunderstood (Moschis, 1996), and that the dominant discourses of ageing that have been accepted by society were associated with negative stereotypes. These included the beliefs that older people were 'over the hill' and 'on the way down', in poor health and dependent on the health care system, somewhat frail or ailing and most were cared for in nursing homes, were socially isolated and had few friends, and rarely expressed a desire to participate in new experiences (Onyx and Benton, 1995; Rowe and Kahn, 1998; Blaikie, 1999). Because of these negative stereotypes, there was a general belief that older adults were incapable of handling the strenuous aspects of travel and needed to be provided with special care, and that their lifestyle should mainly consist of rest and relaxation activities because of their wish to disengage from society (Grant, 2002).

Moschis (1996) challenged this stereotypical picture of the older person who was seen as frail and infirm, and felt that it was not representative of all older people. He concluded that most elderly people remained fairly active and part of their community despite their ailments until at least their late 70s. There is some statistical evidence that their income is dramatically reduced in retirement and that the human body starts to physically wear out after many years of activity to support these negative stereotypes, such as many older people live alone when their children leave home and/or when their spouse has died (Cleaver *et al.*, 2002). Although many older adults fit this profile, others do not, and there is a growing acceptance that the older population is much more diverse, with a greater deal of variability than was previously understood. In fact, this large population segment is not only quite active, but they are also relatively wealthy, possess great vitality and have a keen desire to travel (Watkins, 1994; Moschis *et al.*, 1997). Furthermore, most are physically capable of travelling for pleasure and enjoy relatively youthful activities while on vacation (Muller and O'Cass, 2001).

Subjective age

Subjective age is sometimes referred to as self-perceived age or cognitive age, and is a component of the self-concept that reveals how old one feels, irrespective of a person's chronological age (Wylie, 1974). Wilkes (1992) suggested that subjective age was a more accurate measure than chronological age to help us to better understand how seniors view themselves and their behaviour. Neugarten's landmark studies in the 1960s established that as people approach the latter part of their lives, they express a sense of confidence and mastery as well as a preoccupation with self-utilization. There is a continual search for self-fulfilling activities and experiences as they contemplate how much time they have left to live. One of Neugarten's (1968) respondents supported this premise when he stated: 'It adds a certain anxiety, but I must also say it adds a certain zest in seeing how much pleasure can still be obtained, how many good years one can still arrange, how many new activities can be undertaken' (p. 97). As a result, there is a reaffirmation of older people's value orientation to travel and to explore the world as a tourist before they begin to experience poor health or disability.

This desire to obtain the most they can out of their latter years as they perceive that their time is running out suggests that people are continually assessing their subjective age as being different from their chronological age, and this has been supported by research that has shown that between 60% and 75% of people aged 60 and older felt younger than their chronological age (Markides and Boldt, 1983).

Markides and Boldt (1983) found that the main difference between felt age (subjective age) and actual age (chronological age) was 10.2 years. Seniors typically felt a decade younger than their actual age and placed great importance on having fun and enjoyment in their lives, preferring to experience or enjoy vacation activities with younger people. Males had a greater tendency than females to desire vacationing with much younger age groups, and often coloured their hair and/or underwent cosmetic surgery to enhance their appearance and remove signs of ageing. This age difference becomes larger as one ages, as research by the Menlo Consulting Group found that, on average, US travellers aged 80 often thought of themselves as having a mean age of 65 (Smith and Jenner, 1997). This suggests that people do not perceive themselves as old until they reach at least 75 years or more (Sherman and Cooper, 1988).

These findings suggest that segmenting seniors by how old they 'feel' rather than how old they actually 'are' is a far better approach when marketing tourism products specifically for their needs. There has been extensive research conducted to support the use of the concept of 'subjective age' as a marketing tool for the 'young-at-heart' senior traveller. To support this finding, Cleaver and Muller (2002) surveyed a group of 356 people between 56 and 93 years to ascertain if there were any differences between their subjective and chronological age as a predictor for reasons to travel, personal values and their perceived state of health. Two main groups were found to be significantly different:

1. Younger-at-heart seniors generally felt healthier, sought fun and enjoyment out of life and used travel to fulfil their priorities. They also valued a sense of accomplishment, achievement and personal pride. As a result, the researchers suggested that the tourism product should be marketed to offer various options such as experiencing excitement, thrill, fun and challenge. Strategies that needed to be implemented were to stress the importance of challenging oneself and achieving sensory stimulation, and this concept needed to reflect a self-image of usefulness.

2. Older-at-heart seniors were more concerned about security and danger, travel arrangements falling through and becoming ill while on vacation. A greater proportion of females were in this group, and they were more likely to prefer travelling with either a group of friends or family members (Muller and O'Cass, 2001).

Ageing as a Multidimensional Phenomenon

Previous research has shown that ageing is a multidimensional phenomenon, and that people age biologically, psychologically, socially and even spiritually at different rates (Moschis, 1996). As a result, researchers have found it difficult to place an age group boundary around any specific cohort group and expect to find significant differences between it and any other cohort group. To state it simply: 'People do not always look or act their age!' Yet for practical reasons, especially in the case of travel and leisure services, we often use a lower age limit of 50 or 55 years as a boundary marker to differentiate between middle age and old age.

However, there is some research evidence to suggest that a person's chronological age is a reliable predictor that separates senior travellers from younger non-travellers, specifically in regard to the main reasons for travelling, destination choices and modes of travel (Penalta and Uysal, 1992). Over-50 travellers generally spend more time planning their trips, and significantly more money than under-50 travellers. Furthermore, the over-50 group were more likely to respond to promotions, advertisements and travel packages that were ignored by the under-50 segment. As a result, travel businesses have started to realize that the senior market is an important segment and to shift advertising dollars from other target areas to the 50 years and older segment.

Research on the ageing travel market has found conflicting results. As age increased, there was a tendency for travel to increase in the early years after retirement, and then to decrease later on, especially if a person's health status began to deteriorate or they were very old or frail. On the other hand, however, research with a sample of 1406 adults aged 65 and older who were living in Manitoba, Canada, found that if people increased their educational level as they became older, there was a likelihood that travel to a broad range of distant locations increased with age (Zimmer et al., 1995). Zimmer et al. (1995) concluded: '[U]rban residents who are better educated, have more money, and are predisposed towards spending money on recreation tend to travel further from home, while those with health problems tended to travel to nearby US destinations' (p. 6).

Reece (2004) also noted differences in travel patterns between seniors and non-seniors. He used a 1995 American Travel Survey to examine differences in individual household travel choices between seniors and non-seniors when travelling to South Carolina for leisure purposes. Reece (2004) found similar results to Zimmer et al. (1995) and Horneman et al. (2002), that on average, senior travellers travelled longer distances than younger travellers. Reece also found that, although senior travellers had lower average incomes than younger travellers, they still travelled more often than younger people. This was explained by the fact that, although they had a lower income than younger people, they had greater equity in their own homes and, as a result, had the confidence and greater discretionary income to travel more often than younger people.

Faranda and Schmidt (1999) were critical of the use of only a single variable such as age, as it was not always the most effective measure to use when defining or describing how older travellers differed from younger travellers. Nevertheless, this approach has proved to be popular among tourism researchers. For example, the Travel Industry Association of America released a report in 2000 that compared the differing amount of time spent travelling by older and younger cohort groups, as well as the differing purposes of these trips.

Future researchers need to be careful not to lump all people together as 'older' or 'mature' if they are over an arbitrary age such as 55, 60 or 65. This shows a lack of understanding about what this age group is really like, especially their individual needs, interests and lifestyles (Sherman and Cooper, 1988). It is important to understand that each separate cohort group of older adults has lived through a particular time in history that adds to their distinct characteristics, needs and interests. At the same time, there is individual variability in a person's physiological changes, health status, psychological well-being, socio-economic circumstances, social and family situation and ethnic minority status.

Older aged people include a wide range of chronological ages, from approximately 55 to 100 years or older. In recent years, this wide age range has been segmented into specific age-graded subgroups such as young–old, old–old and oldest of old. One of the consequences of this emphasis on an age-related society is when people of different chronological ages are assigned 'different roles, expectations, opportunities, status, and constraints' (Hooyman and Kiyak, 1988, p. 6). Therefore, it is important to be aware that other variables such as gender, income and education also need to be considered, rather than merely basing future studies on the simple factor of chronological age when catering for the travel needs of older people.

Discussion

A great deal of diversity exists among individuals who are classified as 'older people' according to their chronological age. The traditional stereotypes that existed when older people were commonly referred to as 'over the hill', 'frail and in poor health' and were seen as 'socially isolated' are now largely acknowledged as being incorrect and outdated. In fact, there is stronger evidence to support the fact that many older people are active, vital, enjoy travelling and perceive themselves as much younger than their real age. Therefore, subjective age seems to be a much more accurate measure than chronological age to assist researchers to understand how seniors currently view themselves and the world around them. Studies have confirmed that older people see themselves as approximately 10 years younger than their chronological age, and this gap widens even further as people grow older; they still see themselves as younger, often preferring to enjoy fun experiences with younger people rather than people of their own age. As a result, tourism marketeers need to concentrate on presenting images of older people who are experiencing excitement, fun and challenge, reflecting a self-image of usefulness and that they still like to participate in youth-related leisure activities.

Most of the tourism studies that have been conducted with older adults have generally used 50 or 55 years as the initial marker. This has been found to be a reliable predictor that separates younger travellers from senior travellers. Older travellers are more responsive to advertising promotions and package tours, take more time planning trips and spend significantly more money on trips than people who are under 50. There is substantial evidence to suggest that travel increases after retirement, even for older people who have lower incomes than younger people. However, travel and leisure experiences will decrease if a person's health status deteriorates and/or the person becomes too old or frail. People with increased education will generally travel to more distant locations than younger people.

However, age as a single variable should not be used as the only differentiation between younger and older travellers, as older people as a group are too large and diverse, and can include people ranging from 50 to 100 years. In such a group spanning 50 years there is great diversity in people's health levels, psychological well-being, socio-economic status, social, family and ethnic minority status. Therefore, we also need to consider other socio-demographic variables such as gender, income and education when catering for the tourism and leisure needs of older people.

Other Socio-demographic Variables

Gender

Men and women develop strong sex role identification that enables them to acquire different traits, attitudes and behaviours that are expected of their gender (Cross, 1997). Previous research has shown that older men and women follow different paths as they adapt to the ageing process, with women more successfully adapting to older age than men, who tend to find it more difficult. This is because of men's disengagement from paid work and other public roles in their retirement age (Blau, 1973). Women are more interested in maintaining social networks and activities that promote reciprocal attachments through passive and expressive leisure, as well as cultural and home-based activities (Lawton *et al.*, 1987).

Because women live longer than men, they significantly outnumber men in the older age groups. In the UK, for example, in 1997 there were 1.3 million women compared to 1 million men in the 70–74 age group, and by the time they reached the 80–84 age group the woman/man ratio is almost 2:1, while in Germany it is almost 3:1 (Smith and Jenner, 1977). As a result, women are more likely to experience widowhood, and this transition from wife to widowhood can severely impact on their lifestyle. It was found that continued participation in a number of leisure activities helped widows and widowers to reduce the level of stress associated with the death of their spouse, and at the same time boosted their morale at a difficult time in their lives (Patterson and Carpenter, 1994; Patterson, 1996).

With travel and tourism, gender differences were also noted in many aspects of the lives of men and women. Hawes (1988) was one of the first researchers to study older women and their travel-related lifestyles. He used a sample of women aged 50 and older who were grouped into 5-year age ranges, i.e. 50–54, 55–59, 60–64, 65–69 and 70 and older. Hawes used a representative nationwide sample of 1090 females who returned a questionnaire about their travel-related lifestyle patterns. The main findings were as follows:

1. Women who were in the 55–59 age group were significantly more interested in travelling overseas than any other age group.

2. Exposure to a foreign country predisposes the traveller to want to return to it.

3. Two-thirds of each age group liked the idea of a cabin by a quiet lake as a summer retreat. However, three of the five age groups were not interested in resting and relaxing on a vacation (including some who were 70 years and older), suggesting that they still had the energy and desire to do active things.

4. Approximately 60% of the women felt that the notion of a travel now/pay later vacation was wrong.

5. Only approximately one-third of the women were interested in spending their vacation in, or near, a big city. The 60–64 age group was the only one that was most interested in a big-city environment.

6. The general profile of a woman's travel orientation was: highly educated with high incomes, small household size, active and an acceptance of the uncertainty involved in travel.

7. Approximately one-third of the respondents fell into the following two groups: preferring excitement and adventure, and preferring predictability.

8. Approximately one-fifth of the respondents were dreamers and were content with vicarious experiences and fantasizing through television.

9. The print media was more likely to be effective in reaching the woman traveller compared with television advertising.

Gender differences in travel motivations seem to reflect significant differences in other aspects of the lives of men and women. Gender was found to be the most significant reason for taking a cultural travel experience (Square, 1994), and motivational differences existed between male and female travellers (McGehee *et al.*, 1996).

Lehto *et al.* (2001) analysed secondary data from a French Pleasure Travel Market Survey of 1977. The sample size was 438 travellers who were 50 years and older who preferred long-haul trips (more than 4 days) and preferred to travel outside Europe. The researchers found that females were more sensitive to safety issues than men, and requested greater opportunities to socialize and interact with other people. Women's strong need for socialization and communication was reflected in their strong preferences for local cultural and heritage activities as well as festivals. Joining a group or package travel also provided mature female travellers with ample social opportunities as well as a strong sense of safety and protection. However, older male travellers preferred more instrumental activities that enhanced their health and fitness through outdoor recreation travel, such as golfing, fishing and hiking. Because life expectancy for women is about 6–7 years longer than for men, this adds greater weight to the importance of the healthy, older women travel market for the tourism industry (Lehto *et al.*, 2001).

Statts and Pierfelice (2003) surveyed older people in regard to their immediate and long-range activities following retirement. Using a purposeful sample of 65 retired volunteers (50 were women) the respondents were invited to complete a survey concerning well-being and retirement activities. The average age of the women was 73.8 and the mean number of years retired was 12.8. The men's average age was 75.2 and they had been retired on average for 13.2 years. When the respondents were asked what they did after retirement, travel was the most common response. When they were asked what they would like to do in the next 5 years, travel increased to more than 30% and became by far the most frequent response by this sample of retired people. This study also found that 21% of the sample reported that they travelled immediately after retirement, 18.5% reported travelling in the 5 years after retirement and almost 32% reported that they wanted to travel within the next 5 years. The researchers suggested that travel was a retirement transition activity providing a physical and psychological barrier from work and home life.

This study presented strong support for the belief that travel is a frequently desired and continuing activity for groups of long-term retirees, most of whom are women. Shorter trips are preferred to longer trips for many women who see them as cheaper, as well as reducing the hassles associated with minding young grandchildren and pet ownership. Shorter rather than longer trips might also be seen as cohort-related, because of the greater availability of air travel now than in the previous millennium (Statts and Pierfelice, 2003).

However, travel data suggest that, overall, older women do not travel as much as older men, although this is slowly changing. This was attributed to the fact that many older women are widowed or divorced and do not want to travel as they do not have a partner to travel with. Another factor that inhibits older women from travelling, especially those who live alone, is that they are financially worse off than many men. Therefore, as women outlive men, this creates a pool of women who are interested in travel, but if they do not have a ready travelling companion, they may choose not to travel or may limit their travel to visiting friends and relatives. There is also an emerging trend for widowed people to seek out intergenerational travel options, and to bring grandchildren with them on trips (Smith and Jenner, 1997).

Income

Not only do many older people have the time and the inclination to travel, but they also have the money. In most developed countries, people aged 55 and older possess a relatively large share of discretionary income because most of their investments in their home and family have been completed, and their children are no longer dependent on them (Chon and Singh, 1995; United States Department of Commerce, 1998). In fact, the buying power of many Americans aged 55–64 exceeds what they had during middle age, and in 1995 placed them as the third highest group in median household income ($38,077).

In Australia, baby boomers are overrepresented in the highest household income quintile with 63% of married boomers being dual income couples, while nearly 80% of Australians aged 60 own their own home, and only 4.9% of them have dependent children living at home. Most have greater freedom from mortgage debt and a large accumulation of wealth from their savings (Muller, 1997; Golik, 1999). Cross-cultural studies in Japan by the Ministry of Labour have shown that white-collar workers reached their peak earnings between the ages of 50 and 54, while blue-collar workers reached their peak level a little earlier (Smith and Jenner, 1997).

Blazey (1992) reported that in the USA, citizens older than 50 represented only 25% of the population, yet controlled 75% of the nation's wealth of all stocks, bonds, bank accounts and real estate, indicating that the economic potential of this group to finance travel was huge. According to Norvill (1991), four out of every ten people aged 55 and older undertook a vacation away from home for 5 nights or longer in the past 3 years. In addition, when they travelled they outspent the typical American by approximately $100 per trip. Penalta and Uysal (1992) also noted that the financial health of a large number of older people made them an excellent market for luxury goods and services. As a result, resorts and hotels were specifically designing programmes and activities that targeted older people. Group travel and package tours were also popular with older travellers, as well as the provision for quality travel and travel-related products and services.

A similar trend was noted in Canada, where the 50 and older groups were now controlling 80% of the total personal wealth (Chisholm, 1989). Older adults are now the heaviest consumers of expensive lifestyle products, travel widely and are the leading purchasers of luxury condominiums and luxury cars such as Cadillac and recreational vehicles (RVs). According to Heather Davies, publisher of the Winnipeg weekly newspaper *Seniors Today*, 55% of those who are older than 50 travel two or more times a year, mainly by plane (Chisholm, 1989, p. 25). Toronto resident Patrick O'Connor, 53, travels frequently to Las Vegas and Atlantic City to gamble, and owns a Ford Mustang and a Dodge van. For O'Connor, spending money is part of enjoying life: 'When you reach your fifties, you realise that life is short' (Chisholm, 1989, p. 25).

As the wealth of developing countries increases, so does the potential for early retirement. In the USA, the Bureau of Labour Statistics has forecast that 85% of men and 91% of women aged 65 and older will be retired by 2005. In the age group of 55–64, 30% of men and 46% of women are retired. This is because, after the age of 55, people have fewer large bills to pay and are much less likely to be supporting children or paying off a mortgage. Many have a disposable income that is larger than at any time in their lives, while for others who may have been retrenched earlier than their retirement age, their income might have fallen to a level where it is now below the poverty line.

Ryan (1995) provides a warning that this great wealth of people who are older than 50 might quickly erode away through social change, and that some older people may not be able to travel as easily as first thought. He presents the case that divorce is becoming more commonplace in today's society, resulting in new partners producing children in second marriages while at the same time supporting children from a previous marriage. This, he argues, will result in a delay in the 'empty nest' stage and the need to support children in their educational studies for longer periods of time.

Furthermore, another restriction to travel may be the need to provide constant caregiving for family members who have become sick or disabled. The National Family Caregivers Association (2000) estimated that 54 million individuals provide some sort of caregiving in the USA. The average age of family caregivers is 46; however, 12% are older than 65 years, and about 70–80% are women. The daily demands of caring for a disabled family member take a toll on many family caregivers, and one of the most missed leisure experiences that has been reported was leisure travel. Ory *et al.* (1999) noted that the caregivers of older people with dementia were forced to give up their leisure, including vacations, because of their intensive caregiving responsibilities. Gladwell and Bedini (2004) interviewed 13 caregivers of whom 85% were female, using an 11-item semi-structured interview schedule designed by the researchers. The respondents indicated that since becoming caregivers their leisure was restricted to activities in, or near, their home such as reading, walking, church activities, swimming, gardening and spending time with their family and friends.

Travel was regarded as a significant leisure activity that was restricted because of their caregiving responsibilities. One respondent who cared for her mother with Alzheimer's disease noted: 'We liked to travel . . . now it is impossible' (Gladwell and Bedini, 2004, p. 689). Many of the respondents identified resentment and anger with the changes and loss of leisure travel. For example, one woman who cared for her mother with mobility problems stated: 'the fact that all of a sudden I'm tied to a person, or place, or a thing and I can't come and go as I want. And I think, well, I'm free enough or young enough and healthy enough and I should have some freedom there. So I'll have to admit, I get real angry about it sometimes' (Gladwell and Bedini, 2004, pp. 689–690).

However, overall, the economic statistics suggest that there is a general trend towards more discretionary dollars being budgeted for travel purposes, and this type of leisure activity appears to have become more popular than ever before with older adults (Javalgi *et al.*, 1992).

Education

When baby boomers reach their later years, they will have attained significantly higher levels of formal education than their predecessors. In 1990, about 46% of Americans aged 65 and older had completed less than 4 years of high school, 33% had received a high school diploma and 13% had completed 4 years or more of college (United States Department of Commerce, 1998). In contrast, at present, more than half of all baby boomers have earned at least a high school diploma, and approximately 1:4 have completed 4 years of college (McNeil, 2001). Similarly, Australian baby boomers have more years of formal education than the average Australian, with 27.3% of baby boomers completing a university degree compared with 13% of Australian full-time workers aged 15 and older (Australian Bureau of Statistics, 1996).

Research indicates that people with higher education, income levels, life satisfaction scores and who spend more of their discretionary income on recreation and leisure prefer to travel to destinations that are further away from Canada or the USA (Zimmer *et al.*, 1995).

Discussion

Men and women follow different paths in the adaptation process associated with ageing. Generally, women are more successful in adapting than men because they generally maintain their social networks as well as their hobbies and home-based activities. Men, on the other hand, have difficulties adjusting, mainly because of their disengagement from paid work and their other public roles. Women generally outnumber men in the older age groups in the ratio of 2:1 in the 80 years and older cohort group. As a result, more women reach older adulthood and use leisure more effectively than men. This helps them to reduce their stress levels and to raise their morale during the occurrence of a stressful life event, such as the death of a spouse.

The number of women who prefer to travel overseas as they grow older has increased considerably in the past few years, especially in the 55–59 age group, and these women are more highly educated and have a higher income level than other younger women. In many cases, travel is seen as a transitory activity between paid work and retirement, and provides a psychological barrier from work and home life. When travelling, women prefer shorter than longer trips, are generally more sensitive and aware of safety issues than men and require greater opportunities to socialize and interact with other people. They also display stronger preferences for local cultural and heritage activities and festivals than men. However, in many cases, women are not as confident as men to travel alone, especially as they are more likely to be widowed or divorced and do not have a partner to travel with.

The amount of discretionary income that is left over is also an important factor in older people's ability to travel, but this does not seem to be a problem for baby boomers aged between 55 and 64. For example, in the USA, their buying power generally exceeds what they spend during middle age, and in Canada the older age groups control 80% of total personal wealth. In North America it has been estimated that more than 50% of people aged 50 and older travel two or more times a year, often by plane and are away from home for 5 nights or longer each year.

Education is also a significant factor in determining older people's propensity to travel, especially to destinations that are further away from their home country. Baby boomers are much more highly educated than their older counterparts. In both the USA and Australia, approximately 25% have completed a university or college degree compared with only 13% of the total population aged 15 and older.

Several researchers have issued a word of caution about overinflating the numbers of older people who will travel in the future. Because divorce is becoming increasingly more common in today's society, single-parent families and second marriages are likely to diminish family wealth and restrict leisure travel for older adults with younger children. Caregiving of family loved ones who have become sick or disabled is a further restriction on older people's travel plans, as they may be forced to provide long-term care for family members who have developed chronic health conditions.

Other Factors that Influence Older People's Travel and Leisure Behaviour

Heterogeneity

Several tourism researchers (Shoemaker, 1989; Zimmer *et al.*, 1995) have observed that as a group, the older travel market is extremely diverse and their activity choices include a wide variety of travel attitudes, leisure preferences and other post-retirement activities. Older people are not all the same, and their travel and leisure choices will continue to become more divergent and less accurately represented by the existing stereotypes. For example, Zimmer *et al.* (1995) found that the travel behaviour of seniors in Manitoba, Canada, was relatively heterogeneous, with a number of different destinations being popular. The researchers concluded that other factors such as income, education, rural residency, willingness to spend money on recreation, and health status were as significant as age in influencing older people's choice of destination.

Shoemaker (1989) also argued that the senior market is not one large homogeneous grouping of older people, but a number of separate submarkets each with their own specific needs. He attributed this to the fact that the cohort groups that were born around the same time generally shared common values, attitudes, beliefs and behaviour throughout their lives. These similarities provide the basis for each of these cohort groups to be targeted as a separate and increasingly profitable market segment (Schewe and Noble, 2000).

Seasonality

Seniors are generally not constrained by the school holidays and are not as interested in going to the beach for their summer vacation as are families with young children. Most people travel during the summer months, resulting in attractions being crowded and expensive as are airfares and package tours. The tourist industry is able to offer less expensive rates during the off-season so as to redistribute and balance tourist flows.

Because most seniors are retired and their children have grown up, senior travel is far more seasonal than for travellers as a whole, and as a result older adults travel outside the peak season and generally tend to stay longer than travellers in other age cohort groups. For example, Romsa and Blenman (1989) found that senior German tourists were more likely to take longer vacations for up to 5 months a year between May and September, rather than the traditional annual vacation time of 3 months from June to August. Overall, it was found that in no month of the year was the share of total senior international travel less than 5% or greater than 10%. In contrast, around 30% of total international travel from Europe was the same in August as it was in the beginning of the school holidays (Smith and Jenner, 1997).

Ethnicity

Heterogeneity among the older adult population is affected by factors such as ethnicity and gender: 'To be old and a member of an ethnic minority group, or to be an older woman is to experience environments substantially different from those of a white male. It also means a higher risk of being unhealthy, poor, and inadequately housed' (Hooyman and Kiyak, 1988, p. 474). These select subgroups continue to experience life conditions that lack the dignity and respect expected in other more advanced cultures.

You and O'Leary (2000) observed the heterogeneity of behaviour patterns, particularly in regard to cultural and ethnic factors and their variations in the older travel market. They conducted a meta-analysis research design to compare older Japanese travellers to the USA between 1986 and 1995. In both samples, seniors preferred that people whom they interacted with at their specific destinations spoke their language. In addition, the following leisure activities were consistently unpopular among the Japanese – visiting wild lands, horse riding, hunting and skiing – as these activities were quite unfamiliar to them.

Conclusion

There is general acceptance in the literature that the older travel market is extremely diverse and that their travel and leisure choices are not accurately represented by their existing stereotypes. Tourism researchers have shown that older people are not one large homogeneous group, but a number of different submarkets that should be marketed separately as each cohort group has its own specific needs. For example, older people are not forced to restrict their travel into holiday vacation periods. Because most have retired or their children have grown up, they can afford to travel outside peak times and generally stay longer than travellers in other age cohort groups. As a result, travel agencies are able to offer cheaper prices to older adults because of lower occupancy rates for flights and accommodation. An older person's ethnicity and country of birth also affect their ability to travel and experience enjoyable leisure activities, as the research indicates that there is a higher degree of poverty, inadequate accommodation, poor health and malnutrition in the developing world compared with the more industrially advanced Western societies.

References

Australian Bureau of Statistics (1996) *Australian Social Trends 1996* (Catalogue No. 4102). AGPS, Canberra, Australia.

Blaikie, A. (1999) *Ageing and Popular Culture.* Cambridge University Press, Cambridge, UK.

Blau, Z.S. (1973) *Old Age in a Changing Society.* New Viewpoints, New York.

Blazey, M.A. (1992) Travel and retirement status. *Annals of Travel Research* 19, 771–783.

Chisholm, P. (1989) Postponed pleasures: the over fifties are spending freely on fun, and now the marketplace is beginning to take notice. *Maclean's* 102(9 January), 24–25.

Chon, K. and Singh, A. (1995) Marketing resorts to 2000: review of trends in the USA. *Tourism Management* 16, 463–469.

Cleaver, M. and Muller, T.E. (2002) I want to pretend I'm eleven years younger: subjective age and seniors motives for vacation travel. *Social Indicators Research* 60, 217–241.

Cross, R. (1997) *Why Women Live Longer than Men.* Jossey-Bass, San Francisco, California.

Faranda, W.T. and Schmidt, S.L. (1999) Segmentation and the senior traveller: implications for today's and tomorrow's aging consumer. *Journal of Travel and Tourism Marketing* 8, 3–27.

Gladwell, N.J. and Bedini, L.A. (2004) In search of lost leisure: the impact of care giving on leisure travel. *Tourism Management* 25, 685–693.

Golik, B. (1999) *Not Just over the Hill, Just Enjoying the View: A Close-up Look at the Seniors Market for Tourism in Australia*. Department of Families, Youth and Community Care, Brisbane, Queensland.

Grant, B.C. (2002) Physical activity: not a popular leisure choice in later life. *Society and Leisure* 21, 777–798.

Hawes, D.K. (1988) Travel-related lifestyle profiles of older women. *Journal of Travel Research* 26(Fall), 22–32.

Hooyman, N.R. and Kiyak, H.A. (1988) *Social Gerontology – A Multidisciplinary Perspective*. Allyn & Bacon, Needham Heights, Massachusetts.

Horneman, L., Carter, R.W., Wei, S. and Ruys, H. (2002) Profiling the senior traveller: an Australian perspective. *Journal of Travel Research* 41, 23–37.

Javalgi, R.G., Thomas, E.G. and Rao, S.R. (1992) Consumer behavior in the US travel marketplace: an analysis of senior and non-senior travellers. *Journal of Travel Research* 31, 14–19.

Lawton, M.P., Moss, M. and Fulcomer, M. (1987) Objective and subjective uses of time by older people. *International Journal of Aging and Human Development* 24, 171–188.

Lehto, X.Y., O'Leary, J.T. and Lee, G. (2001) Mature international travellers: an examination of gender and benefits. *Journal of Hospitality and Leisure Marketing* 9, 53–72.

Markides, K.S. and Boldt, J.S. (1983) A structural modelling approach to the measurement and meaning of cognitive age. *Journal of Consumer Research* 19, 292–301.

McGehee, N.G., Loker-Murphy, L. and Uysal, M. (1996) The Australian international pleasure travel market: motivations from a gendered perspective. *The Journal of Tourism Studies* 7, 45–57.

McNeil, R.D. (2001) Bob Dylan and the baby boom generation: the times they are a changin' – again. *Activities, Adaptation and Aging* 25, 45–58.

Moschis, G.P. (1996) *Marketing to Older Consumers*. Quorum Books, Westport, Connecticut.

Moschis, G.P., Lee, E. and Mathur, A. (1997) Targeting the mature market: opportunities and challenges. *Journal of Consumer Marketing* 14, 282–293.

Muller, T. (1997) The benevolent society: value and lifestyle changes among middle-aged baby boomers. In: Kahle, L.R. and Chigouris, L. (eds) *Values, Lifestyles and Psychographics*. Lawrence Erlbaum Associates, Mahwah, New Jersey, pp. 299–316.

Muller, T.E. and O'Cass, A. (2001) Targeting the young at heart: seeing senior vacationers the way they see themselves. *Journal of Vacation Marketing* 7, 285–301.

National Family Caregivers Association (2000) *Caregiver Survey – 2000*. Kensington, Maryland.

Neugarten, B.L. (1968) The awareness of middle age. In: Neugarten, B. L. (ed.) *Middle Age and Ageing*. The University of Chicago Press, Chicago, Illinois, pp. 93–98.

Norvill, H. (1991) The multiple markets of maturing travellers. Paper presented at the conference: Reaching out to the senior market: a tourism and hospitality perspective. Niagara University, Niagara, New York.

Onyx, J. and Benton, P. (1995) Empowerment and aging: toward honoured places for crones and sages. In: Craig, G. and Mayo, M. (eds) *Community Empowerment: A Reader in Participation and Development*. Zed Books, London.

Ory, M.G., Hoffman, R.R., Yee, J.L., Tennstedt, S. and Shultz, R. (1999) Prevalence and impact of caregiving: a detailed comparison between dementia and non-dementia caregivers. *The Gerontologist* 39, 177–185.

Patterson, I.R. (1996) Participation in leisure activities by older adults after a stressful life event: the loss of a spouse. *International Journal of Aging and Human Development* 42, 123–142.

Patterson, I.R. and Carpenter, G. (1994) Participation in leisure activities after the death of a spouse. *Leisure Sciences* 16, 105–118.

Penalta, L.A. and Uysal, M. (1992) Aging and the future travel market. *Parks and Recreation* 27, 96–99.

Reece, W.S. (2004) Are senior leisure travellers different? *Journal of Travel Research* 43, 11–18.

Romsa, G. and Blenman, M. (1989) Vacation patterns of elderly Germans. *Annals of Tourism Research* 16, 178–188.

Rowe, J. and Kahn, R. (1998) *Successful Aging.* Pantheon Books, New York.

Ryan, C. (1995) Learning about tourists from conversations: the over-55s in Majorca. *Tourism Management* 16, 207–215.

Schewe, C.D. and Noble, S.M. (2000) Market segments by cohorts: the value and validity of cohorts in America and abroad. *Journal of Vacation Marketing* 16, 129–142.

Sherman, E. and Cooper, P. (1988) Life satisfaction: the missing focus of marketing to seniors. *Journal of Health Care Marketing* 8, 69–71.

Shoemaker, S. (1989) Segmentation of the senior pleasure travel market. *Journal of Travel Research* 20, 14–21.

Smith, C. and Jenner, P. (1997) The seniors travel market. *Travel and Tourism Analyst* 5, 43–62.

Square, S. (1994) The cultural values of literary tourism. *Annals of Tourism Research* 21, 103–120.

Statts, S. and Pierfelice, L. (2003) Travel: a long-range goal of retired women. *The Journal of Psychology* 137, 483–494.

United States Department of Commerce (1998) *Statistical Abstracts of United States – 1998.* Department of Commerce, Economics and Statistics Administration, Bureau of the Census, Washington, DC.

Watkins, J.F. (1994) Retirees as a new growth industry? Assessing the demographic and social impact. *Review of Business* 15, 9–14.

Wilkes, R.E. (1992) A structural modelling approach to the measurement and meaning of cognitive age. *Journal of Consumer Research* 19, 292–301.

Wylie, R.C. (1974) *The Self Concept.* University of Nebraska Press, Lincoln, Nebraska.

You, X. and O'Leary, J.T. (2000) Age and cohort effects: an examination of older Japanese travellers. In: Chon, K.S. Inagaki, T. and Ohashi, T. (eds) *Japanese Tourists: Socio-economic, Marketing and Psychological Analysis.* The Haworth Press, New York, pp. 21–42.

Zimmer, Z., Brayley, R.E. and Searle, M. (1995) Whether to go and where to go: identification of important influences on senior's decisions to travel. *Journal of Travel Research* 33, 3–10.

4 Contemporary Trends in International Tourism and Travel for Older Adults

---

> The aims of this chapter are to:
>
> - Examine the population growth of older people in selected countries throughout the world.
> - Explore the growth in domestic and international travel by older people.
> - Examine the tourism and leisure-related behaviour of older people in the following countries – USA, Canada, Australia, Europe, UK, Germany, Japan, Israel, Taiwan and Korea.

Introduction

There has been significant growth in the older adult travel and tourism market over the past few years and this rate is expected to grow even more significantly in the 21st century. Most countries are experiencing a significant shift towards a 'greying' population who are more likely to want to travel at much greater rates than ever before. The World Tourism Organization (2001) has estimated that by 2015, the number of international travellers will increase by more than 2 billion people. (In 1999, more than 593 million international travellers were aged 60 and older.) This will be especially true in countries such as the USA, Canada and Australia with their increasing 'baby boomer' cohort group.

The USA senior market is regarded as the fastest-growing segment of travel demand. People who are older than 55 represent 41% of the total population and account for 28% of all overseas trips. Canadians have a higher propensity to travel than Americans and spend twice as much per capita on foreign travel. It has been estimated that 25% of Canadian visitors are older than 55 years, of which 800,000 travelled overseas in 2000. In Japan, 12 million people are older than 65, and it has been estimated that 7.6% of Japanese who travelled overseas in 1990 were older than 60 years (Clench, 1993).

Senior Travel in the USA

Americans over the age of 65 are the fastest-growing segment of American society. In 1900, there were only 3 million people aged 65 and older in the USA; however, by 1950 this had risen to 9%. In 2000, approximately 13% or 32 million were 65 years and older and it has been forecast that by 2050 nearly 21% or 53 million people will be in this age group (Young and Brewer, 2001). This means that older people who are 65 years and older will outnumber teenagers by a 2:1 ratio (MacNeil, 1991; United States Department of Commerce, 1997). In other words, three-quarters of the people who are born in the USA today are expected to live to the age of 65, and half of them will live to the age of 80 (Moschis *et al.*, 1997).

The baby boomer population is also rapidly increasing. Currently, 21% of Americans are aged 55 and older; however, it has been estimated that within 20 years this percentage will increase to 30% (United States Census Bureau, 2000). Moschis *et al.* (1997) noted that approximately 55 million people who are 55 years and older in the USA own more than half of the nation's assets. They also concluded that the main reason the mature market was gaining attention was because of the increasing longevity of the US population. There is a growing realization that when the large 'baby boomer' segment enters the senior category, it will become the largest age segment within the American marketplace (Sellick, 2004).

In the USA, the senior market of the population is also making up a significant segment of the leisure travel and tourism industry (Zimmer *et al.*, 1995; Travel Industry Association of America, 2001). This is because senior travellers have more discretionary income and greater amounts of leisure time compared with younger people. It has been estimated that people who are older than 50 years possess half of the discretionary income in the USA (Lieux *et al.*, 1994), and that older travellers (older than 55 years) have spent about $60 billion out of the $293.7 billion dollar travel industry (Zbar, 1994). Furthermore, 76% of senior travellers take at least one pleasure trip per year, while 60% take two or three (Shoemaker, 1989). Seniors now take more holidays than any other age group and outspend younger people in their leisure activities (Brewer *et al.*, 1995). This suggests that the senior travel market is rapidly increasing because of older people's level of savings and investment income which enable them to have the freedom and the discretionary income to travel.

Recent travel data collected by Collia *et al.* (2003) have highlighted the travel patterns of older adults living in the USA as depicted in the 2001 National Household Travel Survey (NHTS). They used a national household survey of 60,000 respondents from which they selected approximately 9000 who were aged 65 and older as their sample. The data were collected by telephone interviews between March 2001 and May 2002. The researchers found that, overall, older adults took a lower percentage of trips in comparison with the rest of the population of the USA, with approximately 10% of all daily trips and 8% of all long-distance trips.

The family car remained the dominant mode of transportation for Americans, with 90% of older adults conducting their daily and long-distance travel by car. Participation rates of daily travel were 75% for older adults and 91% for younger adults, while participation in long-distance travel was 35% for older, and 40% for younger, adults. Long-distance trips were defined as consisting of 50 miles or longer that commenced from a person's home. The researchers found that 2.6 billion long-distance trips were completed in the USA in 2001, of which only about 8% were undertaken by older adults. Older men tended to take a higher percentage of long-distance trips than older women (53% vs. 47%).

A personal vehicle was by far the most popular mode of choice for long-distance travel by older adults (89.4%), while air travel was the second most used transportation mode (5.3%). Travel by bus was the third most popular transport mode making up 4.3% of all long-distance trips. While older men and women equally preferred trips by air, older women had a significantly higher preference for bus travel than older men and younger travellers. There was more than a twofold percentage increase in trips taken by bus between older women and older men, and a sixfold increase in trips taken by bus between older women and younger adults.

Two-thirds of the long-distance trips taken by older adults were taken primarily for pleasure purposes (66% vs. 49% for younger adults). Pleasure trips consisted mainly of vacations and sightseeing excursions, as well as trips for rest and relaxation, visiting friends and family, and outdoor recreation. More than 50% of long-distance travel was conducted within the state in which the person lived.

Discussion

Older adults who are 65 years and older are the fastest-growing segment of the US population. They generally possess a higher level of discretionary income than the average and as a result they travel extensively, with estimates of 76% of senior Americans taking at least one pleasure trip per year. Most rely very heavily on their personal vehicles for long-distance travel within the USA, with 89.4% using the family car, while only a small percentage utilized air (5.3%) and bus travel (4.3%). However, older Americans are less mobile in comparison with younger adults and tended to take fewer trips, travel shorter distances and have shorter travel times. Older men undertake a higher percentage of long-distance trips than older women, with older women preferring to use bus travel in comparison with older men and younger travellers. Two-thirds of older people (66%) preferred to take trips for pleasure and sightseeing purposes in comparison with younger adults (49%).

Senior Travel Within Canada

Tourism in Canada has grown rapidly since the mid-1980s and, as many of the baby boomer generation are approaching retirement, tourism is beginning to boom. The number of Canadians older than 65 years is expected to grow from 3.2 million to 8.7 million within the next four decades (Driedger, 1994). According to research conducted by the Canadian Tourism Commission (quoted in Driedger, 1994) worldwide tourist arrivals increased by 5.5% a year in the last decade, while revenue jumped by 12% annually. Canadians spent more money per capita on travel than Americans, with 1.6 million Canadians visiting the UK, France, Germany and Italy (Clench, 1993). In Canada itself, a relatively low dollar has kept many Canadians at home, and has been a key stimulant for tourism within Canada as well as encouraging greater numbers of foreign tourists to visit.

Pennington-Gray and Kerstetter (2001) examined changes in preferences for pleasure travel using two different age cohorts of older Canadian adults in 1983 and again in 1995. The two cohorts of older adults used in this study were those aged 55–64, and 65 and older. The data for this study were obtained from two large Canadian surveys that collected their data from phone interviews in 1983 and 1995. The authors found that preferences for travel changed over time. For example, a preference for nightlife and entertainment among the 65 and older age group was a low priority in 1993, but had increased over the 12-year period.

The study by Pennington-Gray and Kerstetter (2001) also found that older adults tended to perceive themselves as younger in age and outlook in 1995 than they did in 1983. As a result, older adults were still interested in seeking novel experiences, personal challenges and new adventures. Overall though, the most important leisure preferences for older adults were visiting national and provincial parks, staying in budget accommodation and shopping trips. The least important preferences for older adults were the attraction of a city's nightlife and entertainment, and going to theme and amusement parks. When segmenting the older market, they found that adults aged 55–64 preferred the following leisure activities – going to the beach for sunbathing and swimming, budget accommodation, shopping, nightlife and entertainment, and theme and amusement parks – than adults 65 years and older. One change that was noted was that the 1995 survey showed that going to the beach for sunbathing and swimming, and the attraction to nightlife and entertainment were more important for adults aged 65 and older than was previously indicated in the 1983 study.

Discussion

A Canadian study examined the differences between two cohort groups of older people aged 55–64, and older than 65, and found that there were significant differences in the leisure activities that were enjoyed during two different time periods 12 years apart. Canadians generally preferred to visit national and provincial parks, to shop and to stay in budget accommodation. The least important preferences for people were for nightlife and entertainment activities, and visiting theme and amusement parks. However, going to the beach and nightlife entertainment increased in popularity among people older than 65 in 1995 than in the previous study conducted in 1983. This may suggest that older people no longer regard themselves as being 'old' when they reach 65 years, and do not feel as constrained by society's negative stereotypes as they did previously. Age does not seem to be a barrier that restricts older people, and it is now more acceptable to seek out and enjoy exciting and novel leisure experiences.

Senior Domestic and Outbound Travel in Australia

In 2002, the number of people who were 65 years and older totalled approximately 2.5 million and comprised 12% of the Australian population. The Australian Bureau of Statistics (1999) projected that this figure will rise to almost one-quarter (24%) of the Australian population by 2051. A similar trend to the USA and Canada has been found with senior travellers making a significant contribution to the domestic tourism market in Australia as well. Approximately 16.7 million domestic overnight trips were undertaken by senior travellers (aged 55 and older) in 2002, and this accounted for 22% of all domestic overnight trips in Australia. This figure is expected to substantially increase as the baby boomer generation accelerates Australia's ageing population from around 2010 and beyond (Bureau of Tourism Research, 1999).

As noted in Table 4.1, senior overnight travellers spent a total of 91.5 million nights travelling in Australia, and this accounted for 31% of total nights spent by all domestic overnight visitors. This equated to an average of 5.5 nights, which was higher than the average length of stay of 3.5 nights

Table 4.1. Domestic overnight trips, visitor nights and expenditure in Australia, 2002. (From Hossain *et al.*, 2003.)

	Non-senior 15–54 years	Younger senior 55–64 years	Older senior 65+ years	Total 55–65+ years
Overnight trips (millions)	58.6	9.2	7.5	16.7
Visitor nights (million)	207.1	44.7	46.8	91.5
Average length of stay (nights)	3.5	4.9	6.2	5.5
Total expenditure ($ billion)	31.4	5.1	3.5	8.5
Average expenditure per trip ($)	536	551	458	509
Average expenditure per night ($)	152	113	74	93

spent by non-seniors. This finding was supported by other overseas studies that found that senior travellers stayed in one location longer than travellers in any other age cohort group (Shoemaker, 1989; Fleischer and Seiler, 2002).

Older people have the money to travel, and in 1994 it was estimated that Australia's 2.97 million older people spent $895 million annually on domestic travel, and this was expected to grow to $2.3 billion by 2051 (Australian Bureau of Statistics, 1996). Senior travellers who were aged between 55 and 64 spent more money on their trips than older, senior travellers who were aged 65 and older. Of the $8.5 billion expenditure by senior travellers on overnight trips in 2002, younger seniors spent $5.1 billion, which was much higher than the amount spent by older seniors ($3.4 billion). Younger senior travellers also spent more on average per trip ($551) and staying overnight ($113), while older senior travellers spent $458 per trip and $74 per night, respectively. This shows that in general older people have the time and money to spend on holiday travel, although the spending pattern of cohort groups reduces the older the age of the group. This was attributed to having more free time in retirement, and their priority of spending a larger proportion of their discretionary income on travel and leisure than any other types of activities (Horneman *et al.*, 2002).

The proportions of older males and females who were travelling were found to be similar; however, more males (53.4%) than females (46.6%) travelled overnight in the younger senior group (55–64 years). The reverse situation was found to be true for the older senior group (65 years and older), with females (54.2%) outnumbering males (45.8%) as overnight travellers. The majority of senior overnight travellers were couples (76%) and around 58% were retired on a pension, while only 5% were working on a full- or part-time basis. The main reasons for travelling were to have a holiday or to visit friends and relatives. Most senior travellers (46%) stayed with friends or relatives for an average of 5.4 nights. The second most popular form of accommodation was at a hotel, resort, motel or motor inn (27%) at which older travellers spent on average 3.6 nights. Only 9% of senior travellers stayed in caravan parks, commercial camping grounds or camped with an average length of stay of 8.5 nights.

In 2002, senior travellers made an estimated 663,000 outbound trips (22%). They spent around 15.8 million nights away from home with the average trip length of 25 nights, which is slightly longer than younger outbound travellers (22 nights). Senior outbound travellers spent just over $4.0 billion on overseas trips in 2000 with an average expenditure of nearly $6100 per trip. This was 21% higher than the average trip expenditure by younger outbound travellers. Therefore, the data show that senior outbound travellers tended to stay away from Australia longer (25 days compared with 22 days), and spent more on their trips ($6057 compared with $5024) than younger outbound travellers.

Horneman *et al.* (2002) studied senior travellers who were aged 60 and older and lived in Queensland. The researchers examined their travel preferences, demographic and psychographic characteristics, and travel motivations, and attempted to identify the types of services, products and facilities that they preferred. A sample of 724 senior cardholders was randomly selected from a database. More than half of the seniors who were surveyed were between 65 and 74 years, most were either married or widowed and had completed a high school education.

They found that out of 12 holiday attraction types that were investigated, seniors preferred visiting areas with a natural or rural setting that had a historical context rather than attractions with a more developed focus. Their most important motivations for travel included:

- travelling while their health was good (46%);
- spending time with family and friends (43%);
- visiting places they have always wanted to see (36%); and
- having a break from their normal routine (21%).

There was also a tendency for seniors to travel for personal satisfaction rather than to fulfil the expectations of others.

In this study, most of the seniors who were surveyed (80%) fell into three distinct market segments based on their preferred holiday type and were named the Conservatives, Pioneers and Aussies:

- Conservatives made up 45% of the total senior sample. They sought a reliable holiday package and were drawn to cities and urban-based attractions. They enjoyed family type fun and were happy to be involved in typical Aussie-type activities. Opportunities for shopping should be made available to them as well as tours of nearby attractions.
- Pioneers represented 25% of the market segment. They were younger and better-educated seniors, still active, and sought out adventure and new experiences, but with a level of assured safety and security

involved. They liked to be independent and preferred self-learning and exploration to guided activities. They were also attracted to rural and bush settings as well as historical and cultural perspectives.

- Aussies represented 15% of the senior demographic data, and valued family interaction and involvement in their holidays. Comfort, security and familiarity with a holiday destination was essential because Aussies had less income, and tended to make their own entertainment rather than want to be entertained.

This study found that there were three distinct market segments within the senior travel market that have different characteristics, needs and wants. Although they differed, one common theme emerged, that they wanted safety and security in their travel, and the assurance that they would be satisfied with their tourist experience. However, many seniors also wanted new and challenging soft adventure experiences, holidays in a natural and/or rural setting as well as opportunities to be with their family.

Discussion

In 2002, senior travellers accounted for approximately 22% of all domestic overnight trips within Australia, spending $895 million annually and being away from home for an average of 5.5 nights. The majority wanted to take a holiday or to visit friends and relatives. Only 9% of senior Australians preferred to stay in caravan parks or commercial camping grounds with an average length of stay of 8.5 nights. Seniors generally preferred to visit areas in a natural or rural setting that had some historical context. Above all, seniors wanted to feel secure when they travelled, to experience new and challenging activities and environments, as well as the opportunity to be with their family. Overall, senior outbound travellers spent just over $4 billion on overseas trips, with an average expenditure of nearly $6100 per trip. This was nearly 21% higher than for younger outbound travellers (average of $5024), and they stayed away from home longer – for 25 days compared with 22 days for younger outbound travellers.

Senior Travel in Europe

In 2000, the total population of Western Europe was a little over 300 million, with the number of people aged 55 and older significantly increasing to around 100 million (Viant, 1993). In northern Europe, the population growth of the 55 and older group is expected to reach 29% by 2010, while the population growth of the 65 and older age group is also expected to increase from 11.1% in the early 1960s to 16.2% in 2010 (International

Labour Organization, 1997). In Malta, for example, the propensity to travel for people aged between 55 and 59 increased from 1.91 in 1990 to 2.35 in 1995 and then to 3.00 in 2000.

However, overall, Europe's share of global tourism has steadily diminished over the years, which has lowered its balance of payments because of the growing propensity of Europeans to take their holidays outside their own country. On the other hand, there is a generally well-supported belief that Europe will become an attractive location for retired tourists in the future. This is because it has well-developed transport and accommodation facilities, and a well-organized and efficient travel industry (Viant, 1993).

In 1992, the ETDC conducted an ATI survey of eight different European countries that were heavily involved in senior travel: Austria, France, Germany, the Netherlands, Spain, Sweden, Switzerland and the UK. The report made the following points: seniors accounted for 1:5 domestic and international trips in Europe; travel propensity declined with increasing age; Germany and the UK had the largest senior domestic markets, while seniors in Scandinavia and Spain showed the highest propensity to travel; Germany and the UK were the largest senior international markets; the UK was the leading market for overseas travel; senior travel was significantly less concentrated in peak times; there was a higher proportion of senior trips that preferred all-inclusive tours (42%); and an even higher proportion of senior trips (64%) that emphasized the need for suitable accommodation.

This report was written in 1992, and forecast that future growth of domestic trips by European seniors would reach 255 million in 2000, which was an 80% increase on 1990. It also made the point that the travel industry lacked accurate information about seniors and on the whole did not appreciate the size and growth potential of this market, with several countries virtually ignoring the economic impact of senior travel. This has resulted in a disappointing performance by the European travel industry overall, which has lagged well behind North America in developing effective promotional policies for senior travel (Viant, 1993).

Discussion

In northern Europe, the number of older adults aged 65 and older is increasing and is expected to grow from 11.1% in the 1960s to around 16.2% in 2010. Europe's share of global tourism dollars has diminished over the years, which some sectors of the tourism industry have attributed to ignorance and a lack of information about the size and growth potential of the senior market. As a result, the promotional strategies that have been used to attract the senior market have lagged well behind the USA.

Germany and the UK were the largest senior domestic and international markets, while seniors in Scandinavia and Spain showed the greatest propensity to travel.

Senior Travel in the UK

The number and proportion of older people in the UK has also grown over the years. For example, it has been forecast that the proportion of those aged 50 and older will grow from 30% (20 million people) in 2001 to 37% (25 million) in 2011 compared with the total population of the UK (Office for National Statistics, 1999). The most rapid growth will be in the 55–59 age group, which is expected to increase from just below 3 million people in 1997 to just over 4 million in 2005, which is a growth rate of 31%. The growth in senior travel to the UK has grown steadily during the period from 1994 to 1996 for the 55–64 age group, with 1.6 million travelling in 1994, to 1.9 million in 1995 and to just over 2 million in 1996. Senior residents who travelled abroad had increased from 17.4% in 1994 to 17.9% in 1995 and 18.1% in 1996. The most popular destination for seniors was Europe, with the number of senior international overseas visits from the UK estimated at 4.25 million trips of which 1.22 million travelled to Spain alone (Viant, 1993).

You and O'Leary (1999) studied the diversity and heterogeneity of the UK outbound travellers market and segmented it based on push and pull travel factors. They used data from the UK Pleasure Travel Market Consumer Survey (1996) that included 1208 personal in-home interviews with long-haul travellers. They defined a long-haul trip as a trip of 4 nights or more by plane outside Europe and the Mediterranean. Of the 1208 respondents, the sample was delimited to 405, who were 50 years and older, and indicated that they had travelled in the last 3 years. The overall socio-demographic profile was as follows:

- The average age was 61 years.
- The majority had less than a university education (75.8%) and were mostly married (68.9%).
- The largest occupational category was retired or unemployed (39%).
- 78% had a monthly household income of around £400.
- 51.4% were male and 48.6% female.
- The average number of pleasure trips in the last 3 years was 6.4.
- The average number of pleasure trips by plane in the last 3 years was 4.2.
- The average number of pleasure trips to long-haul destinations in the last 3 years was 1.9.
- The average expenditure per person during the most recent trip was around £73 per day.

A cluster analysis was used to differentiate between the three distinct groupings among older travellers:

1. Passive visitors (19%): the most important push force was to visit
friends and relatives (76%), and being together with families (61.3%).
The most important destination attributes were good public transportation (32%), good standards of hygiene and cleanliness (37.3%), personal safety (46.7%) and opportunities to meet and socialize with people
(28%). They also appeared to have lower levels of involvement in leisure
participation, preferring to stay put once they arrived at their chosen
destination. However, they achieved moderate participation rates in
nature-based sightseeing such as visiting national parks (58.8%), driving
to scenic places (56.1%) and sightseeing in cities (50.7%). The average
expenditure per day per person was significantly lower than the other
two groups (mean = £50.67).

2. Enthusiastic go-getters (40%): this group was the most enthusiastic
about pleasure travel and the most active of all the groups. They participated in a wide range of activities with significantly higher overall activity participation rates than the other two groups. They had the highest
involvement rates in nature-based sightseeing (76.4%), driving to scenic
places (75.2%), observing wildlife and birdwatching (52.2%) and visiting mountainous areas (51.6%). They also liked to get to know local
people (78.3%), enjoy local festivals (37.0%) and visit historical places
(60.2%). This was the youngest of the three groups with an average age
of 60 and average expenditure per day of £74.9 per person.

3. Culture hounds (41%): they achieved the highest ratings for their
interest in arts and cultural activities (56%), and visiting historical or
archaeological places (41.1%). They regarded looking at outstanding
scenery and meeting local people as important, as well as enjoying visiting places of historical interests (60.9%), visiting museums and galleries
(58.6%), going to local cultural events and festivals (57.4%), getting
to know local people (59.8%) and attending local festivals and fairs
(44.1%). This group appeared to have a significantly higher formal educational level, with 35.5% reporting that they had at least some college
education.

The authors concluded that both push and pull forces played an important role in interpreting travel decision making and destination choices.
The three groups reported lowest participation rates in high-energy sports
such as alpine skiing, diving and surfing. Furthermore, all groups reported
higher participation rates in shopping, dining out in restaurants and sightseeing in the major cities. Socializing was also rated as very important across
all segments of the older market. Seniors were also more concerned about
safety than non-seniors, and would not visit places they considered volatile
or risky, especially if they have high crime rates or poor travel facilities and/
or infrastructure.

Suggestions were made about marketing strategies for each of the three groups. For passive visitors, there is a need to emphasize family ties as well as encouraging friendliness and socialization opportunities with local communities. For the go-getters, marketing needs to emphasize the variety of leisure activities that represent good value and that would appeal to this group at particular destinations. For the culture hounds, a marketing programme should focus on the various cultural aspects of the destination as well as information on good destination facilities.

Discussion

In the UK, the fastest population growth in the older adult population was in the 55–59 age group, with a growth rate of 31% between 1997 and 2005. As a result, the growth of senior travel within the UK has grown steadily from 1.6 million to just over 2 million in 1996. Seniors who travelled abroad have also increased from 17.4% in 1994 to 18.1% in 1996. The average number of pleasure trips by air travel in the last 3 years was 4.2 trips while to long-haul destinations was 1.9 trips. The highest participation in leisure activities was for shopping, dining in restaurants and sightseeing in cities. Socializing with other people was also rated as very important, as were concerns about safety and security while travelling.

Senior Travel in Germany

Germany is facing a massive increase in the number of elderly people in the near future. The German National Office of Statistics estimated that the number of people aged 60 and older would grow from 12 million in 1985 (21% of the population) to 16 million in 2030 (38% of the estimated population) (Lohmann and Merzbach, 1997). In 1999, people aged 50 and older made up more than 41% of all travellers (this represented an increase from 33% in 1972). However, in the age group of 60–84, growth is expected to be from 16.3 million to 19.1 million, an increase of 17%, with the biggest growth in the 65–69 age group. This suggests that the main growth potential from the German tourist market will come from the older age group rather than the baby boomer segment in the USA and Australia.

Romsa and Biennan (1989) studied the vacation patterns of elderly Germans. They surveyed over 3000 Germans who were 14 years and older and who had undertaken a vacation in 1979. They selected two older cohort groups (60–69 years, and 70 years and older) for comparison with younger age groups. They found that undertaking a vacation as a leisure or recreational experience declined with age. Over 30% of Germans who were 70 years and older had never taken a vacation compared with only 9% in the 30–39 age group. Furthermore, older travellers placed a greater priority on visiting friends or relatives, and on their health, than younger respondents. Their data also showed that 61% of older vacationers tended to prefer domestic vacations rather than international ones. The most popular choice of transportation for the 60–69 age group was evenly split between the car and the train; however, for travellers aged 70 and older, rail and bus travel was more important than the car. In addition, retirement also allowed older travellers more flexibility in regard to the length of their vacation and the time when it could be undertaken. Older people appeared to enjoy many of the same types of activities as the general population, except that they were more health conscious. However, transportation was a prime consideration, with bus or train connections considered as essential. Older adults further emphasized the importance of inexpensive short trips or mini-vacations that could be taken during the week rather than on weekends.

In a further survey, Lohmann and Danielsson (2001) used regression analysis (travel analysis) data to monitor the holiday travel behaviour, opinions and attitudes of older Germans. Data were based on face-to-face interviews with a representative sample of more than 7500 respondents. They found that seniors travelled more than they did in the 1970s and that the travel propensity of the older than 60 age group increased by 76%. With trip organization, 68% of Germans aged 70 and older organized their main holiday trip themselves. This was because many were experienced travellers who felt comfortable travelling extensively.

The authors concluded that older adults did not change their travel behaviour because they turned 65 or because they had retired. They described their actual travel behaviour in relation to their former travel behaviour and observed that it did not change much at all as they aged. They found that once people have passed the 50-year mark, this generation tended to maintain a consistent set of travel behaviours that were stable and predictable over time (Lohmann and Danielsson, 2001).

Discussion

The largest population increase in Germany will originate from those aged 60 and older, who have been estimated to increase from 33% in 2025 to nearly 40% in 2050. Domestic travel is more popular for older Germans, with travel propensity for people who were 60 years and older increasing by more than 76% than in the 1970s. The main choice of transport was evenly split between the automobile and the train; however, for people aged 70 and older, train and bus travel were equally seen as the most popular. Older people were found to be more experienced travellers who organized their main holiday trip themselves, suggesting that they maintain a consistent, stable and predictable set of travel behaviours after the age of 50.

Senior Travel in Israel

The population of Israel is also ageing, with the senior population older than 55 years expected to grow from 16.5% in 1999 to 22% in 2020. The 65 and older age group is also expected to rise from 9.8% to 13.2% over the same period (Israeli Central Bureau of Statistics, 1999).

To ascertain the determinants of vacation travel in Israel, Fleischer and Seiler (2002) used a random sample of 373 seniors who lived in Israel (240 people aged between 55 and 65, and 133 aged between 66 and 75). Respondents were asked about their vacation patterns and preferences in the preceding year, their present vacation behaviour in comparison with their past behaviour, and their socio-demographic and work status profiles using a simple utility maximizing consumer choice model.

Fleischer and Seiler (2002) found that older adults who had previously taken a vacation and had higher incomes took longer vacations than individuals with lower incomes. However, as individuals grew older, especially after they retired, the number of vacation days began to decrease, which was attributed to their deteriorating health. Differences were noted between younger and older senior travellers, with income found to be a significant predictor of vacation travel for the younger age group, while health and safety concerns were more significant for the older age group.

Another study by Cai *et al.* (2001) identified the characteristics and travel behaviour of older adults and compared them with a younger segment of inbound tourists who arrived in Israel in 1997. The total sample consisted of 12,790 respondents who were divided into two age groups: seniors and non-seniors. Approximately 25% of the tourists surveyed were 55 years and older, with the majority from Europe (61%) and the USA (32%). The main religious affiliations among seniors were Catholics (30%), Protestants (30%), Jews (27%) and non-affiliated (6%).

The main reason that these seniors gave for visiting Israel was to do with religion, as 35% of the senior market indicated that undertaking a pilgrimage was the main purpose for their trip. Sightseeing (19%) and visiting relatives (18%) were given as the next main reasons for travel, followed by holiday or leisure (15%). Significantly, larger proportions of seniors than younger tourists stated that pilgrimage, sightseeing/touring and/or visiting relatives was the main purpose of their visit. Around 48% of seniors reported that their current trip was their first visit to Israel compared with 56% of younger tourists. Seniors (37%) tended to rely more on travel agents and less on other information sources for trip planning. Only 5% of seniors used information sources from an electronic database compared with 12% of younger travellers. Most seniors travelled in pairs (50%), while 40% travelled alone and only 8% travelled in a group of three or more people. A senior tourist spent on average approximately 7% more money than tourists under 50 years during their visit to Israel ($1266 vs. $1179).

Discussion

Israel's population is ageing, with the older than 55 age group predicted to increase from 16.5% in 1999 to 22% in 2020. Income was found to be a significant predictor of vacation travel for older people, while safety and health was more significant for the older group. As a result, senior travellers are very important to the Israeli tourist industry. Seniors from USA and Europe are the main visitors to Israel and are more likely to be Catholic, Protestant or Jewish, and much more likely to be on a pilgrimage, sightseeing or visiting relatives than younger tourists. A large percentage of older tourists had been to Israel before, travelled with one companion, obtained information from a travel agency and purchased a travel package. Only a small percentage of seniors visiting Israel received information from an electronic database, suggesting that older people do not yet feel comfortable about making bookings for trips on the internet.

Senior Travel in Asia

Japan

Japan's population is rapidly ageing as a result of a shift from high to low birth and death rates. By 2025 the 50 years and older age group is expected to increase by nearly 15 million or 23% of the total population, especially for the 55–59 age group, which is expected to increase from 8.2 million to just over 10 million (United Nations, 2000). By 2050 it has been estimated that 1 in 3 Japanese people will be elderly citizens. At the same time, the younger age groups are shrinking with the 20–24 age group declining by 2.1 million in 2005 compared with 1997.

Nozawa (1992) noted that Japan was shifting to become an elderly society as the proportion of people aged 60 and older was gradually increasing. In particular, there has been a spectacular increase in the number of older Japanese tourists, with Japan ranking third in international tourism expenditures, which were $30,716 million in 1994 (World Tourism Organization, 2001), comprising 10.1% of the world's total (Japan Travel Bureau, 1995). Older Japanese have more discretionary income and leisure time, and spend approximately 30,000 yen (US$230) more than the average Japanese traveller on their trips, preferring to stay longer at a single destination than younger Japanese people. They are also more quality-conscious and concerned about the content and value of their tour than its actual price (Kurokawa, 1990).

In Japan, age affects travel in many ways. For example, a younger person is more inclined to travel abroad than an older person, who reaches an age where he or she is likely to be in less robust health. The lifestyle of elderly Japanese men typically centres on work, while younger Japanese men have a desire to achieve a better balance between work and free time. Thus, cohort membership influences the demand for international travel. Sakai *et al.* (2000) used regression analysis to conclude that age and cohort effects were significant determinants of international travel for both Japanese men and women. Japanese women, in particular, who have reached the age of 60 were more inclined to travel than women in their 20s. For both men and women, travel propensities after the age of 60 were higher than for any other age group; however, they actually travelled less for various reasons. These included concern about language barriers, distaste for foreign food, anxiety about their personal health and dislike for foreign travel (Japan Travel Bureau, 1995).

You and O'Leary (2000) conducted a longitudinal analysis for 10 years to compare two different age groups of Japanese travellers (55–64 years vs. 45–55 years) to ascertain if there were any changes in travel behaviour and vacation activity participation patterns. Two large data-sets of Japanese outbound travel data were collected in 1986 and 1995, and compared to observe any changing trends. The results found that seniors who were surveyed in 1995 were much more active and participated in a wider variety of activities than their 1986 counterparts. The 1995 group had higher participation levels in culture and heritage, more visiting friends and relatives, higher nature-based activity participation and were more interested in sightseeing around the coastal areas. They also preferred to stay at a specific destination longer (described as a 'hub and spoke' travel style) and to explore one area rather than rushing off to different places, as seniors did in 1986. Seniors in 1995 were found to be more sophisticated travellers and preferred less escorted and guided tours compared with their counterparts in 1986. They liked greater flexibility when travelling overseas, appreciated travelling as a lifestyle and felt that money spent on overseas travel was well spent, compared with the previous study.

The authors concluded that there was still a high demand for security and safety among older Japanese travellers when they travelled overseas. Cultural and heritage products had a strong appeal to older Japanese travellers, while shopping was still an inseparable part of the overseas travel package. Although escorted tours were still seen as important, increasing numbers of older travellers appreciated and demanded more flexibility while at their specific destinations.

Discussion

Japan is rapidly becoming an ageing society and by 2025 the number of people who are older than 50 is expected to increase by nearly 15 million or 23% of the total population. The older Japanese adult has more discretionary income and free time, spends more and stays away for longer periods of time than the younger Japanese person. Travel propensities for men and women older than 60 have increased in recent times; however, they still express concerns about language barriers, foreign food and their health. Seniors are now more active and participate in a much wider variety of activities, are more sophisticated travellers and prefer to be more independent and rely less on escorted and guided tours. Older Japanese tourists still place a high preference on safety and security, prefer to visit cultural and heritage sites and enjoy shopping as an important leisure activity.

Taiwan

Taiwan is considered an elderly society. The elderly population has been estimated to be 2.8 million people, or 12% who are older than 60. It has been projected that the elderly population will increase to 20% of the total population by 2033 (Ministry of Interior, 2001). Taiwanese senior citizens aged 60 and older accounted for 10.7% of the total number of outbound travellers, with the major destinations being other Asian countries (82%) and North America (11%) (Chinese Tourism Bureau, 2002).

Huang and Tsai (2003) studied senior travel behaviour in Taiwan. They surveyed a convenience sample of approximately 4000 respondents aged 55 and older in the cities of Taipei and Kaohsiung. They found that the senior travel market was a vital market for Taiwan because many Chinese senior citizens had the time to travel and were willing to spend an appreciable amount of their income for this purpose. The main motivations for those who travelled were rest and relaxation (35.6%), to meet and socialize with people and to spend time with their immediate family (20.1%). The all-inclusive package tour with a more elegant, less regimented, itinerary was the most popular type of package tour.

Package tours were found to be the most popular form of travel because of their convenience (60.9%) as well as providing security for tourists with possible language problems (18.3%). As a result, the travel agent business in Taiwan was a highly competitive field of employment, with approximately 2464 travel agencies in May 2002 serving more than 23 million people. These agents made air travel arrangements for 7.18 million outbound travellers in 2001.

In general, senior travellers from Taiwan preferred historical and beautiful sites, good restaurants and hotels as well as airline facilities with adequate travel safety and reasonable prices. The authors also found that Taiwanese senior travellers preferred to buy all-inclusive package tours from travel agents because they were convenient; however, at the same time they also demanded quality tour content and services.

Discussion

At present the older population (60 years and older) in Taiwan is 12%; however, it has been projected that this percentage will increase to 20% of the total population by 2033. Many senior citizens have the time to travel and want to spend an appreciable amount of their income for this purpose. Inclusive package tours purchased from travel agents are the most popular form of travel because of their convenience, security and as a means of overcoming language problems. Travel agents are very competitive, with approximately 2464 travel agencies in May 2002 serving more than 23 million people. Older Taiwanese travellers prefer to visit historical and beautiful sites, eat at good restaurants and hotels with reasonable prices and are very safety conscious.

Korea

South Koreans were not permitted to leave their country for outbound pleasure travel until 1983, when only nationals who were aged 50 and older were allowed to leave the country as tourists. In 1987, the age constraint was lowered to 30 years and in 1989 the age restriction was completely removed. As a result, outbound departures had increased to over 4 million a year by 1995.

Kim *et al.* (1996) studied the travel attitudes and motivations of Korean tourists about taking overseas trips. The data were collected through secondary analysis of the Pleasure Travel Market Survey that was conducted by Tourism Canada in 1991. This survey used personal, in-home interviews of 1200 Koreans who were aged 18 and older and who had taken an overseas vacation in the last 3 years, or intended to take a trip during the next 2 years.

The researchers compared two age groups, those between 18 and 34 years with those older than 35. *t*-tests were used to ascertain that the older group rated 'relationships' higher than the younger group. Chi-square analysis concluded that the older group was more likely to have a larger number of overseas travel experiences than the younger group. This study also found that Korean travellers were more likely to choose Oceania and Europe than the USA for overseas holiday trips, especially to achieve their main travel needs related to self-esteem requirements.

Discussion

It was not until 1989 that the government of South Korea allowed nationals to leave the country for the first time as tourists. Generally they prefer to travel to Oceania and European countries rather than the USA. Older Koreans place great emphasis on relationships and prefer to travel with their family to explore their particular cultural interests.

Conclusion

The senior market is set for a dynamic expansion. All countries that were studied in this chapter estimated that older adults were the fastest-growing segment of their tourist market. As the years pass by, many older people feel much younger in their 50s and 60s than their parents did, and as a result choose to be more healthy and active, to experience new and challenging cultural experiences in different overseas countries before they become too old and their health starts to decline. Today's seniors are also much better educated, healthier and have a higher disposable income than previous generations. Many older people are now waiting until they retire to undertake international trips. For example, although people aged 55 and older make up only one-fifth of the US population, they account for almost half of the long-haul trips. It has been estimated that the vast majority of senior American travellers took at least two trips outside the USA, and that almost one-quarter took four trips or more over a 3-year period. Australians, Germans and the British prefer to take more domestic trips than overseas ones, with Australians spending an estimated $10.8 billion on domestic trips in 2002. The Asian countries of Japan, Taiwan and Korea are also projecting older populations in the 21st century, resulting in increased numbers of older tourists who are becoming more experienced as they travel regularly. As a result, many Asian travellers are becoming more confident and independent although package tours are still popular. They want to be more active and healthy during their travels, preferring to shop, visit cultural and historical sites, eat out at restaurants as well as placing a high priority on travel safety and security.

References

Australian Bureau of Statistics (1996) *Australian Social Trends 1996* (Catalogue No. 4102). AGPS, Canberra, Australia.

Australian Bureau of Statistics (1999) *Older People: Australia – A Social Report* (Catalogue No. 4109.0). AGPS, Canberra, Australia.

Brewer, K.P., Poffley, J.K. and Pederson, E.B. (1995) Travel interests among special seniors: continuing care retirement community residents. *Journal of Travel and Tourism Marketing* 4, 93–98.

Bureau of Tourism Research (1999) Domestic tourism monitor. Bureau of Tourism Research, Canberra, Australia.

Cai, L.A., Schwartz, Z. and Cohen, E. (2001) Senior tourists in the holy land. *Journal of Teaching in Travel and Tourism* 1, 19–33.

Chinese Tourism Bureau (2002) Outbound departures of nationals of the Republic of China by age, 2001. Available at: http://www.totbroc.gov.tw/tourism report2001/chinese/sep 0403.htm

Clench, C. (1993) The European senior travel market: a golden opportunity for the travel and tourism industry. *World Travel and Tourism Review* 3, 135–138.

Collia, D.V., Sharp, J. and Giesbrecht, L. (2003) The 2001 national household travel survey: a look into the travel patterns of older Americans. *Journal of Safety Research* 34, 461–470.

Driedger, D. (1994) Amazing greys: old images of aging are changing in an era when seniors are living longer, healthier, wealthier and more independently than they ever have before. *Macleans* 107, January 10, 26–29.

Fleischer, A. and Seiler, E. (2002) Determinants of vacation travel among Israeli seniors: theory and evidence. *Applied Economics* 34, 431–440.

Horneman, L., Carter, R.W., Wei, S. and Ruys, H. (2002) Profiling the senior traveller: an Australian perspective. *Journal of Travel Research* 41, 23–37.

Hossain, A., Bailey, G. and Lubulwa, M. (2003) *Characteristics and Travel Patterns of Older Australians: Impact of Population Ageing on Tourism.* Bureau of Tourism Research, Canberra, Australia.

Huang, L. and Tsai, H.-T. (2003) The study of senior traveller behaviour in Taiwan. *Tourism Management* 24, 561–574.

International Labour Organization (1997) *Economically Active Population 1995–2010.* STAT working paper 96–5, Volume 5, International Labour Office Bureau of Statistics, Geneva.

Israeli Central Bureau of Statistics (1999) Israel in figures. Available at: http:www. cbs.gov.il/Israel_in_figures/population.html

Japan Travel Bureau (1995) *All about Japanese Overseas Travellers.* Japan Travel Bureau, Tokyo.

Kim, Y.J., Pearce, P.L., Morrison, A.L. and O'Leary, J.T. (1996) Mature versus youth travellers: the Korean market. *Asia-Pacific Journal of Tourism Research* 1, 102–112.

Kurokawa, M. (1990) Japanese full-moon travel market. *Weekly Travel Journal,* 30 July, 38.

Lieux, E.M., Weaver, P.A. and McCleary, P.A. (1994) Lodging preferences of the senior tourism market. *Annals of Tourism Research* 21, 712–728.

Lohmann, M. and Danielsson, J. (2001) Predicting travel patterns of the senior citizens: how the past may provide a key to the future. *Journal of Vacation Marketing* 7, 357–366.

Lohmann, M. and Merzbach, G. (1997) Senior citizen's tourism: a simple approach to determine their future travel behaviour. *The Tourist Review* 3, 4–12.

MacNeil, R.D. (1991) The recreation profession and the age revolution: times they are a changin'. *Illinois Parks and Recreation* 22, September/October, 22–24.

Ministry of Interior (2001) The statistical analysis on major indicators of the elderly. Available at: http://www.moi.gov.tw/W3/stat/topic/topic136.htm

Moschis, G.P., Lee, E. and Mathur, A. (1997) Targeting the mature market: opportunities and challenges. *Journal of Consumer Marketing* 14, 282–293.

Nozawa, H. (1992) A marketing analysis of Japanese outbound travel. *Tourism Management,* 226–234.

Office for National Statistics (1999) *Special Focus on Older People,* Summer, No. 100. The Stationery Office, London.

Pennington-Gray, L. and Kerstetter, D.L. (2001) Examining travel preferences of older Canadian adults over time. *Journal of Hospitality and Leisure Marketing* 8, 131–145.

Romsa, G. and Biennan, M. (1989) Vacation patterns of the elderly German. *Annals of Tourism Research* 16, 178–188.

Sakai, M., Brown, J. and Mak, J. (2000) Population aging and Japanese international travel in the 21st century. *Journal of Travel Research* 38, 212–220.

Sellick, M.C. (2004) Discovery, connection, nostalgia: key travel motives within the senior market. *Journal of Travel and Tourism Marketing* 17, 55–71.

Shoemaker, S. (1989) Segmentation of the senior pleasure travel market. *Journal of Travel Research* 27(3), 14–21.

Travel Industry Association of America (2001) *Newsline: February, 2001.* Travel Industry Association of America, Washington, DC.

United Nations, Division for Social Policy and Development, Department of Economic and Social Affairs (2000) The Sex and Age Distribution of the World Populations, 1998 revision. Available at: http://www.un.org/esa/population/publications/ageing/Graph.pdf

United States Census Bureau (2000) *Census 2000: Projections of the Total Resident Population by 5-year Age Groups.* US Census Bureau, Washington, DC.

United States Department of Commerce (1997) *How We're Changing: The State of the Nation – 1997.* US Department of Commerce, Bureau of the Census, Washington, DC.

Viant, A. (1993) Enticing the elderly to travel: an exercise in Euro-management. *Tourism Management* 14, 50–60.

World Tourism Organization (2001) *Tourism 2020 Vision: Global Forecasts and Profiles of Market Segments, 7.* World Tourism Organization, Madrid, Spain.

You, X. and O'Leary, J.T. (1999) Destination behaviour of older UK travellers. *Tourism Recreation Research* 24, 23–34.

You, X. and O'Leary, J.T. (2000) Age and cohort effects: an examination of older Japanese travellers. *Journal of Travel and Tourism Marketing* 9, 21–42.

Young, C.A. and Brewer, K.P. (2001) Marketing continuing care retirement communities: a model of resident's perceptions of quality. *Journal of Hospitality and Leisure Marketing* 9, 133–151.

Zbar, J.D. (1994) More than a cool bus ride needed to sway seniors. *Advertising Age,* June 27, 34, 37.

Zimmer, Z., Brayley, R.E. and Searle, M. (1995) Whether to go and where to go: identification of important influences on senior's decisions to travel. *Journal of Travel Research* 33(3), 3–10.

5 Information Sources on Tourism and Travel for Older People

The aims of this chapter are to:

- Discuss the main types of information sources that are used by older adults in selecting a tourist destination.
- Examine the influence of the mass media on trip decision making for older adults.
- Critique the lack of senior models in advertising campaigns for travel products that are aimed at the older market.
- Examine the changing role of travel agents in providing international travel for seniors.
- Explore the increased use of the internet by older adults for travel purposes.

Introduction

The tourism and leisure industry is increasingly targeting people aged 65 and older because many have greater amounts of free time and discretionary income to spend on travel, and as a result older adults have become a significant growth market. Although many baby boomers are approaching 65 years, many perceive themselves as increasingly self-confident and, as a result, feel younger in age and outlook, are more in control of their lives and

©I. Patterson 2006. *Growing Older: Tourism and Leisure Behaviour of Older Adults* (I. Patterson)

so they still want to travel (Peterson, 1998). They seek out new experiences and creative personal challenges in their travel and leisure experiences, and have become skilful and knowledgeable consumers who seek value for their money. This chapter discusses the types of information sources that older adults use when making decisions about tourist and travel destinations. Some of the important questions that will be asked in this chapter are: How do older people make decisions about where they want to go in their travels? What information sources do they use when making these decisions?

Information Sources and the Older Traveller

Mansfield (1992) classified information sources for travel into two main types:

- formal information sources such as travel agents, brochures, travelogues, guidebooks and maps; and
- informal information sources from friends and relatives.

One of the first studies that identified the main information sources that elderly travellers use when making vacation decisions was by Phillips and Sterntha (1977). They argued that older people tended to use a wide selection of the mass media to compensate for a reduction in their interpersonal contacts. They found that older consumers depended more on the mass media than younger consumers and on peak media sources (such as newspapers) more than the broadcast media (such as television).

However, a further study by Capella and Greco (1989) found conflicting results to the study by Phillips and Sterntha (1977). Capella and Greco administered a questionnaire to 94 respondents who were older than 60 in the central area of New York state. They found that family and friends played the most important role as an information source in helping to determine a vacation destination for the 60 years and older market. The print media was also found to be important, while the electronic media was found to be beneficial. As expected, past experience was also a very important determinant when making decisions about a likely travel destination (see Table 5.1).

Table 5.1 shows that family, neighbours, magazines and newspapers were the most important sources of information, while for three of these sources in particular (family, neighbours and newspapers) gender and social class also played a significant role. Upper-class males relied more on their family and personal sources, while females relied more on newspapers for information. Generally, lower-class people (particularly females) who were in poorer health relied more on the print media such as magazines and newspapers as well as their neighbours for information about vacation destinations (Capella and Greco, 1989).

Table 5.1. Perceived importance of pre-purchase information sources for elderly consumers. (From Capella and Greco, 1989, p. 150.)

Information source	Mean importance score[a]
Family	3.62
Past experience	3.55
Friends	2.77
Magazines	2.52
Newspapers	2.34
Television	2.21
Consumer publications	2.15
Direct mail	2.13
Point of purchase displays	1.89
Neighbours	1.79
Radio	1.63
Travel agents	1.51

[a]5 = extremely important; 1 = not important at all.

Kim *et al.* (1996) examined the potential relationships between travel motivations and information search behaviour. They posed the question: Were more active travellers likely to consult certain types of travel information sources and not others? They used a mailing list of people aged 55 and older in the USA, and out of 3000 questionnaires that were mailed, 914 usable questionnaires were returned(31% response rate). The researchers used linear structural equation modelling as the main method for data analysis. Three distinct information-seeking groups were confirmed and named:

• Knowledge-seeking travellers were the most active among groups that wanted to experience new things, visit museums and historical sites, seek intellectual enrichment and visit new places. These travellers were more likely to consult official information sources such as state tourist information offices, Chambers of Commerce/Convention and Visitor's Bureaux at a specific destination before they made their travel plans.

• Escape group of travellers sought warm-weather activities to escape the cold weather and everyday routine, and preferred rest and relaxation to other more active leisure activities. These travellers were less likely to search for travel information.

• Kinship-seeking travellers who travelled to spend time with friends and immediate family. These travellers were not interested in searching for travel information.

The print media was found to be the most significant information source used by the older market as a whole, suggesting that this source of information needed to be funded to a greater degree than other information sources.

Word-of-mouth Information Sources

Several researchers (Javalgi *et al.*, 1992; Fodness and Murray, 1997) found that personal experience and word-of-mouth recommendations were the two most powerful information sources that were used in making travel decisions for older travellers. Fall and Knutson (2001) surveyed 235 travellers who were 55 years and older and who travelled for pleasure within the state of Michigan, USA. They were asked to rate 19 different information sources in regard to how useful each was when making pleasure travel decisions (see Table 5.2).

Fall and Knutson (2001) found that two-thirds (66.2%) of their sample preferred to use travel information from word-of-mouth sources such as friends or relatives. Highway Welcome Centres (42.7%), Commerce/ Convention and Visitor's Bureaux (43.3%) and travel publications from the state (33.5%) also received higher ratings for providing specific travel information. This was attributed to older people's strong trust in government institutions to provide accurate and reliable travel information.

Table 5.2. Information sources useful for older travellers. (From Fall and Knutson, 2001, p. 105.)

	Means	Standard deviation	Useful (%)
Word of mouth (friend or relative)	3.73	1.11	66.2
Mass media (alpha = 0.88)			
Magazine feature article	3.02	1.05	31.3
Newspaper feature article	3.01	1.10	32.6
Television feature story	2.98	1.17	35.2
Television advertisement	2.59	1.08	18.1
Newspaper advertisement	2.45	0.97	12.9
Magazine advertisement	2.40	0.94	10.7
Radio advertisement	2.27	0.97	9.9
New media (alpha = 0.76)			
internet website	2.49	1.44	26.6
CD ROM	1.82	1.10	9.9
Tourism-specific media (alpha = 0.80)			
Highway Welcome Centre	3.34	1.16	42.7
Chamber of Commerce	3.24	1.25	43.3
State Travel Publication	2.94	1.25	33.5
Brochures/direct mail	2.89	1.31	34.2
Automobile Club	2.63	1.41	30.9
Travel channel	2.42	1.27	21.5
Travel agent	2.36	1.26	18.5
Trade show	2.10	1.14	12.0

n = 235.

Another important finding from this research was that feature stories in magazines (31.3%), newspapers (32.6%) and television (35.2%) were more useful in making travel decisions than paid advertisements. This was because older people preferred to read stories and view pictures in greater detail about specific destinations they were interested in. Paid advertisements were generally not found to be useful in making travel decisions; however, 18.1% did state that television advertisements were helpful, but only 9.9% felt the same about radio advertisements. The worth of newspaper advertisements (12.9%) and magazine advertisements (10.7%) was also quite low. Interestingly, 26.6% did state that websites were very useful in making travel decisions. When asked to name the single most important media source, the internet was mentioned as second only to word-of-mouth recommendations made by family and friends.

Discussion

The two most important sources that older adults use when making decisions about travel are word-of-mouth sources, particularly from relatives and friends, and from people's personal experiences. Although word-of-mouth sources are the most preferred, feature stories in magazines, newspapers and television documentaries are also popular. However, paid advertisements in the mass media are rated lower in importance in influencing older people's decisions about holiday destinations. Internet sites are becoming more popular as older people are developing more confidence in using computers. They provide more detailed information and cheaper online bookings, although there is still a great deal of distrust about using the internet for credit card bookings. As a result, many older adults still prefer to use travel agents as their main provider of travel information, bookings and financial exchanges.

Travel Agents as an Information Source

Travel agents serve both as information providers and as planning/booking providers for a large number of travellers particularly when planning international overseas travel (Oppermann, 1997). Travel agencies have emerged as one of the top three information sources used by tourists for overseas travel, and for travelling to destinations that people had not previously visited (Duke and Persia, 1993; Mihalik et al., 1995).

It was not until the 1980s that any serious research was conducted about how consumers perceived the role of the travel agent and the reasons why they chose a particular agency to make travel bookings. Bitner and Booms (1982) were the first to predict that the role of the travel agent needed to change in the future–from the traditional role of a clerk to a salesperson and, ultimately, to a travel counsellor. They suggested that if travel agents were to survive, they needed to adopt the following radical changes: the use of more aggressive marketing techniques to segment the market and to better communicate with their clients; to have a better command of product line and profitability analysis; to expand their use of highly sophisticated information systems and equipment; to gain a thorough knowledge of travel destinations and requirements of each of the market segments as well as an understanding of how to interact and successfully negotiate with their suppliers. Sheldon (1986) examined the role of the travel agent from an economic perspective, and reaffirmed that a travel agent's main function was to reduce information and transaction costs for consumers as well as promotional expenditure for suppliers. Sheldon found that basic package tours provided a bigger discount to the consumer (15%) than did all-inclusive tours (3%) in his study.

Kendall and Booms (1989) studied the way consumers use, choose and respond to communications from retail travel agencies. They administered a questionnaire to 660 respondents in the Seattle region using a random digit dialling technique, as well as conducting several focus group workshops to discuss issues associated with their views on travel agencies. The authors found that word-of-mouth communication was relied on quite heavily, and clearly some agencies had developed many loyal clients. The researchers found that consumers will sometimes call a travel agency that is listed in an advertisement to compare basic information and prices but will always use their regular agency for actual bookings and payments.

The researchers concluded that travel agents needed to be knowledgeable about the needs and expectations of their clients, especially in regard to the types of restaurants they preferred, local attractions or side trips, leisure activities to be undertaken, destinations, hotels and resorts as well as transportation. Finally, the authors found that consumers rated the importance of all types of information sources higher than their own physical comfort when visiting an agency. In regard to their physical needs, some clients were particularly attracted by the specific location of the retail operation and the pleasantness of the office decor, while others just preferred to use the telephone to deal with the agency. They concluded that travel agents needed to develop more sophisticated marketing techniques and have a thorough understanding of consumer needs to effectively compete in the current travel marketplace.

Richards (1995) was interested in researching whether travel agents were interested in providing customers with information by helping them to bridge the information gap. This was because consumers were now becoming more skilled in accessing specialized product knowledge through their own sources and, as a result, were increasingly more advanced than travel agents in their means of information retrieval. Oppermann (1997) focused on residents' perceptions of travel agency service attributes and compared them to travel agents' beliefs about what customers found to be important. He collected responses from 266 travel agents and 400 New Zealand residents and concluded that there was a wide gap between residents' perceptions and travel agents' beliefs. He argued that travel agents needed to be more aware about client needs in order to remain competitive and ensure long-term viability. Oppermann (1997) felt that travel agents needed to lift their performance because they were coming under increasing pressure from other competitors in the travel industry. For example, the increased availability of tourism information on the internet, coupled with direct booking and payment facilities, was now seen to be detrimental to travel agencies in general. As a result, Oppermann cited several authors who forecast the demise of travel agencies because of the increasing competition from the internet. Lewis *et al.* (1998), for example, expressed concern about the future of travel agents given the increasing trend towards information technology. This was because they noted that there had been a significant reduction in agency commissions paid by airlines to travel agencies, and the increasing use of the internet by consumers to obtain travel information and make direct airline reservations. Changing customer demands and travel patterns of seniors have resulted in increased expectations in terms of value and convenience, as well as the emergence of increasingly knowledgeable consumers who are becoming more proficient users of information technology.

As previously noted, the traditional centralized industry structure is currently under attack from travel providers who are directly accessing their customers. This has become increasingly evident in the airline industry where carriers such as Southwest Airlines in the USA sell most of the tickets without the use of travel agents. Even established airlines such as American and United are now using more direct channels such as line services, the internet and toll-free telephone numbers to reach their customers. Eliminating the human aspect minimizes costs for airlines and, as a result, they can offer discount fares that are exclusively available to online users as well as promoting the use of electronic ticketing (Lewis *et al.*, 1998).

However, although they are under threat, travel agents are still providing important services to travel consumers. They act as information brokers by passing on information from suppliers of travel products to consumers. They process transactions by printing tickets or forwarding money, and often act as advisers to travellers. Aspects such as trust and social contact are still important to some consumers, particularly when planning leisure travel, and face-to-face communication with an agent at a physical retail location is still seen as important for many travellers. In the future, because of the highly competitive nature of the travel industry and declining commissions paid by airlines, this will probably lead to the widespread consolidation of many travel agencies. The success of travel agents will depend entirely on their ability to 'capture the market's loyalty, ensure access to travel information while providing value-added services, and develop winning product strategies supported by information technology' (Lewis *et al.*, 1998, p. 25).

Discussion

In the past, travel agents have provided important services for older travellers, especially if they were travelling overseas. Many older adults still prefer word-of-mouth communications with their travel agent, many of whom have built up a loyal clientele over the years, and still rely on travel agents for information and advice. Several authors have challenged the traditional role of the travel agent, stating that it needed to change from that of a salesperson and clerical worker to a type of travel counsellor if they still wanted to remain competitive. This was because of the increasing threat from online bookings and internet services, especially in the airline and hospitality industries. A good travel agent needs to develop sophisticated marketing techniques and detailed information about travel destinations, as well as gaining a better understanding of the specific travel needs of different segments of the older adult market.

Advertising as an Information Source

Advertising agencies have come under constant criticism because of their underrepresentation of people 60 years and older in print advertisements and television commercials (Greco, 1989). They have justified their actions on the outdated belief that older people do not wish to be identified as a separate and definable market segment (French and Fox, 1985). There is a growing number of active and healthy seniors who identify themselves as being middle-aged rather than people who are 65 years and older. Muller and O'Cass (2001) used the term 'subjective age' to describe an aspect of the self-concept that emphasizes how one feels, irrespective of one's chronological age. They found that half the number of seniors in their study who were between 56 and 93 years ($n = 356$) felt up to 9 years younger than their actual age, while the other half felt younger by 10 years or more.

Greco (1989) researched the views of advertising practitioners about the use of older people (65 and older) as central figures in advertisements for selected products and services directed at an older audience. A self-administered questionnaire was mailed to 286 executives from 143 advertising agencies that included attitudinal and product market-related questions about the use of elderly people in advertising. Only 112 (40%) completed the questionnaire. The survey found that the only categories that were recommended for the use of an elderly central character to reach an older audience were for health products, financial services and insurance as well as travel and vacations. This was because one of the problems that advertising agencies face is that many of their products are also consumed by younger members of the population. They concluded that if target markets were found to be significantly different, directing a message through the use of older models would result in more positive reactions. For example,

younger audiences were seen to be sheltered from elderly orientated advertisements in magazines such as *Prime Time, Modern Maturity* and *50Plus*.

Slowly there are signs emerging that there is a growing acceptance of the
use of older models in the advertising industry. For example, the Ford Modelling Agency has created a 'Classic Women' department to meet the growing
demand that advertising agencies have for older models. Older models are
now being used in advertisements for Ponds cold cream, Clairol and Adorn
hairspray, resulting in these companies nearly doubling their business compared to the previous year. A host of new products for the older than 55 age
group are coming on to the market including skin treatment products from
Revlon, lip treatment from Elizabeth Arden as well as Clairol Silk and Silver
hair colour that are positioning themselves in the market for older women.
Both Amtrak and Alaska Division of Tourism have expanded their marketing to include the 55 years and older market by including both younger and
older travellers in their vacation advertisements. The media are also publish-
ing articles on ageing from a positive viewpoint, with an emphasis on healthy
eating, luxurious travel and retirement housing options (Fannin, 1985).

Discussion

Over the years, older adult models (older than 55) have been underrepresented in most print advertising and television commercials. This was
explained by the general belief that older people do not feel older, and
that their subjective age was lower than their chronological age. As a result,
the majority of older adults do not relate to older-age models. However,
recent research has indicated that older-age models should be used more in
advertisements for health, financial, insurance and travel services to attract
older markets. There are now signs that this is starting to occur with specific
products coming onto the market for the older than 55 age group, and
several advertising companies are now using more older models in their
tourism and travel advertisements.

Brochures as an Information Source

The travel industry is becoming increasingly aware of the emerging grey
market and many of the operators in the UK are offering specially designed
older packages such as 'Leisurely Days' from First Choice, 'Golden Years'
from Airtours and 'Golden Times' from Cosmos. However, there is some
research evidence (Pritchard and Morgan, 1996; Peterson, 1999; Dann,
2001) to suggest that market researchers do not really understand older
consumers. They perceive them as only being responsive to price induce-
ments and are too old to be persuaded to change their buying behaviour
by trying out new products or switching brands. On the other hand, many

people aged 60 and older feel that they are too young to go on a typical senior's package.

Many of the brochures promoted by tourism operators show very few images and models of tourists who are aged 45 and older. In others that specialize in older adults, they are often portrayed as passive, non-threatening members of the community who appear in the photograph's background so as to provide some 'local colour' (Pritchard and Morgan, 1996). A comparative study was conducted by Dann (2001) of brochures that were provided by six of the principal tourism operators in the UK (Saga's European and the Mediterranean, Thomson's Young at Heart, Cosmos's Golden Times, JMC's Golden Circle, Airtours' Golden Years and First Choice's Leisurely Days) to ascertain what was the main message being transmitted, especially for people aged 50 and older.

The brochures showed that leisure activities were largely depicted as controlled by company personnel. This suggested that there was little time to 'fraternize with the natives', with the majority of photos depicting older tourists in local settings. This indicated to Dann that tour operators did not know how to authentically represent this older segment of people who were narrowly portrayed as undertaking a very limited range of leisure activities. These brochures were dominated by activities that used stereotypical leisure activities that were seen as only being appropriate for older people such as ballroom dancing, bingo, card games and lawn bowls. For example, the brochure for First Choice's 'Leisurely Days' stated in the text that they offered card and board games, competitions and quizzes, parties, tea dances and sing-alongs – all being passive leisure activities and none being active or physically challenging. Their motto was 'You name it, we'll do our best to organise it', emphasizing the need for control and supervision by the tourism operator at all times (Pritchard and Morgan, 1996).

Furthermore, the brochures also portrayed older women participating in a narrow range of leisure activities that were even more limited than those for older men. With the exception of keep fit activities and dancing, very few women were portrayed in any active leisure pursuits. Dann (2001) also found that the brochures clearly excluded the depiction of people with disabilities, and of gays and minority groups. Of the 1487 pictures contained in the six catalogues, only one showed an elderly male tourist with a walking stick suggesting that all older guests must be fit enough to participate in physical activities organized for them. In the depiction of couples, the overwhelming majority were heterosexual couples, with 16 images portraying same-sex couples and only 1 of these 16 involving men, and all except 2 depicting young people. In regard to minority groups, there were only two cases where non-whites were featured, and both of them assumed servile roles. Dann (2001) concluded that 'the message is clearly that blacks do not belong to an elderly white clientele in a holiday setting' (p. 30).

Dann (2001) concluded from his assessment of the main tourist brochures that private sector operators tended to treat those older than

50 as indistinguishable from the remainder of the mass market to which they catered for. Most of the time, the elderly were depicted as an essentially conservative, white, heterosexual group featured in 'placeless tourist enclaves, out of contact with locals . . . and engaged in a series of activities organised for their own good' (p. 31). Older tourists were texturally and pictorially depicted as interacting among themselves, having to make do with supervised shopping and sightseeing excursions and pressured into participating in numerous overseen pursuits: 'If they desire escape and freedom, they are provided with regimentation' (p. 31). Therefore, Dann (2001) concluded that this growing segment of the population was being more and more controlled by the travel industry, which was simply exchanging one form of social incarceration for another.

Ylanne-McEwan (2000) also investigated how travel companies market their holidays for those older than 50 through holiday brochures in the UK. She collected copies of holiday brochures that targeted people older than 50 from travel agencies and carefully analysed them to identify common themes. Her overall impression was similar to Dann's – that these holiday brochures appeared to be targeting healthy and active travellers who sought the company of other people of a similar age, and who enjoyed group activities. These holidays are characterized as active, glamorous, adventurous and romantic, and they were seen as providing an escape from gloomy, mundane, everyday realities at home such as bill paying and the winter weather. Although images in these brochures identified fun-loving and fun-seeking active individuals, they also depicted a somewhat homogeneous group with similar interests that were dependent upon other holidaymakers and their resort hosts. For example, ballroom dancing and afternoon teas with free biscuits seemed to be the major attractions that were highlighted, with an emphasis placed on communalism and being part of a group.

Although images of older travellers suggested a positive and active identity, older people were subjected to discriminating treatment when they applied for holiday insurance as they generally had to pay higher premiums because insurance companies presumed that increased health problems would occur with advancing years. This reflected a fundamental problem for the tourist industry because of its attempt to promote a 'positive ageing' image while at the same time denying the realities of ill health that may accompany old age (Ylanne-McEwan, 2000).

Discussion

Brochures that target older people indicate that there are very few elderly people who are actually shown in the holiday photos, and that company personnel who organize activities for them tend to rigidly control and enforce a narrow range of mainly passive leisure activities upon them, such as shopping, sightseeing and communal activities like dancing. Older people who use holiday brochures in the UK were found through content analysis to be indistinguishable from other age groups, and were portrayed as mainly white, heterosexuals, interacting only among themselves and generally participating in a limited number of leisure activities that were organized for them. Suggestions for change included the need for the inclusion of more senior models in brochures, and the depiction of older people in positive rather than negative ways.

Magazines as an Information Source

A growing volume of research has investigated the effectiveness of various marketing approaches in magazines that aim to attract seniors to travel (Mathur *et al.*, 1998). This was explored through the use of content analysis on magazine advertisements, especially in regard to the marketing of travel destinations. Peterson (1998) used this type of analysis when comparing models who were 65 years and older with models who were 45 years and younger in magazine advertisements that were sponsored by foreign tourism marketeers. Peterson hypothesized that older consumers will be depicted less frequently, and betrayed as negative, weak, helpless, confused or uninformed in comparison to magazine advertisements showing younger consumers. He conducted a content analysis of 32 international tourism magazines between 1992 and 1996. A total of 1194 foreign tourism advertisements were identified and categorized into three age groups: less than 45 years, between 45 and 64 years, 65 years and older. The advertisements were also categorized as favourable or unfavourable in relation to the display of physical or mental competence/incompetence in these roles (see Table 5.3).

Table 5.3 shows that there were fewer older models in the 65 years and older group than in the other two age groupings, and it was noticeable that the older age group was portrayed more unfavourably than the younger age groups. This study found strong evidence to conclude that seniors were less frequently and less favourably mentioned, even for offerings that appeared to be focused on this particular age group. In other words, younger models were judged more positively than the older ones, which was significantly

Table 5.3. Frequencies of models by age group, portrayed in a favourable or unfavourable manner. (From Peterson, 1998, p. 11)

Age grouping	Favourable (%)	Unfavourable (%)	Total (%)
Less than 45	93 (87.7)[a]	13 (12.3)	106 (100)
45–64	45 (76.3)[a]	14 (23.7)	59 (100)
65 and older	12 (60)	8 (40)	20 (100)
Total	150 (81.1)	35 (18.9)	185 (100)

[a]Significant at the 0.05 level.

different at the 0.05 level. In addition, the proportion of favourable models for the 65 years and older segment was smaller than the proportions for the other two segments. This confirmed that tourism marketeers have neglected seniors in their advertisements and, if depicted, they were portrayed in an unfavourable manner. This unfavourable image of seniors was seen by Peterson (1998) as an unproductive strategy in attracting the older and more affluent sector of the market. This tended to reinforce the negative image of older people rather than depicting them in a more positive light.

Discussion

Peterson (1998) conducted content analysis to test the effectiveness of magazine advertisements in attracting seniors to travel. He compared advertisements using older and younger models, and found that advertisements used older models less frequently and less favourably. He concluded that this was unproductive as the older market was an expanding one, and the use of unfavourable images of older people only supported the outdated use of negative stereotypes.

Television

Peterson conducted further research on the effect of television commercials on senior travel. In 1999 he hypothesized that most television commercials pitched at seniors tended to show younger models, even for products and services that mainly appealed to older consumers. This approach was justified by marketeers who believed that senior models were inappropriate for their advertisements, and if older models were to be used this was likely to result in diminished demand for the firm's products within the senior market. On the other hand, other researchers have concluded that depicting older people in a positive way can be an effective tactic for penetrating this segment and gaining a larger market share (Greco, 1989; Millman and Erffmeyer, 1989).

A further study by Peterson and McQuitty (2001) used content analysis of hotel and motel commercials shown on three major American television networks, one local television station and five cable channels in 1999. They confirmed similar results to their previous findings, that advertisements portrayed older people less frequently and less favourably than younger people. Peterson and McQuitty (2001) concluded that because of this finding, the industry was damaging customer relation programmes and their financial position by underutilizing seniors and portraying them in a negative image. They recommended that the hotel and motel industry needed to portray seniors as significant people who were capable, knowledgeable and motivated (p. 48).

Peterson and Sautter (2003) further examined television commercials to determine the implications of congenial vs instrumental behaviour in the scripting of commercials that targeted older markets. Congenial behaviour was seen as worthwhile in itself, an end rather than a means (i.e. a leisure activity). On the other hand, instrumental behaviour was defined as the means to an end, and was aimed at getting things done (i.e. the act of purchasing consumer goods). This is because many people judge others by the degree to which they engage in instrumental or productive activity, such as work. They hypothesized that television commercials that portray seniors as primarily engaging in instrumental behaviour will enhance their image, whereas if congenial portrayals of seniors tend to predominate, the effect will result in the lowering of the senior's self-image.

This study utilized a content analysis method that examined a number of television commercials from the three dominant television networks in the USA, one local television station and seven cable companies in 1998. A total of 1276 commercials were identified in which the primary models were assigned to one of three age groups: less than 45 years, 45–64 years, 65 years and older. A panel of analysts indicated that the primary models were engaging in either congenial or instrumental behaviour (see Table 5.4).

The results confirmed the hypothesis that seniors were more frequently portrayed in congenial behaviour than were younger people. Furthermore, this research also found that instrumental behaviour betrayal was more likely to be perceived as favourable in comparison with congenial behaviour, which was depicted as less favourable. The researchers concluded that the sponsors of television commercials may be forfeiting a market share of the older market because they were depicting older people in negative roles that were perceived as largely congenial and less favourable.

Discussion

Peterson and his colleagues (1998, 2001, 2003) conducted several content analyses of magazine advertisements and television commercials on

Table 5.4. Portrayals of congenial and instrumental behaviour by age group. (From Peterson and Sautter, 2003, p. 113.)

Age grouping	Congenial number (%)	Instrumental number (%)	Total number (%)
Less than 45	114 (51.6)[a]	107 (48.4)	221 (46.3)[a]
45–64	113 (59.8)[a]	76 (40.2)	189 (39.6)[a]
65 and older	45 (67.2)[a]	22 (32.8)	67 (14.1)
Total	272 (57)	205 (43)	477 (100)

[a]Signifies a proportion less significantly larger than the next largest proportion according to a *t*-test at the 0.05 level of significance.

different travel destinations, and found that older models were portrayed less frequently and less favourably than younger models. This confirmed the generally held belief that tourism marketeers were ignoring senior models, while at the same time depicting them in an unfavourable and negative light. They strongly advocated that older people should be seen as capable, knowledgeable and motivated individuals rather than weak, helpless and confused. A further study examined the categories of congenial vs. instrumental behaviour as it related to the portrayal of older people in television advertisements and their effect on tourism services. They found that senior models were seen more often in congenial behaviour that was seen as unfavourable, and negatively affected the self-image of older people. This supports the view that older people prefer more passive and sensory pleasures that were typical of traditional elderly travellers, rather than self-enrichment and learning new things, which are more typical of a modern baby boomer population.

The Growth of Computers and Internet Technology

An increasing number of older people are now using a computer. For example, about 30% of Americans aged 55 and older owned a computer in 1996 (Adler, 1996). Adler further stated that more than 60% of older adults who owned a computer loved to play online games. A number of older adults freely interact with others by exchanging emails and playing online games, and at the same time they share common interests and develop new relationships. Baby boomers who are now aged between 42 and 60 will rapidly increase the percentage of computer users in the future. This is because baby boomers have been characterized as being well educated and wealthy and, as a result, generally have favourable attitudes towards the use of computers.

A study by White *et al.* (1999) at Duke University concluded that teaching older adults to use computers to access the internet and email has resulted in a trend towards reduced loneliness. White *et al.* (1999) found that computers have a beneficial effect on older people's psychosocial well-being as well as expanding their social support network. White *et al.* also noted that involvement in a network of online support and chat groups helped older people to feel connected to society and was a strong predictor of lower levels of perceived life stress.

Age is an important demographic variable in terms of the likelihood of older adults using the internet for a browsing search for specific information, purchasing and perceptions of security. A study by the Georgia Tech Research Corporation (GTRC, 1998) found that mature individuals were less likely to use search engines to reach an internet site than through traditional means such as by reading magazines and newspapers. This study also found a significant relationship between a traveller's age and his or her likelihood of making purchases over the internet. As individuals age, they appear to be more suspicious of the quality of products available, and almost 50% of potential travellers older than 50 years cited the quality of the goods as a problem when making purchases over the internet. Mature individuals were also less likely to admit that they would use their credit cards over the internet (GTRC, 1998).

Morrell *et al.* (2000) conducted a study to document usage of the world-wide web among a sample of 381 (151 men and 230 women) in different age groups in south-eastern Michigan. The breakdown in age groups was 108 middle-aged (40–59), 181 young–old adults (60–74) and 92 old–older adults (75–92). Two versions of the web-use questionnaire were mailed to respondents: one directed towards current users of the web and the other directed to non-users. Only 9 of the 92 old–older adults indicated that they were current web users. Users were found to be younger, better educated, more likely to own a computer, have a higher household income and to live with someone who was a non-user. The authors concluded that age was a good predictor of web use, and the reason that the old–older age group did not use the web was because of a lack of computer access and knowledge about using the web.

Several organizations have recognized the need to provide older people with greater knowledge about using a computer and the web. As a result of this demand, SeniorNet was formed to provide education for older adults so as to enable them to gain greater access to computer tech-nology (Grodsky and Gilbert, 1998). SeniorNet began in 1986 as a research study that was aimed at encouraging seniors to use a computer. The study found that under the right conditions, older adults adapted well to using digital technology. As a result, SeniorNet soon established an infrastructure of learning centres specifically designed for older adults that has grown into a national network of 128 learning centres covering 35 states in the USA. Adults who are 50 years and older enrol in inexpensive 8-week classes ranging from an introduction to computers to creating your own web page. These classes are peer-taught by more than 1800 older adult volunteers who have taught more than 120,000 older adults over the years to use computers and the internet.

The mission of SeniorNet is centred on inclusion and independence, and classes are places in which comfort and community are stressed and older students are encouraged to ask questions and work at their own pace. By going online, older adults can also locate new friends and gain support in difficult times. For example, SeniorNet has a grief support discussion group where people can find comfort and support when necessary. Other intergenerational projects, such as 'Living Archives' launched in 1993, have enabled school students to interact with seniors and, at the same time, encouraged participation by older adults in this form of electronic classroom. The project focuses on specific topics such as the Second World War, the 1950s, civil rights, space travel and the women's movement. This has enabled a high school student in Alabama to communicate with a holocaust survivor in Arizona, or a senior citizen who marched with Dr Martin Luther King Jr. to share that experience with students across the country (Grodsky and Gilbert, 1998).

Older Adults and the Use of the Internet for Travel Purposes

The internet is a technological innovation that has a profound influence on all facets of people's lives. The internet is gaining rapidly on other forms of media such as television and newspapers in terms of time spent on these types of media (Heichler, 1997). The travel industry has consistently been identified as one of the main industries that is most likely to be affected by the growth of the internet. Machlis (1997) stated that travel was the single largest revenue generator among consumers on the internet, totalling US$800 million in 1997.

Weber and Roehl (1999) aimed to provide a profile of consumers who purchased travel via the internet. These researchers at GTRC conducted a web survey in 1997 to track the growth and changes of the web user base. The survey was conducted online with participants completing questionnaires that were posted on the web. Their study found that age and education were significant variables, and that people who were younger (25 years and younger) or older (older than 55 years) were less likely to purchase travel arrangements online than people in other age groups. In addition, respondents with 4-year college degrees or postgraduate qualifications were more likely to purchase travel online than people with lower educational levels. Travel purchasers were also more likely to have previously been online for 4 or more years. The most frequently cited reasons for not purchasing products online were credit card fraud, no assessment of product quality, privacy issues and preference to purchase locally. The researchers concluded that the major challenges facing online travel retailers were to address the issues of credit card security and data access. Consumers must feel confident that the information being provided was safe and could be used ethically and appropriately (Weber and Roehl, 1999).

A further study by Bonn *et al.* (2000) used a sample size of almost 14,000 travellers who were interviewed during a recent trip to Tampa, Florida. The researchers divided the sample population into three representative age groups: generation X'ers, baby boomers and mature travellers. A small number of travellers from England, Canada, Germany and Brazil (11.2%) completed the questionnaire, while 88.8% of the total sample were residents of the USA. The authors found that the US respondents, particularly generation X'ers and baby boomers, consistently stated that they were the most likely users of internet services in the travel area. Mature travellers were less likely to make use of the internet to book a trip as the trend line in their study indicated nearly flat growth until 1999. However, future growth in internet usage among mature travellers is likely to expand as a result of the continuing maturation of the baby boomer population, rather than any change in behaviour patterns of present-day mature travellers.

These latest figures are encouraging, with seniors who now use the internet increasing by 47% between 2000 and 2004. In a February 2004 survey, 22% of Americans aged 65 and older have access to the internet and this has increased from 15% in 2000. This translates to about 8 million Americans who are aged 65 and older who now use the internet. In contrast, 58% of Americans aged 50–64, 75% aged 30–49, and 77% aged 18–29 currently go online. In particular, 41% had made travel reservations online at the end of 2003. This is a 16% increase since 2000 and has a growth rate of 64% (AScribe Health News Services, 2004).

A report titled 'Older Americans and the internet' stated that despite the significant gains among seniors, 'most Americans aged 65 and older live lives far removed from the internet, know few people who use e-mail or surf the Web, and cannot imagine why they would spend money and time learning how to use the computer' (AScribe Health News Services, 2004, p. 2). However, this is quickly changing as a growing group of younger baby boomers in the 50–60 age group have become significantly more attached to the internet. Lee Rainie, author of this report concluded: 'internet users are gaining momentum. Internet users in their 50's who work, shop, and keep in touch with friends and family online will age into, and transform the wired senior population' (AScribe Health News Services, 2004, p. 2).

Discussion

In 1998, people who were older than 50 years and who were intent on travelling were more likely to use the traditional advertising media such as magazines and newspapers. This was because they lacked knowledge and access to computers, and were not sufficiently confident to use the web. However, there are many benefits of using the internet such as developing an increased social support network with improved contacts with friends, relatives and family members through email services. Surfing the web can increase older adults' knowledge and skills and help them to re-establish and maintain their sense of empowerment and confidence. Finally, cognitive improvement through the learning of new technologies has also been discovered, as research has found that older adults substantially increase their ability to feel mentally alert, challenged and useful (Lee *et al.*, 2003). Through the growth of organizations such as SeniorNet, older people are learning how to use computers and the internet in relaxed and comfortable settings close to their homes. This has encouraged wider usage such as through intergenerational projects in which schoolchildren can now instantaneously interact with seniors through the use of electronic classrooms.

Although younger consumers are more likely to make online bookings for travel purposes, older people are becoming increasingly more confident to use this form of information technology. Perceived problems still exist with aspects such as credit card security, quality control and privacy issues. However, the number of people aged 65 and older in the USA who are using the internet has increased from 15% in 2000 to 22% in 2004, an increase of 8 million Americans. This will further increase with the growth in the number of baby boomers who are proficient in their use of the internet, and who prefer to take advantage of its services in regard to online purchases. This has already encouraged the use of discount fares such as for international travel; however, it has placed greater pressure on the future role of the travel agent, and may eventually eliminate them in their role as broker in these travel transactions.

Conclusion

Over the last decade, the older market has emerged as an extremely important one because of its increased purchasing power for most consumer goods and services. This has resulted in increasing attention by the mass media and the advertising industry in particular. Evidence from research has shown that the lesser use of older models in advertising and television commercials has not been commensurate with the growing importance of this segment throughout the world. It is important that seniors be used and seen as positive role models in the media, and shown as productive, vital and energetic people.

For older people, the most important sources of information about where, how and when to visit are primarily through personal sources such as family and friends. Thus, word-of-mouth communication through satisfied customers seems to be the key element in influencing elderly people's decisions about their preferred holiday destinations. Magazines and newspapers play a secondary role in the information acquisition process. Over the last 5 years the use of the internet and of online booking services has become more popular, and has started to reduce the role of the travel agent as an adviser and booking agent. Older people are now overcoming their fear of failure by learning how to use computers and the internet. They no longer feel that they are too old to learn, and that the internet is difficult to master. Courses have been established through organizations such as SeniorNet that are now providing low-cost classes in local community settings. This has substantially increased the number of older people using internet services so as to instantaneously communicate with their family and friends. However, there still is growing resistance to booking travel services online because of credit card fraud, quality control of products and privacy issues.

References

Adler, J. (1996) Older adults and computers and the internet use. Available at: www. seniornet.org/research/survey2.html

AScribe Health News Services (2004) 22 percent of Americans aged 65 and older go online: many more are shopping, doing health research, making travel reservations. *Pew Internet and American Life Project* March 25, 1–2.

Bitner, M.J. and Booms, B.H. (1982) Trends in travel and tourism marketing: the changing structure of distribution channels. *Journal of Travel Research* 21, 39–44.

Bonn, M.A., Furr, H.L. and Hausman, A. (2000) Employing internet technology to investigate and purchase travel services: a comparison of X'ers, boomers and mature market segments. *Tourism Analysis* 5, 137–143.

Capella, L.M. and Greco, A.J. (1989) Information sources of elderly for vacation decisions. *Annals of Tourism Research* 14, 148–151.

Dann, G.M. (2001) Targeting seniors through the language of tourism. *Journal of Hospitality and Leisure Marketing* 8, 5–35.

Duke, C.R. and Persia, M.A. (1993) Effects of distribution channel level on tour purchasing attributes and information sources. *Journal of Travel and Tourism Marketing* 2, 37–56.

Fall, L.T. and Knutson, B.J. (2001) Personal values and media usefulness of mature travellers. *Journal of Hospitality and Leisure Marketing* 8, 97–111.

Fannin, R. (1985) The greening of the maturity market. *Marketing and Media Decisions* 20, 72–81.

Fodness, D. and Murray, B. (1997) Tourist information search. *Annals of Tourism Research* 24, 503–523.

French, W.A. and Fox, R. (1985) Segmenting the senior citizen market. *The Journal of Consumer Marketing* 2, 61–74.

Greco, A.J. (1989). Representation of the elderly in advertising: crisis or inconsequence? *The Journal of Consumer Marketing* 6, 37–44.

Grodsky, T. and Gilbert, G.C. (1998) Seniors travel the information superhighway. *Parks and Recreation* 33, 70–74.

GTRC (1998) *GVU's 10th WWW User Survey.* Georgia State University Press, Atlanta, Georgia.

Heichler, E. (1997) internet lacks content for women. *Computerworld* 31, 64.

Javalgi, R.G., Thomas, E.G. and Rao, S.R. (1992) Consumer behavior in the US travel marketplace: an analysis of senior and non-senior travellers. *Journal of Travel Research* 31, 14–19.

Kendall, K. and Booms, B. (1989) Consumer perceptions of travel agents: communications, images, needs, and expectations. *Journal of Travel Research* 33, 29–37.

Kim, Y., Weaver, P. and McCleary, K. (1996) A structural equation model: the relationship between travel motivation and information sources in the senior travel market. *Journal of Vacation Marketing* 3, 55–66.

Lee, B., Godbey, G. and Sawyer, S. (2003) The changing roles of computers and internet in the leisure lives of older adults. *Parks and Recreation* 38, 22–25.

Lewis, I., Semeijn, J. and Talalayevsky, A. (1998) The impact of information technology on travel agents. *Transportation Journal* 37, 20–25.

Machlis, S. (1997) Profits elude travel sites. *Computerworld* 32, 53–54.

Mansfield, Y. (1992) From motivation to actual travel. *Annals of Tourism Research* 19, 399–419.

Mathur, A., Sherman, E. and Schiffman, L.G. (1998) Opportunities for marketing travel services to new-age elderly. *Journal of Services Marketing* 12, 265–277.

Mihalik, B.J., Uysal, M. and Pan, M.-C. (1995) A comparison of information sources used by vacationing Germans and Japanese. *Hospitality Research Journal* 18/19, 39–46.

Millman, R.E. and Erffmeyer, R.C. (1989) Improving advertising aimed at seniors. *Journal of Advertising Research* 29, 31–36.

Morrell, R.W., Mayhorn, C.B. and Bennett, J. (2000) A survey of World Wide Web use in middle-aged and older adults. *Human Factors* 42, 175–184.

Muller, T.E. and O'Cass, A. (2001) Targeting the young at heart: seeing senior vacationers the way they see themselves. *Journal of Vacation Marketing* 7, 285–301.

Oppermann, M. (1997) Service attributes of travel agencies: a comparative perspective of users and providers. *Journal of Vacation Marketing* 4, 265–281.

Peterson, R.T. (1998) The depiction of seniors in international tourism magazine advertisements: a content analysis. *Journal of International Hospitality, Leisure and Tourism Management* 1, 3–17.

Peterson, R.T. (1999) Depiction of seniors in packaged food commercials: a content and analysis. *Journal of Food Products Marketing* 5, 26–47.

Peterson, R.T. and McQuitty, S. (2001) The depiction of seniors in hotel and motel television commercials. *Journal of Hospitality and Leisure Marketing* 8, 37–49.

Peterson, R.T. and Sautter, E. (2003) A review of the depiction of senior citizen instrumental and congenial behaviour in television commercials. *Journal of Hospitality and Leisure Marketing* 10, 101–120.

Phillips, L.W. and Sterntha, B. (1977) Age differences in information processing: a perspective on the aged consumer. *Journal of Marketing Research* 14, 444–457.

Pritchard, A. and Morgan, N. (1996) Selling the Celtic arc to the USA: a comparative analysis of the destination brochure images used in the marketing of Ireland, Scotland and Wales. *Journal of Vacation Marketing* 2, 346–365.

Richards, G. (1995) Retailing travel products: bridging the information gap. *Progress in Tourism and Hospitality Research* 1, 17–19.

Sheldon, P.J. (1986) The tour operator industry: an analysis. *Annals of Tourism Research* 13, 349–365.

Weber, K. and Roehl, W.S. (1999) Profiling people searching for and purchasing travel products on the World Wide Web. *Journal of Travel Research* 37, 291–298.

White, H., McConnell, E., Clipp, E. and Bynum, L. (1999) Surfing the net in later life: a review of the literature and pilot study of computer use and quality of life. *Journal of Applied Gerontology* 8, 358–378.

Ylanne-McEwan, V. (2000) Golden times for golden agers: selling holidays as lifestyle for the over 50s. *Journal of Communication* Summer, 83–99.

6 Modes of Tourism and Leisure Travel by Older Adults

The aims of this chapter are to:

- Describe the most popular modes of transport used by older adults for leisure travel.
- Discuss characteristics of the drive market as the most popular mode of leisure travel for older adults.
- Analyse the use of recreational vehicles to establish temporary communities.
- Investigate the growing trend of a segment of older people known as 'snowbirds' to move to warmer climates.
- Suggest strategies that the motorcoach industry might use to increase usage by older adults.
- Investigate the growth in luxury cruise shipping for the wealthy baby boomer and older adult market.

Introduction

The automobile is the most preferred mode of pleasure travel for older people in western societies (Javalgi *et al.*, 1992; Eby and Molnar, 2001). In the USA, the car is the most popular form of vacation travel, with 59% of older adults travelling in their family car when they take trips for pleasure. Airline travel runs a distant second to car trips, with 28% of older adults using plane travel,

Table 6.1. Mode of travel for senior (55–64 years) and non-senior pleasure travellers (under 55 years). (From Javalgi *et al.*, 1992, p. 17.)

	Travel characteristics		
	Non-senior group	Senior group	
Mode of travel	Under 55 (%)	55–64 years (%)	65+ years (%)
Automobile	73.7	65.4	58.3
Plane	16.9	20.7	22.4
Train	1.4	1.1	1.6
Bus	3.8	6.9	17.1
Truck/van/RV	9.0	10.6	9.3
Other	2.7	2.7	5.4

followed by travel in a rented car (8%), or motor home (2%), and finally bus and train services (1%) (see Table 6.1). However, older adults are more likely than average to travel by bus, with 6% of adults aged 65 and older taking a vacation trip on a tour bus, which makes them four times more likely than the average to do so (Dortch, 1995). Wei and Ruys (1998) found similar results for Australia, with the two most preferred modes of travel being the family car (57.3%) and airlines (37.4%) for people who are aged 60 and older.

Javalgi *et al.* (1992) concluded that the popularity of the automobile starts to decrease as the age of the respondents increases after the age of 65, which is related to a general decline in health as a person ages and may not have the stamina to drive long distances any more. An examination of the types of destinations associated with different modes of travel found that older adults mainly use the automobile to visit children, relatives and to attend entertainment and functions related to their work organizations (Teaff and Turpin, 1996). Overall, seniors as a group have a higher preference for public transport in comparison to the general population.

Although bus travel is not the most popular mode of transportation for taking pleasure trips, it increases in importance as a person ages. Javalgi *et al.* (1992) interpreted this increase in bus travel to an increased use of package tours by people aged 55 and older, because package tours generally incorporate travel by bus and/or plane. There may be a number of reasons for the increased use of public transport, such as the desire to let someone else do the driving, sight problems, frailty forcing people to substitute private cars for public transport, as well as for reasons of cost.

When considering international travel trips that were undertaken by seniors (Smith and Jenner, 1997), almost one-third were made by aeroplane (31%), with a slight preference for scheduled flights (17%) compared to charter flights (14%). The next most popular form of transport was by car (27%) while almost a quarter (24%) favoured the use of coaches and buses for international trips. This was because coach travel is generally seen as cheaper than air travel and is perceived to be a safer way of travelling, with formalities taken care of by a courier or guide. Cruise ships were also a popular senior pastime in the UK, with the average age of cruise passengers in 1996 being 56.3 years (Smith and Jenner, 1997).

The Drive Market and the Older Traveller

The drive market has been defined by Prideaux *et al.* (2001) as 'tourism that centres on travelling from an origin point to a destination by car that is either privately owned or rented, and engaging in tourism related activities during the journey' (p. 211). The drive market includes day-trippers, overnight travellers, intrastate and interstate travellers as well as international travellers. Drive tourists also include travellers visiting friends and relatives as well as those staying in private accommodation (Prideaux *et al.*, 2001).

Research has found that tourist travel by automobile is common for people of all ages, and for older people, approximately two-thirds have used the personal automobile as their main mode of transport for holidays (Javalgi *et al.*, 1992). Eby and Molnar (2001) investigated the main factors that are important in the choice of destination for overnight automobile trips to determine how these factors vary between different age groups. The authors used a previous survey entitled 'The Overnight Automobile Travel Survey' and mailed it to 15,000 randomly selected names from a national consumer database that included all states. A total of 1380 usable surveys were returned from all 50 states in the USA. Respondents provided ratings in reference to their most recent overnight automobile trip.

Eby and Molnar (2001) found that older people travel for different reasons than younger people. The main motivations for respondents 65 years and older was for social interaction (28.5%), and this was the only age group that reported it more frequently than for relaxation (17.3%) and recreation reasons (13.6%). Older travellers were also more likely than younger people to select education and health as other important motivations for travel. Furthermore, travel time was less important for the oldest age group who were less concerned about stops and delays along the travel route. This was because they were less concerned than younger people about their final destination, as most were retired and had more free time available. Older people also placed a higher importance on safety, particularly in regard to the route and the conditions of the road, than younger people. Eby and Molnar (2001) concluded that a possible marketing strategy would be to analyse all possible routes and suggest the safest ones for older drivers to take. The older age group also placed less importance on entertainment, sports and recreation for overall trip satisfaction than younger people.

Prideaux *et al.* (2001) investigated the senior drive market in Australia, defining seniors as people who were aged 60 and older. The Bureau of

Tourism Research (1999) reported that in Australia seniors rely heavily on the car for holiday travel but at a lower rate (57.3%) than the national average (78.9%). In Australia, where distance is a significant factor, the lower percentage use of cars by seniors may be the result of a shift in preference to air travel because of the physical difficulties and mental concentration that is needed to drive long distances which deteriorates as a person ages.

The authors mailed a questionnaire to a random sample of 1250 seniors who were holders of a Seniors Business Discount Card or a Seniors Card in Queensland, Australia. The response rate was 36.6% (457 respondents) while 20.4% valid responses (51 respondents) were received from service providers. The sample consisted of 55% females and 45% males. A total of 60.3% were living in a married or *de facto* relationship with a partner, and the majority of respondents (59.1%) relied on the government retirement pension for a substantial proportion of their income.

The most popular mode of transport for travel to a holiday destination was by private car (57.3%), followed by the aeroplane (37.4%). Surprisingly, service providers believed that tour coaches and long-distance trains were more heavily patronized by seniors; however, the reverse was found to be true. While holidaying at a specific destination, seniors relied on their car as the primary mode of transport (61.5%), followed by public transport (24.4%) and tour coaches (9.8%). The most popular time for travel was from mid-July to September (74.4%), which are the cooler months, and they avoid the heat of summer (December to February) in Australia.

The most important information sources that were used to assist in choosing travel destinations were word of mouth from family, friends and other seniors (60.4%), pamphlets and brochures (58.3%), travel agents (57.1%), travel brochures (56.4%) and the Seniors Card Business and Discount Directory (55.1%). Therefore, it was apparent from these findings that seniors used a number of information sources, with emphasis on the print media in preference to the electronic media.

Long-distance touring has been looked upon as one of the most popular activities undertaken by senior travellers. However, distance alone does not solely define automobile touring, and other aspects need to be considered such as the distance travelled, the type of accommodation used, and attitudes towards the driving experience. For senior travellers, the accommodation preference is often based on the type of vehicle used, such as the North American recreational vehicle (RV), the motor home, the Australian caravan, or simply carrying tents and camping equipment (Pearce, 1999).

For senior travellers, the time frame for automobile touring patterns often extends well beyond the 2- to 3-week vacation period and many may stay away for extended periods of time and pursue a flexible itinerary. Black and Rutledge (1995) reported that 42% of self-drive travellers left home for extended holidays of more than 2 weeks, while 20% toured for more than 35 days. Further data that were collected indicated that in many locations 50% of the visitors were over 60 years and 10% were over 65 years.

McCarthy (1996) surveyed caravan park users in Queensland, Australia, and found that these residents were generally aged 45 and older. He used a sample of 1359 people that was drawn from an 11,000 person Queensland Visitor Survey. He categorized the senior self-drive travellers into three main segments that closely resembled categories that were developed by Shoemaker (1989) in a compatible study in the USA. The groups were as follows:

1. A touring passing-through group (48.6%) travelled further than the other two groups, were more interested in 'going' than getting there and they enjoyed the constant movement and travel.
2. A cultural and nature-orientated activity group (16.9%) were mainly interested in rainforests, national parks and the Great Barrier Reef.
3. A low-impact recreational group (34.6%) were essentially a coastal Queensland fishing and boating group who had a limited touring pattern.

Pearce (1999) concluded that older long-distance tourists who towed caravans or used camping equipment took on additional responsibilities apart from driving and navigating, such as vehicle maintenance, setting up camp, budgeting and banking, food purchase and preparation, laundry and correspondence were required. McHugh and Mings (1992) found that there was a clear gender differentiation between men and women when touring for long distances, with males focused on the vehicle and equipment maintenance while females attended to food, laundry, banking and correspondence.

Discussion

The automobile is the most popular mode of pleasure travel for older people, with almost 60% using the family car, followed by airline travel (28%), rental car hire (8%), motor home and caravan (2%) while only 1% used bus and train services. The automobile provides a self-contained social environment that is used by older travellers who often travel long distances in a confined spaced over a long period of time to visit family and friends. Long-distance drive touring is popular in Australia because of the large distances between capital cities. Travel time is less important for older drivers who are less concerned about stops and delays along the travel route, and are more prepared to take side trips because most are retired and can take their time. Because of this, many older people stay away from their home for extended periods of up to 5 weeks and mainly travel in the off-season when it is cooler and cheaper for accommodation. However, it is the campground or caravan park itself that provides the potential for attracting high levels of social interaction and friendship with people of similar ages and interests.

Recreational Vehicles and Older Travellers

Over the last 20 years, tent camping has substantially declined and has been replaced by caravans and RVs. Recently, concerns about international air travel after the terrorist attacks of 11 September 2001 encouraged more people to buy RVs and travel around their own country. RVs and caravans provide more 'creature comforts' than basic survival living, which is a common feature of tent camping. About 70% of the RVs that are built are towable while the rest are motorized (self-propelled). Towable RVs include travel trailers, folding camping trailers and truck campers. Motorized RVs are motor homes, van campers (vans with sleeping, kitchen and toilet facilities), van conversions (multi-use vans modified in appearance for recreational use) and bus (motorcoach) conversions (Janiskee, 1990).

At present, RV sales are also booming in the USA, and are especially popular with the younger and more affluent baby boomers. Many modern RVs have been described as 'homes on wheels', with the larger ones having bath and kitchen facilities, CD players and tape decks, and some even a satellite dish for television. Recently, the industry has been winning over the sporting set with vehicles that include not only living quarters but also loading ramps and cargo space for jet skis, kayaks and dune buggies (Conover, 1998). Since 1980 RV ownership has increased by 50% among householders who are aged 55 and older, and it has been estimated that by 2010 the number of people who own RVs will have risen to nearly 8 million households (Blais, 2002). The number of RVs is expected to increase by as much as 20% between 2000 and 2010 compared with 10% for all other vacation travel modes, as the baby boomer generation enters the prime RV buying years (Dortch, 1995). It has been estimated that many baby boomers when they turn 50, which is the typical age of motor home buyers, will decide to buy an RV at the rate of 350,000 each month (Rawe, 2003). Tugend (2005) reported that the typical RV owner is 49 years old, married, with an annual income of approximately $56,000, according to a 2001 University of Michigan study commissioned by the Recreation Vehicle Industry Association. They are more likely to own their own homes and spend their disposable income on travelling within the continent of America, travelling for an average of 4500 miles and vacationing for 4–5 weeks annually.

Motorized RVs come in three main models:

- Class A version is the most popular. It looks like a bus, has wide views and can be as long as 30 ft and sleep up to six people. Among the possible luxuries are granite countertops, queen-size beds, plasma televisions and home theatres. Costs vary from $50,000 up to $1 million.
- Class B motor homes look more like a family van. They are cheaper than similar car models and sleep up to four people. They are generally priced in the $50,000 range.

- Class C models are generally shorter than those in Class A, but have more sleeping space as part hangs over the driver's area, accommodating up to eight people (Tugend, 2005).

Adler and Springen (1988) suggested that RV camping has provided the chance to balance two of America's most powerful cultural impulses: the urge for wanderlust and middle-class self-satisfaction.

Advantages of RV living

- RVs are relatively inexpensive, spacious and luxurious trailers that can be purchased relatively cheaply compared to a permanent home. Taxes are also generally lower in comparison to permanent residences. Heating expenses are often eliminated, while water, sewage and electricity costs are generally much cheaper.
- Social advantages also exist, as older travellers can choose locations based upon their personal preferences and develop a network of new friends and acquaintances.
- Older travellers openly admit to the freedom and fun this type of life-style as they feel they have the right to it because of their hard work and responsibility prior to retirement.
- The advantages of this type of lifestyle are redefined in favour of a mobile life, such as the separation from relatives and immediate family is often justified as desirable. Their former permanent homes are seen as continual time wasters and 'money pits' such as mowing lawns, shovelling driveways, painting and household repairs 'no longer hang heavily around their necks' (Jobes, 1984, p. 192).

RVs offer freedom, flexibility and control (Blais, 2002). Some owners stated that they would use their RV as an escape vehicle in case of terrorism, while others wanted a stress-free vacation away from the hassles and worries of group travel and to bring a little bit of home with them. RV travel is less structured than going to a motel. One RV owner, Urban Arbour, stated:

> You don't have to take a plane and make reservations. With the amenities right there, life is very convenient, we enjoy all the scenery, you are very free and can stop whenever you want … with packing its easy, you have everything – food, equipment such as jacks, spare gas cans, tools, radio equipment, CB radio, cell phones and necessary papers such as passports, ownership records, and insurance.

His wife Ginny also stated:

> You do your own cooking. You eat light, and get accustomed to it. We take certain basics and fill the freezer with meat and things like that. We stock

up on canned foods such as soup and spices and buy fresh vegetables as we go. It's pretty easy.

(Conover, 1998, p. 14)

Disadvantages of RV living

There are several disadvantages that need to be carefully weighed up before this type of lifestyle is seriously adopted:

- the problem of finding a good mechanic and spare parts in rural areas if the RV breaks down and needs major repairs;
- frustration of finding required facilities in unfamiliar areas, such as a post office, restaurants and mechanical repair shops;
- crowded and full RV parks, with very few close to major city centres;
- signs, poles and trees that project into roadways; and
- selecting an RV park from a directory and finding that it has closed down or been inappropriately located such as next to a railway line (Blais, 2002).

RVs and resort camping

Over the last 20 years, large-scale commercial campgrounds have played an increasingly important role in RV travel (Janiskee, 1990). Over this time, tent camping has substantially declined and most campers now use recreational vehicles that are seen as 'more amenities orientated'. About two-thirds of RV camping are in public campgrounds, of which it has been estimated that there are approximately 8500 nationwide (Blais, 2002). Many provide modern facilities and services that are very plush in comparison with the rustic standards of the past. Most RV campers want the campgrounds to have paved roads, safe drinking water, hot showers and flushing toilets, electrical hook ups, shade and picnic tables (McEwan and More, 1986).

In the early 1980s, approximately 85% of commercial grounds in the USA were suitable for RV use. The ground was level, free of obstructions and equipped with both water and electricity. Because most RV owners require extra comfort and convenience, a variety of higher-order amenities have been provided such as recreation centres, portable gas sales, swimming pools, playground equipment, boat rentals, barbecue facilities, coin-operated games and RV repair services (Janiskee, 1990). At present, more than three-quarters of RV owners who use campgrounds stay for fewer than 11 days each year; however, nearly one-quarter of campers stay for longer than 25 days, and tens of thousands of retirees use their RV for months at a time, and some all the year round (National Park Service, 1986).

With a growing number of RVs on the road, concern has been expressed that there are not enough campgrounds to cater for this increased usage. At certain times of the year, especially in summer, most campgrounds are full; however, at other times of the year they have around 50% occupancy. During heavy booking times, there is no other alternative than to do what is called 'boondocking', which refers to free or low-cost camping that has occurred in the past in such places as public streets and shopping centre parking areas. It has been reported that several stores such as Wal-Mart encourage RVs to park overnight in their parking lots. A spokesman for Wal-Mart stated:

> Generally we limit it to one night. We do it as a convenience for people who come in late at night, shop with us, and then leave in the morning. Generally RV'ers are good folks and good customers. Many follow routes where Wal-Mart's are handy because we have prescription drug stores, optical departments, and other items crucial to them. They are very courteous and often check in at the courtesy desk to let us know they are parked in the back of the lot.
>
> (Blais, 2002, p. 6)

Over the past few years there has been a growing trend towards campgrounds of greater size and complexity. Several of these offer over 3000 RV sites and provide settings for resort-style family camping, which is especially appealing to campers who place a high priority on comfort and socializing, and regard campgrounds as trip destinations rather than stops along the way. Many are designed to function as camping resorts, with many providing new amenities that are comparable to hotel resorts, having their own compact cluster of residences, distinctive neighbourhoods, a street system, shops, recreation and parking areas, police and fire protection, rubbish collection and church services. Because of their urban-like functions, these RV-orientated large campgrounds and parks have been termed 'campground towns' (Janiskee, 1990).

Categories of RV users

The status of RV owners is determined by how much time they spend in their 'rigs':

- People who consider their rigs as their permanent residence are termed *full-timers* residing in them for most of the year. Many full-timers are also described as 'snowbirds', which is a term applied to people who temporarily reside in warm and sunny climates during the winter, and more northern, cooler locations during the summer in the USA.
- People who spend at least 4 months in their RV each year are called *seasonal travellers*. They generally maintain permanent residences and

their primary interaction is around their home although they frequently become part of a mobile community once they are committed
to seasonal travel.

• People who use their rigs as recreational homes are called *vacation travellers*. These range from people who use their rigs for a few weekends a
year to people who travel for two or three extended vacations each year.

(Jobes, 1984, pp. 184–185)

Full-time Older Travellers and Temporary Communities

Full-timers fear having to give up their mobility and are clearly travellers
who are free to go anywhere and are seen as different from the majority of retirees who are settled in one location. Generally they are prepared
to forego the security of a permanent residence to become constantly drifting mobile travellers. Full-time travellers are generally respected by other
travellers for their commitment to this type of lifestyle, and their friends
are usually formed from their well-developed travel networks (Jobes, 1984).

Full-timers stay at a number of temporary communities throughout the
year in a variety of locations. This type of lifestyle is particularly attractive
to people who have recently retired, particularly men who are single and
have largely adopted this type of lifestyle because they generally enjoy the
responsibility of selecting this type of vehicle, and overseeing its general
operation and maintenance. Conversely, women are more likely to provide
assistance in organizing informal gatherings, shopping and food prepara-
tions (Jobes, 1984). One of these full-time travellers, Tom, describes his
experiences in his RV:

> Tom was an independent contractor who became tired of travelling on
> Omaha's icy streets in winter. Thus in the spring of 1995 we bought a
> used rig and went to South Texas. We visited relatives, played a little golf,
> toured, and got acquainted with the climate of the desert. At the end of
> the summer we sold our home, moved into the RV, and haven't looked
> back since. Since the fall of 1995 we have driven about 140,000 miles,
> we have been to all 48 states, six Canadian provinces, Mexico and Belize
> (without the motor home). We have parked on or near the properties of
> 19 relatives in 15 states and 23 friends in 15 states and provinces. Those
> trips ranged from one night to more than 90 nights. We also spent nights
> in what seems to be innumerable RV parks. As we move our home about
> the country we try to travel about 175 miles per day, we get a reserva-
> tion ahead only for crowded or busy areas, and when we park, we try to
> sample the local music, culture, and food.
>
> (Blais, 2002, p. 9)

Temporary communities are often communities of special interests, of
people who consciously come together because of their shared interests,

values and preferred behaviours. Travellers are free to choose when and where they will go and with whom, although to the outsider it may seem quite structured and predictable. The locations may change periodically, but the interaction networks tend to remain relatively stable. Much of their free time is spent playing cards, sharing meals and conversing, and people who are injured or become ill are taken in and supported until they recover. Mobile travellers develop their own unique language and refer to themselves as gypsies, vagabonds or nomads, and their language often includes technical jargon that is associated with their 'rigs'. This perceived freedom also reflects that the person is experiencing a successful retirement and that they are economically secure to live a life of leisure.

An example of a temporary community of RV users with a special interest are the 'Care-A-Vanners', which is a Christian organization titled 'Habitat for Humanity' that travels around the USA and volunteers to build homes for the poor. With as many as 6000 volunteers as members, up to 1400 people have been known to collaborate at certain times to build as many as 25 houses in a single week. Gurwitt (2003) described this as follows:

> In a warm afternoon in early November, eight Care-A-Vanners park their RV's in a small fenced in field of grass. Aside from a slab of concrete where they have set out folding chairs to serve as a patio and gathering space, the site is featureless. The eight RV's form a tiny settlement set back from the busy road out front. The RV's are all comfortable but unpretentious models, generally larger and longer than the basic table becomes-a-bed variety. . . . Liz and Bill from Florida took to the road, however as much as they liked being nomads, they developed a gnawing sense they wanted to do more than just travel; that's why are they decided to try out a Habitat build.
>
> (p. 29)

Liz also stated at the end of her experience:

> For the first time in my life, I'd surely understand what a team effort can do . . . we learned a lot, laughed a lot, and made the building look like a house . . . we have decided to sign up for two new builds and do a couple of two-week stints in Miami and Santa Fe. It was without a doubt our best social RV experience.
>
> (Gurwitt, 2003, p. 32)

Seasonal Older Travellers

In the USA and Canada, the term 'snowbird' has been used to describe the seasonal traveller. The name comes from the migration of large numbers of geese and ducks from the icy cold climate of northern North America to warmer locations in the south. Snowbird is the name of the song sung by Anne Murray that begins with the words: 'Spread your tiny wings and

fly away, and take the snow back with you, where it came from on that day'
(Coates *et al.*, 2002). These lyrics also apply to the large human migration
from Canada and northern USA, who escape from snow shovelling, sub-
zero temperatures and winter nights to enjoy the warmer climate of south-
ern USA and Mexico where they can play golf, swim and obtain a suntan.
They tend to go to familiar locations such as South Florida, the Rio Grande
Valley in Texas, Phoenix and Tucson in Arizona, the California desert, Baja
California and west central Mexico.

This annual movement of hundreds of thousands of northern residents into the southern districts of the USA and Mexico represents a highly
significant social phenomenon. The total number of snowbirds is sketchy;
however, Smith *et al.* (2000) quote figures from the Canadian Tourism
Research Institute that state that 45% of Canadians expected to take a winter
trip in the sun in 1999. This was an increase of almost 30% over the number
of those who intended to take a similar vacation in 1998, and the highest total
number in the past 6 years. Statistics Canada estimated that in 1999 over 14
million Canadians spent one or more nights in the USA. Out of this number,
641,000 stayed in the USA longer than 21 days. Of these, 79.6% went for pleasure, recreation or a holiday, while 12.9% went to visit friends and relatives.
The majority of snowbirds go to the key destination states of Arizona, California, Florida and Texas, and the largest number of them, between 300,000
and 375,000, go to Florida. The sharp decline in the Canadian dollar in the
1990s has resulted in shorter trips and alternative destinations such as Mexico that are offering lower overall costs. Between 1992 and 1999, the number
of Canadians who visited Mexico has risen by 58% (Coates *et al.*, 2002).

Smith *et al.* (2000) reported that one of the most popular destinations
in Mexico is the Mayan Riviera, a 130 km corridor of tropical vegetation
south of Cancun, with white beaches and upscale resorts, which is becoming
the fastest-growing vacation playground for Canadians. Florida is not prov-
ing as popular as it used to be, and in 1998 the number of Canadian visitors
fell to 1.72 million, a reduction of 18% from the previous year. This has
been attributed to the difference in dollar values between the two countries. Large numbers of snowbirds still flock to Florida but the state seems
to have lost its large international tourist market. Other states such as Las
Vegas and Texas are capitalizing on a more adventurous Canadian market.
Texas has developed an effective coupon programme called Buckaroo Bucks
($) to offer large discounts for Canadian families, resulting in 58% more
Canadians visiting Texas in the fourth quarter of 1998 compared with the
first quarter (Smith *et al.*, 2000).

McHugh and Mings (1992) undertook a detailed study of Canadian
snowbirds who had seasonally migrated to Phoenix in their RVs. Statistics
Canada published data on Canadian travel to the USA in 1988. Table 6.2
presents data on tourist travel to the Sunbelt states in 1988. Arizona had
189,900 person visits from Canada and ranked seventh among the eight
Sunbelt states with more than 100,000 person visits. During the winter of

Table 6.2. Travel by Canadians to the Sunbelt states of the USA, 1988. (From McHugh and Mings, 1992, p. 259.)

State	Total person visits	Nights per visit	October/ March	April/ September
			Time of trip (%)	
Florida	1,899,000	19.9	60.4	39.6
California	880,300	9.4	43.6	51.4
Nevada	550,800	4.5	61.5	38.4
Georgia	387,000	2.3	56.0	44.0
South Carolina	371,200	5.2	44.5	55.5
North Carolina	273,100	2.3	67.6	32.4
Arizona	189,900	16.1	67.6	32.4
Texas	166,800	9.7	52.2	47.8

1993–1994 these numbers had risen to an estimated 220,000 (Mings and McHugh, 1995). The mean length of visits to Arizona among Canadian visitors in 1988 was 16.1 days, which was much longer than for other Sunbelt states, with the exception of Florida for 19.9 days. In addition, Canadians who travelled to Arizona were more concentrated in the autumn and winter seasons than in any other Sunbelt state.

Phoenix represents one of the largest concentrations of RV resorts in the USA. In the winter of 1987 and 1988, McHugh and Mings (1992) administered a survey questionnaire in nine Phoenix RV resorts using a sample size of 1056 RV households (942 American and 114 Canadian). The authors found that seasonal migration of RVs was a lifestyle primarily for white, middle-income, retired and married couples. Three-quarters were between 60 and 74 years, with a small proportion who were under 60 years, while others were older than 75 years. The vast majority were married couples with both the respondent and spouse being retired. A small percentage of Canadians (10.6%) had children or other family members residing in Arizona, and a somewhat larger group (27%) had close friends who were Arizona residents. Most RV travellers know many people in the RV resort, with American respondents knowing an average of 75 people, while Canadians knew an average of 42 people.

These authors attributed this to RV resorts in Phoenix having a small town social atmosphere, creating many socializing opportunities among residents with an emphasis on group-orientated leisure activities (McHugh and Mings, 1992; Mings and McHugh, 1995). Less than 5% of Canadian RV travellers anticipated that they would want to make a permanent move to Phoenix, while more than 80% reported that this was very unlikely. Deterrents to permanent migration for Canadians included a general sense of national pride and allegiance to Canada; family, friends and economic ties in their home communities; climatic and environmental preferences; and difficulties associated with obtaining permanent resident visas in the USA (McHugh and Mings, 1992).

In a further study, Mings and McHugh (1995) investigated the nature of snowbird lifestyles while residing in Arizona during the winter months. They used a longitudinal research design, interviewing 12 couples from three large Phoenix-area RV resorts. All couples agreed to continue meeting regularly in the future to review changes to their lives over the previous year. The authors found that outdoor activities were popular with snowbirds such as desert sightseeing, walking, golfing and swimming – all these activities were virtually impossible during the winter in their home states. The RV lifestyle was seen to be the most distinctive in regard to the very large amount of time and attention given to a wide variety of leisure activities. Another advantage was the importance of social interaction among RV travellers. Most were outgoing, group-orientated people with a strong preference for leisure activities that allowed them to socialize. Card playing, dancing, bus tours, potluck dinners and shuffleboard were stated as their most popular activities. Another common trait of the RV lifestyle was the high levels of geographic mobility, such as their preference for local sightseeing and overnight excursions. For some people, the resort in Arizona was used as a home base for short trips to nearby attractions such as casinos in Nevada, the beaches of California and the border towns of Mexico.

Most winter residents were very involved in leisure activities for a large percentage of their waking hours and on most days. The resorts themselves organized and managed events such as pancake breakfasts, talent nights, dance and art classes, tennis, golf and pool. When they returned home, the range of leisure activities was much more limited and the pace of participation slowed down considerably. Furthermore, at home all their friends and neighbours were not retired, whereas in Phoenix most people were full-time pleasure seekers. As a result, snowbirds generally welcomed a lifestyle that included periods of high activity where they enjoyed easy access to leisure facilities and programming as well as the ready availability of leisure partners in the RV resort in Phoenix. On return to their home city in Canada, there was a period of relative calm and a slower-paced lifestyle with a reduction in the number of leisure activities that people engaged in.

In Australia, seasonal travellers are referred to as 'grey nomads' or 'grey voyagers', and are generally aged over 55, retired and want to travel around Australia in their own time and at their own pace. The Bureau of Tourism Research estimates that over 200,000 caravan trips were taken for more than a 6-week duration in a single year by Australian retirees (Carter, 2002). Because of this, the caravan industry is thriving as many older people are travelling around Australia. Its growth rate is around 15% a year, contributing about $AUS2 billion to the Australian economy every year. In 2002, the sale of caravans increased by 17%, with more than 80% of these sales attributed to the older age groups (Brannelly, 2003).

Mings (1997) travelled to Australia to investigate the grey nomad movement there and to see if there were any similarities or differences between snowbirds and grey nomad populations. He interviewed 306 couples in 41 caravan parks between Mossman and South Mission Beach, in Queensland, Australia. The profile of a grey nomad was:

- Age 62.5 years for women and 65.5 years for men.
- Only 3% resided permanently in the caravan park, with the majority from New South Wales, Victoria and South Australia.
- Mainly middle-class incomes, for males the most common occupation was tradesmen/technicians (45%) and for women it was home duties (33%).
- Positive reasons about the grey nomad lifestyle: 82% stated that weather was warm/dry, there was an appreciation for the outdoors such as the rainforests/beaches/the Reef, 14% were impressed by friendliness of people they had met.
- Negative reasons: 40% could not think of anything they disliked – some mentioned the insects (sandflies), humid weather, overcrowdedness and the Queensland traffic.
- Daily activities included walking, swimming, fishing, golf and lawn bowls.
- Sightseeing was mentioned by 95% of couples, while reading, socializing, relaxing and dining out were also popular leisure activities.

Mings concluded that there were major differences between American RV resorts and Australian caravan parks. There was appreciably less social interaction in Queensland caravan parks, with 76% stating that they did not know any other caravanners in the park. There were few group-orientated leisure activities such as dances, classes, dinners and sporting tournaments compared with American RV resorts. They stayed an average of 35 days in Queensland caravan parks compared with 4.4 months on average in Phoenix RV resorts. The return rate was 2.2 times compared with 5.9 visits in Phoenix.

Mings (1997) concluded that a true community of sunbirds in Queensland does not exist. This is because Australian grey nomads prefer to travel greater distances at a more leisurely pace, sometimes between 300 and 500 km per day rather than staying for long periods at one caravan park. In fact, 70% had travelled around Australia at least once previously. They like sightseeing along the way and are not in a rush to get to their particular destination. This is because they plan to be on the road for a considerable amount of time with a mean of 128 days (4 months), and are more mobile than North Americans. They have higher levels of local and regional mobility and an average of 323 km per week travelling around town, with shorter day trips also being popular. Walking was also a preferred physical activity with 54% indicating that they walked around the caravan park, to the beaches, and went bushwalking.

A more recent study by Onyx and Leonard (2005) looked at grey nomads and their main motivations to travel within Australia. The authors used an ethnographic methodology while they travelled around Australia in a motor home, over a 10-week period. In their travels, they asked respondents to fill in a brief questionnaire on their demographic information and this was followed up by in-depth interviews with couples, usually in a small group format. Overall, 418 older adults (215 males and 203 females) participated in their study of which 93% were couples and 7% were males travelling alone. The average age was 64.5 for males and 61.3 for females. They were evenly spread with 34% living in a major urban city, 33% from a regional city and 33% from a rural area. The majority (74%) were travelling in a caravan towed by a four-wheel drive, 7% in a motor home, while others were in campervans, reconditioned buses or cars with trailers.

The main motivations for travelling around Australia were:

1. Freedom – to go at one's own pace, to be independent and make one's choices about where to go. 'We don't travel more than 200 kilometres per day because we've got the time now. You've got time to smell the flowers as they say' (female, 52 years).

2. Adventure – discovering new places and a diversity of landforms. 'There is still a lot of frontiers left . . . you can go out in the desert, be miles from anywhere and you can go places with a 4wd that not too many people have been . . . yes, adventure, and the people you meet in places like this. It's fantastic' (male, 68 years).

3. Beauty – the scenery, desert, sunsets, rich birdlife, seeing the stars at night, to wonder at the vastness and diversity of the country. 'Just seeing Australia, like just seeing the sun go down on those rocks . . . look at the colour, isn't it beautiful' (couple, both 63 years).

4. Learning – about the history of various towns and geophysical landforms. 'I paint as I travel, learning about the culture, the history, the geography, the animals and birds, I've taken hundreds of photos of different birds of which I do paintings . . . some are in galleries' (male, 69 years).

5. Social networks – the majority travelled with their spouse and although meeting other people was important, they still had their own company. Word of mouth was important to find out from other people the best places to visit and stay. 'Once you camp somewhere and you get to know your neighbour and you really talk to them. We've kept in contact with a few of them . . . from all walks of life' (female, 60 years).

These results of Onyx and Leonard's (2005) study suggest that in Australia the grey nomad lifestyle is quite different from the North American snowbird. Older Australians love the sense of freedom and adventure of travelling around Australia. They do not like staying in caravan parks, especially longer than 1 week, and they generally avoid the commercialized tourist resorts on the coast. They also do not seem to form any lasting friendships with people they meet on their trip. Finally, they do not like to be organized or managed, and prefer to do 'their own thing'. This may be the result of a strong reaction against the bureaucratic controls that many Australians faced in their previous work life.

Discussion

RV living offers an alternative style of living for retired people. As a result, older people often decide to become part of temporary communities of people with similar values, statuses and interests that are associated with a mobile lifestyle. An example of seasonal travellers are Canadians who travel to Sunbelt destinations in the USA on a massive scale, mainly during the winter season and are referred to as 'snowbirds' because they flock in larger numbers to warmer climates.

Phoenix is a major summer destination for those from the western provinces of Canada, particularly British Columbia. Phoenix is well known for its concentration of large-scale RV resorts that have evolved into winter retirement communities for large numbers of Americans and Canadians. However, Canadians are generally only interested in seasonal visits or shorter vacation trips because of their strong attachment to their homes, but they start to develop stronger ties to destinations they visit on a more regular basis over time.

Mexico has emerged as a major destination for snowbirds and winter travellers, and is likely to become a more attractive location in the future because of the decline in the exchange rate of the Canadian dollar. Baby boomers who are approaching retirement are increasingly beginning to relocate their investment income from northern to southern locations and to spend at least part of the year in a warm, sunny climate.

In Australia, the grey nomad movement is growing as older people are deciding to travel around Australia at increasing rates. Statistics indicate that approximately 200,000 grey nomads undertook long-distance trips for at least a 6-week duration during a single year. Australian grey nomads differ from North American snowbirds in that older Australians like to take their time and drive longer distances, prefer to keep to themselves and have reduced social interaction, and are not really interested in being organized into group leisure and educational activities in caravan parks. They prefer to do their own thing, and have a sense of freedom and adventure.

The Motorcoach Tour Industry and the Older Traveller

According to the American Bus Association (2001), 25 million passengers boarded 624,000 motorcoach charter and tour buses in 1996. Of these passengers, it has been estimated that between 50% and 70% were senior citizens (Chacko and Nebel, 1993; Marshall, 1997). Tour coaches have been defined as 'any coach license to operate scheduled tours that includes an itinerary and all tickets are commercially available for purchase' (Prideaux *et al.*, 2004, p. 67). In Australia, the State Government transport authority exercises control over the operation of tour coaches, and usually requires them to be approved vehicles and registered to a licensed tour operator.

Most of the early research on coach travel concentrated on the demographic profile of people who were attracted to coach trips, and what this mode of travel offered people in terms of travel experience. For example, Arnold (1979) found a distinctive demographic profile of the typical coach patrons, who he concluded were mainly older and female. Shearings Holidays (1990), one of Britain's oldest suppliers of coach holidays, concluded that nearly two-thirds came from the cohort group aged 60 and older. In the USA, Cunningham and Wood (1985) estimated that the average age of coach users was 54 and one-third had retired from work. Marshall (1997) also reported that older travellers accounted for 70% of all bus trips. Chacko and Nebel (1993) found that over 50% of motorcoach tour patrons were senior citizens, and because of this high percentage of usage, they felt that coach operators needed to review their itineraries and make them more attractive for older people. This was because of the likelihood that if coach services were not improved, seniors would be more inclined to substitute coach travel with airline services. This study clearly illustrated the importance of the senior citizen market to motorcoach group tour operators and the need for increased concerns about future threats from the airline industry.

Baloglu and Shoemaker (2001) examined the differences between motorcoach users and non-users. They collected data from randomly selected residents in Pennsylvania aged 55 and older. A questionnaire was mailed to respondents, of whom only 193 replied (out of 2000 surveys that were mailed originally), and 171 non-respondents were interviewed over the telephone by a professional market research firm. The results showed that seniors who were more likely to take a motorcoach tour were mainly concerned about the price of travel services. Further analysis found that motorcoach travellers preferred trips that were filled with lots of activities such as visiting historical sites, beautiful scenery, availability of shopping trips, facilities for physical activities, and walking paths or other places for exercise. One senior citizen responded to a fellow passenger's complaint about doing too many activities: 'This is a bus trip where the goal is to see as many things as possible. If he wants to rest, he should have gone on a vacation' (Baloglu and Shoemaker, 2001, p. 16).

Baloglu and Shoemaker also concluded that older motorcoach travellers tended to use travel as a means for building friendships. Because of this trend, the researchers suggested that there was a need to employ well-trained tour guides to facilitate interaction between passengers, as well as providing them with lots of free time to get to know other passengers. Other suggestions included the need for motorcoach operators to constantly seek out new destinations as older travellers are less likely to want to return to the same place on a regular basis. A final recommendation was that tour bus operators needed to better promote their companies and the destinations they visited, as branding and positioning in the market was seen as critical for the survival of the industry.

Thus, the senior market is a viable option for bus operators because older people are willing and able to travel during the off-peak season to a variety of destinations. There is a general pattern of coach excursionists travelling as a couple, normally as husband and wife. When questioned about what attracted them to coach travel, clients stressed that it took away the worry of route planning and driving, arranging accommodation and visits to specific attractions (Dean, 1993). Quiroga's (1990) study of Latin American travellers touring Europe found that the physical and psychological security provided by tourist coaches offered a unique blend of novelty, adventure and safety. Dean (1993) studied coach trips in central-southern England and found that the range of destinations on offer increased the traveller's geographical horizons for a range of recreational experiences and allowed them to travel at comparatively lower prices.

Hsu (2001) was interested in studying seniors' motorcoach tour choice behaviour. She mailed a survey to 817 randomly selected customers who had used a Kansas tour operator over the past 12 months. Hsu found that six factors emerged as important choice attributes for seniors travelling on motorcoach tours. Of the six, reputation as well as health and safety were rated as extremely important. The other four – flexible schedule, operator services and referrals, promotional materials, social activities – were rated as important. The reputation and reliability of the tour operator was also seen as extremely important. Hsu concluded that health and safety concerns should be the top priority when developing a favourable image among senior travellers. Blazey (1992) also reported that older travellers had major fears about their safety. Often the tour provider had to deal with health care issues and emergencies during a trip, and therefore it was important that policies and procedures were developed and clearly communicated to tour guides and bus drivers to ensure that proper implementation occurred when it was required.

Seniors also valued having some flexibility with their tour itinerary. Lago and Poffley (1993) found that seniors wanted the freedom to come and go, and make decisions about what leisure activities they wanted to participate in. The attractive and comprehensive tour information that lists the types of social activities included in the tour package was also seen as important. Wilite et al. (1988) concluded that any marketing mix that was directed at older adults needed to emphasize older people's concern for safety, their physical needs and abilities as well as the provision of detailed information in the advertising material.

In a further study, Hsu and Lee (2002) set out to determine the characteristics of different segments of senior motorcoach travellers. A research instrument was developed to assess the importance of 55 motorcoach tour operator and tour package selection attributes. The questionnaire was mailed to 2000 randomly selected people whose names were provided by tour providers in the state of Kansas, USA. Out of this total, 817 were returned and found to be usable. Of these, approximately 50% of respondents were between 65 and 74 (47.2%), married (52.4%) and with their highest level of education being attendance at high school (42.9%). The majority of respondents were female (75.4%) and retired (81.3%). The researchers segmented the senior motorcoach tour market into three distinguishable groups:

- Dependents (53%): at the top of their list was health and safety concerns. Require a 1–800 telephone number, name recognition very important, and tour was recommended by friends and travel agent. They tend to be older retired people without a college degree and have lower incomes.

To target the 'dependents' segment, operators need to promote themselves as specialists in conducting older senior motorcoach tours. Toll-free telephone numbers need to be provided to answer questions or concerns from prospective travellers. Tours need to be reasonably priced to stay within the dependent's price range. This was the largest group with the highest returns so there was a need expressed to develop expertise in catering for the special needs of this group.

- Sociables (18%): rated social activities as important selection criteria. This group saw evening entertainment and group activities as very important in addition to safety and health concerns. They also rated attractiveness and comprehensiveness of promotional materials more important than the recommendations from travel agents and friends or relatives. This group mainly consisted of younger seniors with higher incomes than the other two market segments.

To target the 'sociables' segment, promotional materials need to be professionally prepared, as well as stating all the social activities planned for the trip. Because they are younger seniors, more physically active social programmes should be included in the itinerary. It must be affordable and provide value for money, even though this group had higher incomes than the other two market segments.

- Independents (29%): other than health and safety issues, the independents rated only the 1–800 telephone number and name recognition as important. This group had a higher level of education, were younger and earned a moderate income.

The 'independents' are more interested in planning some of the activities and exploring destinations on their own. Information should be provided about specific destinations and local culture in the form of a welcome kit, and free time should be allowed for independent exploration.

Based on the results of this study, tour operators need to target a particular market segment and provide specialized packages of offerings and marketing strategies to meet the specific needs of each market segment. For example, research found that the traveller aged 45–55 was interested in having more free time, more choices and fewer long uninterrupted motorcoach segments when they travelled. The report stated: 'It is likely that the approach to traditional tour programs will not have to be completely abandoned, but rather altered to evolve into a more boomer-friendly product' (Sparrow, 1998, p. 6).

In Australia, the demand for coach travel is relatively low and, as a result, the senior market has had very little experience in using coach travel. Prideaux *et al.* (2004) examined and compared a number of tour coach attributes against the perceptions that tour coach operators had about the needs of seniors using an identical group of attributes. A questionnaire was sent to a random sample of 1250 Senior Card and Seniors Business Discount Cardholders. A total of 366 replies were found to be usable, while a similar survey of tour coach operators generated 32 valid responses.

Almost two-thirds of respondents (61.5%) indicated that they used private vehicles for travel around a holiday destination area, quite a significant number used public transport (24.4%). The period from July to September was the most popular time for travelling (53.1%), while the summer period (January to March) was the least popular (15.2%). The most popular holiday attractions were natural ones such as parks, beaches and gardens (41.5%); however, the use of public transport (including coaches) to travel to these areas was much less popular. With their ranking of preferred coach attributes, seniors rated comfort as the primary attribute compared to operators who ranked comfort in only fifth place. Coach operators also failed to identify the desire of seniors for quality overnight accommodation and meals. Seniors indicated that comfort and social experiences were relatively more important than other aspects of the trip, while coach operators overestimated the importance of an information guide that was given out at the start of the trip, and time spent at sites they visited was regarded as an important part of the coach trip.

In regard to holiday preferences, Prideaux *et al.* (2004) found that over 46% chose a 'reliable package as their holiday preference', followed by 'places where people rarely go' (24.6%) and a 'real Aussie family environment' (16.8%). Few respondents chose 'taking in the sites and dining in luxury', an 'exclusive retreat' or 'places with good time people' as their preferred choice. The authors concluded that tour coach operators have misjudged the reasons why seniors use coach travel when visiting particular destinations. In the future, coach operators must develop products and provide levels of service that encourage seniors to substitute existing forms of travel for coach tours. This study found apparent differences between the desires of customers and the perceptions of coach operators, indicating that there is a need for operators to regularly review their travel itineraries on the basis of high-quality research so as to implement any modifications that may be needed.

Discussion

Motorcoach trips are a popular means of travel for older adults, with several researchers noting that between 50% and 70% of passengers were seniors. Lower prices for travel is a major factor in their choice of travel, and popular preferences for trips include shopping, sightseeing and looking at beautiful scenery, as well as visiting historical and cultural sites. Most coach travellers also enjoy the chance for social interaction and making new friends, and therefore the personality of the tour guide is important in facilitating passenger interaction. Older adults generally travel together as a couple, enjoy the reduced stress of not having to organize their own trip and the security of travelling together at a comparatively lower cost than other forms of transport. Safety is a major issue, especially in regard to the coach driver's ability to deal with emergencies such as health care problems. Research indicates that older people like some flexibility in their tour itinerary, to have some freedom to come and go, and make choices about the types of leisure activities they prefer while on tour.

Tour companies need to concentrate their efforts on targeting specific segments of the older market and on attempting to provide for their individual needs. For example, many baby boomers prefer more free time, flexible itineraries, short trips, to be more independent and have fewer uninterrupted segments of the trip. Coach travellers also like comfort when they travel as well as quality overnight accommodation and meals. Therefore, coach operators need to regularly review their itineraries, offer shorter trips, provide more choice and free time, and attempt to cater for the individual needs of older people if they are to successfully compete with other forms of transport such as the airline industry.

Cruise Tourism and the Older Traveller

Cruise tourism refers to a holiday spent on a water-based vessel or cruise liner for leisure purposes. The ship (or cruise liner) usually travels to a number of destinations where passengers generally disembark for short periods of time to visit land-based sites for shopping and/or sightseeing purposes. These cruise ships are well equipped with entertainment and sporting facilities, and passengers are provided with full board accommodation. The cruise ship industry is regarded as the fastest-growing segment of the leisure travel industry, with the number of North American passengers reaching 5 million in 1999 with an occupancy rate of 91%, which was forecast to reach a record-breaking 8.3 million by 2003 (Sloan, 1999).

The main advantages of ocean cruising are:

- Allowing people to see interesting parts of the world without having to pack and unpack, as people are able to experience an exotic location and then go back to their ship, which is essentially a deluxe hotel.

- Providing access to places that are inaccessible by land. For example, Alaska is a difficult place to visit because groups have to be flown into geographically difficult locations and the quality of the hotels is not high. Ocean cruising along the Alaskan coastline overcomes these major problems.
- Many of the new ships offer outstanding leisure and entertainment facilities. For example, the new Royal Caribbean passenger ship *Explorer of the Seas* has three swimming pools, an extensive fitness centre or spa, dozens of boutiques and nightclubs, miniature golf, a sports court with a full-size basketball court, a video games room, an in-line skating track, a rock-climbing wall, a golf simulator that allows passengers to play some of the top golf courses in the world, and an ice skating rink that is used for free skating during the day and as a venue for an elaborate ice show in the evening.
- Everything is included and people know what it is going to cost before they start their trip, including accommodation, food, onboard activities and entertainment (Waldrop-Bay, 2000).

The majority of all-inclusive cruise ships are small luxury vessels that attract 'empty nesters' and seniors with higher disposable incomes. The reason that passengers gave for taking this type of trip was that they wanted to slow down the pace of their lives and have other people handle things for them. In the future, the older sector of the market will comprise a different type of senior citizen, one with an increasing income and greater flexibility of travelling time, which will provide greater impetus for cruise shipping. It is expected that the impact of the new state-of-the-art cruise vessels that have been specifically designed for the American market will lead to an increased demand among older people (Page, 1987; Fost, 1992).

Cruise ships are now providing the maximum in leisure and entertainment facilities, utilizing existing multi-purpose lounges and surplus deck space. The new style of ships will be 40,000 t, carrying between 1200 and 1500 passengers in double cabins with their own showers and toilets, with 70% possessing a sea view. Public areas will include casinos, bars, lavish discos, theatres, etc., and there is likely to be even greater emphasis on shopping. This will reduce the need to call at ports purely for shopping or recreational purposes, and allow the possibility of choosing a greater range of ports for senior or cultural attractions.

Cruise ships have responded to consumer demand by offering speciality theme cruises such as bridge, dancing, golf, as well as musical and archaeological interests to cater for older people's needs and interests. Elderhostel offers a 12-day Chesapeake Bay cruise for history buffs, nature lovers and beauty seekers. The tour price in 2003 was from $3130 to $3700, and this included all lectures, field trips, accommodation and meals.

Other smaller, expensive vessels offer exploration-type cruises for baby boomers who are mainly interested in adventure tourism experiences. For example, Royal Viking Line offers a 20-day trip round the tip of South America duing which passengers can go piranha fishing, tour river systems and land at Cape Horn. Other specialist operators attract retired people through trips to Antarctica, Galapagos, Greenland, Iceland and the Chilean Fjords, because many older people want to visit remote islands that are inaccessible by other means of transport. A combination of flying and cruising is seen as a further development, and the cruise industry hopes that this will result in an expansion of this market, particularly to South-east Asia.

Fost (1992) discussed the growing need for single seniors to seek companionship when they travel. Because of the large number of single and widowed women, older single men are continually in demand. The Royal Cruise Line offers mature men a change to cruise for free as 'hosts':

> Hosts schmooze, play bridge, and dance with women who travel unattached. . . . The cruise line requires hosts had to bring a tux and a white dinner jacket, and often requires them to spend up to five hours a day working . . . one guy with a pacemaker had to drop out of the program because it was too gruelling . . . many women book the cruise solely because of the hosts.
>
> (Fost, 1992, p. 47)

As an interesting new idea that Linquist and Golub (2004) have advocated is that cruise ships might be considered a viable alternative to assisted living facilities in the community for the frail, older adult. This is because cruise ships have their own apartment-like living arrangements, 24-h medical staff available, and help can be arranged with activities of daily living such as bathing and meals.

Discussion

Cruise tourism is a popular form of leisure travel, especially for the older and wealthier person. Cruise ships are now responding to consumer demand by providing the best entertainment and state-of-the-art facilities, and are attempting to cater for the changing leisure interests of baby boomers and older adults through the provision of theme and adventure-type cruises. Cruises have often been regarded as a popular means of relaxing and meeting other single people, especially for the large number of widowed women in society. However, because of a shortage of older single men, shipping lines are now providing opportunities to these men to travel free of charge and act as hosts for women. This has resulted in increasing numbers of older people taking cruises as a leisure travel activity, and may also be used as assisted living facilities for the more frail older person.

Conclusion

Drive tourism is a significant form of tourism with a high rate of participation by older adults. Today's cohort of older people who are retired
are largely dependent on some form of government-funded pension.
However, in the future, baby boomers will be more reliant on their own
superannuation schemes and less on welfare and, as a result, will have
higher incomes in retirement. The senior market is rapidly changing in
terms of pre-retirement travel experiences as well as improved levels of
health, fitness and disposable income, as increasing numbers of baby
boomers retire. Because of this trend, many retired people are buying
RVs and caravans at an increasing rate and are travelling to warmer climates in the USA and Australia on a massive scale, mainly during the
winter season. They are commonly referred to as 'snowbirds' or 'grey
nomads' because they flock in larger numbers to warmer climates, and
are older travellers who feel free to go anywhere and become constantly
drifting mobile travellers.

In the future, baby boomers are more likely to use the airline industry in greater numbers than older adults do presently. However, for
many older people who are on restricted incomes, they will be forced to
use bus or train services, especially if they are unable to continue driving
because of certain medical conditions. On the other hand, the increasing wealth of this significant market sector will present several opportunities for the private sector to introduce new products and higher service
standards. Expectations of the baby boomer generation will differ from
the demands of current users of coach tours. At present, older adults are
more likely than the average to take tour bus vacations. This is because
they favour packaged trips that relieve them of the hassles of finding
their own way, carrying their luggage and paying tips. Will baby boomers
also favour packaged trips? Based on this research, it is unlikely, as baby
boomers are generally more experienced travellers, healthier, fitter, and
are more likely to prefer independent travel in their RVs and caravans
rather than packaged tours. Motorcoach companies will need to respond
to these changes and adjust their products and services accordingly to
meet the diverse needs of new baby boomer customers in the future if
they are to survive. Cruise ships are an excellent example of an industry that has responded quickly and appropriately to older consumer
needs. They are providing a range of different types of cruises such as
theme and adventure cruises, in a variety of different-sized vessels that
have the latest technologies and entertainment facilities to attract the
more wealthy baby boomer generation. As a result, the number of passengers who take cruises each year in North America is increasing with
new record-breaking figures.

References

Adler, J. and Springen, K. (1988) These folks are really on a roll. *Newsweek* 114(1 August), 58–59.

American Bus Association (2001) Motorcoach industry facts. Available at: http// www.buses.org/industry/

Arnold, S. (1979) Passenger profile of coach users. *The Chartered Institute of Transport Journal* 38, 266–269.

Baloglu, S. and Shoemaker, S. (2001) Prediction of senior travellers motorcoach use from demographic, psychological, and psychographic characteristics. *Journal of Travel Research* 40, 12–18.

Black, N. and Rutledge, J. (1995) *Tourism in North West Queensland: The Authentic Australian Adventure.* James Cook University Press, Townsville, Australia.

Blais, P. (2002) On the road again: they're big; they're slow; they're often the vehicle of choice for tourists. *Planning* 68, 6–11.

Blazey, M.A. (1992) Travel and retirement status. *Annals of Tourism Research* 19, 771–783.

Brannelly, L. (2003) Grey nomads keep caravan industry rolling along. *Australasian Business Intelligence* 13 July, 1008.

Bureau of Tourism Research (1999) Domestic tourism monitor. Bureau of Transport Research, Canberra.

Carter, P. (2002) Domestic caravanning and camping: results from the 2000 National Visitor Survey. *Tourism Research Report* 4(2), 1–27.

Chacko, H. and Nebel, E. (1993) The group tour industry: an analysis of motorcoach tour operators. *Journal of Travel and Tourism Marketing* 2, 69–83.

Coates, K.S., Healy, R. and Morrison, W.R. (2002) Tracking the snow birds: seasonal migration from Canada to the USA and Mexico. *American Review of Canadian Studies* 32, 433–452.

Conover, K.A. (1998) Get up and go in your own RV: owners tell just why this mode of travel has so much appeal. *Christian Science Monitor* 16 April, 14–17.

Cunningham, L.F. and Wood, W. (1985) An analysis of the intercity bus tour passenger market. *Transportation Research Forum* 26, 265–272.

Dean, C.J. (1993) Travel by excursion coach in the United Kingdom. *Journal of Travel Research* Spring, 59–64.

Dortch, S. (1995) Vacation vehicles. *American Demographics* 17, 4–5.

Eby, D.W. and Molnar, L.J. (2001) Age-related decision factors in destination choice for United States driving tourists. *Journal of Hospitality and Leisure Marketing* 9, 97–111.

Fost, D. (1992) Cruising at 60 is no fun alone. *American Demographics* 14, 47.

Gurwitt, R. (2003) Have tools will travel: meet the Care-A-Vanners. *Mother Jones* 28, 28–32.

Hsu, C.H. (2001) Importance and dimensionality of senior motorcoach traveller choice attributes. *Journal of Hospitality and Leisure Marketing* 8, 51–70.

Hsu, C.H. and Lee, E-J. (2002) Segmentation of senior motorcoach travellers. *Journal of Travel Research* 40, 364–373.

Janiskee, R.L. (1990) Resort camping in America. *Annals of Tourism Research* 17, 385–407.

Javalgi, R., Thomas, E. and Rao, S. (1992) Consumer behavior in the U.S. pleasure travel market: an analysis of senior and nonsenior travellers. *Journal of Travel Research* 31, 14–19.

Jobes, P.C. (1984) Old-timers and new mobile lifestyles. *Annals of Tourism Research* 11, 181–198.

Lago, D. and Poffley, J.K. (1993) The aging population and the hospitality industry in 2010: important trends and probable services. *Hospitality Research Journal* 17, 29–47.

Linquist, L.A. and Golub, R.M. (2004) Cruise ship care: a proposed alternative to assisted living facilities. *Journal of the American Geriatrics Society* 52(11), 1951–1954.

McCarthy, T. (1996) Understanding senior caravan travellers in Queensland: a segmentation approach. Unpublished B. Admin. (Tourism) Hons. Thesis.

McEwan, D. and More, T.A. (1986) Recreation quality and the market for tent camping. *Journal of Park and Recreation Administration* 4, 83–95.

McHugh, K.E. and Mings, R.C. (1992) Canadian snowbirds in Arizona. *Journal of Applied Recreation Research* 17, 255–277.

Marshall, A. (1997). Seniors have big travel budgets but need accommodation. *Hotel and Motel Management* 212(7 April), 17.

Mings, R.C. (1997) Tracking 'snowbirds' in Australia: winter sun seekers in far north Queensland. *Australian Geographical Studies* 35(2), 168–182.

Mings, R.C. and McHugh, K.E. (1995) Wintering in the American Sunbelt: linking place and behaviour. *Journal of Tourism Studies* 6, 56–62.

National Park Service (1986) *1982–1983 Nationwide Recreation Survey*. Government Printing Service, Washington, DC.

Onyx, J. and Leonard, R. (2005) Australian grey nomads and American snowbirds: similarities and differences. *Journal of Tourism Studies* 16(1), 61–68.

Page, K. (1987) The future of cruise shipping. *Tourism Management* June, 166–168.

Pearce, P.L. (1999) Touring for pleasure: studies of the senior self-drive travel market. *Tourism Recreation Research* 24, 35–42.

Prideaux, B., Wei, S. and Ruys, H. (2001) The senior drive tour market in Australia. *Journal of Vacation Marketing* 7, 209–219.

Prideaux, B., Wei, S. and Ruys, H. (2004) Tour coach operations in the Australian seniors market. *Journal of Hospitality and Tourism Management* 11, 65–77.

Quiroga, I. (1990) Characteristics of package tours in Europe. *Annals of Tourism Research* 17, 185–207.

Rawe, J. (2003) Not your dad's RV: seating togetherness and wary of flying, active families find today's slick recreational vehicles are just the ticket. Their sales are surging. *Time* 161 (7 April), 2–4.

Shoemaker, S. (1989) Segmentation of the senior pleasure travel market. *Journal of Travel Research* 17, 14–18.

Shearings Holidays (1990) *Coach Holidays: The 'Cinderella' Sector.* Shearings Holidays, Wigan, UK.

Sloan, G. (1999) Trips, crowds and prices: on the up and up. *USA Today* 22 October, 1D.

Smith, C. and Jenner, P. (1997) The seniors travel market. *Travel and Tourism Analyst* 5, 43–62.

Smith, G., O'Hara, J., McClelland, S. and Ferguson, S. (2000) Flocking south: after years at home with their sagging loins, millions of Canadians have caught the winter travel bug. *MacLean's* 31 January, 60.

Sparrow, H. (1998) Industry news: group travel industry is preparing for boomers. *The Group Travel Leader* 6 December.

Teaff, J.D. and Turpin, T. (1996) Travel and the elderly. *Parks and Recreation* 31, 16–19.

Tugend, A. (2005) RV's find a new fan base: the baby boomers. *New York Times, Late Edition* 16 January, 3.8.

Waldrop-Bay, H. (2000) Seaworthy rewards. *Incentive* 174, 107–111.

Wei, S. and Ruys, H. (1998) Industry and senior perception survey. Brisbane: Office of the Ageing, Department of families, youth and community care, Queensland Government.

Wilite, B., Hamilton, K. and Reilley, L. (1988) Recreational travel and the elderly: marketing strategies with a normalization perspective? *Activities, Adaptation and Aging* 12, 59–72.

7   Different Travel Markets: Group Package Tours for Older Adults

---

The aims of this chapter are to:

- Classify the different types of package tours that are used by older adults.
- Examine the important role of the tour guide in package tours.
- Explore the reasons why package tour groups are popular among older adults.
- Investigate the growing trend towards special interest package tours.
- Formulate specific recommendations about the travel needs of older travellers for the benefit of package tour operators.

Introduction

Package tours help to bridge the gap between the travel industry and the leisure needs of a growing number of older people. Group package tours are generally offered by travel agencies and are popular because they take the pressure off older adults who do not have the capacity or desire to travel independently. The travel agency helps to minimize problems, as seniors do not have to worry about such items as ticket purchases and accommodation details, and can fully concentrate on the trip experience itself. Travelling with others encourages social interaction and sharing, and this provides a heightened sense of enjoyment. Minimizing problems on the return trip also allows participants to retain positive psychological feelings about the experience. Package tours also provide the means by which the group comes together after the trip to share their recollections through slides, videos and informal gatherings. This adds to the leisure experience and encourages future group travel experiences (Hudson and Rich, 1993).

What Are Package Tours?

Travel behaviour can be categorized in three main types: escorted or guided tours, group package tours and fully independent travel.

1. Escorted tours are divided into two subtypes, fully escorted tours and partially escorted tours, depending on the amount of use made of tour guides. With an escorted tour, the function of the tour guide is generally indispensable and can be a crucial variable in the success or failure of a group package tour.
2. Package tours are categorized into two main subtypes, complete and partial packages, depending on the amount of pre-arranged travel services that are required, such as ground transfers, hotel arrangements and meals.
3. Fully independent tourists make all their travel arrangements by themselves and follow a personally determined schedule (Yamamoto and Gill, 1999).

The escorted or guided tour

One of the first research studies that studied the sociology of the package tour was Schmidt (1979), who referred to it as a 'guided tour'. Although his paper was largely theoretical in nature, it was based on extensive fieldwork experiences that included direct participant observation and interviews with tour guides, tourists, travel agents, coordinators of conventions and tourist bureaus, and travel researchers. Schmidt (1979) defined a guided tour as 'all forms of tourism where the itinerary is fixed and known beforehand and which involves some degree of planning and direct participation by agents apart from the tourists themselves' (p. 441).

Schmidt (1979) outlined the various advantages of a guided tour. Guided tours solve the problem about what to see in a limited amount of time. A large geographical area can be condensed into a selective smorgasbord of the most important tourist attractions, which are arranged into a package of highlights that is seen in the shortest amount of time. Psychological security is provided through an organized itinerary so that the entire group knows beforehand where they will be going and what hotels they will be staying in. Economic simplification and security are also facilitated because tourists know beforehand the cost of the entire trip, and in addition many of the expenses are discounted such as group airfares and hotel accommodation.

Tour coordinators and guides act as buffers between the tourists and the social environment, arranging transport, interpreting and handling problems when they arise so as to minimize friction between tourists themselves, and this encourages in-group solidarity. Guided tours serve as a legitimate mechanism for leisure by providing for both active and educational experiences. They often manage to facilitate and combine opportunities for adventure, novelty, escape and educational experiences within safe limits. At the same time, the tour guide acts as a buffer between the tourist and the unknown and often threatening environment (Schmidt, 1979, pp. 442–447).

The tour guide

One of the first academic studies on the role of the tour guide was by Holloway (1981), who was interested in the relationship between guides and passengers during one-day coach tours. Holloway's study was based on his personal observations and interviews with these tour guides. Holloway found that the tour guide was crucial not only in fostering group interaction but also providing security and protection in the face of difficulties encountered in the host country, as well as acting as a cultural broker. The guides themselves stated that the essential element of any trip experience was how the group interacted with each other, and this was closely linked to the success of the trip.

Therefore, tour guides have a dual function: first, to provide an insulating function for tourists to the external environment, and secondly, to help to internally integrate a group of tourists among themselves. Because of this, tour guides need to be competent in both their knowledge and presentation skills so as to help integrate tourists into a particular setting. Tour guides also help to integrate the group itself, and soon friendships are initiated and a group feeling is generated as tourists meet and provide an important means of social support through their relationships with other tourists. Tour guides are often instigators of this sociability through their use of humour and friendliness, which help to promote an amiable and friendly atmosphere. Finally, the tour guide also provides a type of insulation from the external environment through the provision of information and explanations that allow tourists to become familiar with the traditions and history of a particular culture. This helps to protect tourists from mixing and meeting with residents from the country that they are actually visiting (Schmidt, 1979).

The package tour

Cohen (1972) was the first researcher to study the dynamics of package tour groups and conclude that their main function was to transplant the tourist into a foreign country inside an environmental bubble that limited their contact with the local population. As a result, the tour group often develops a unique atmosphere of camaraderie and solidarity that is built up because of the high physical proximity of tourists, especially on coach tours where they are forced to share the same confined physical space (bus seats, dining tables, hotels, etc.) for most of the trip. In fact, several package tour groups such as the Toledo-based Grand Tour cater specifically for single seniors to travel together. These seniors enjoy travelling but lack travel companions or have a difficult time organizing and coordinating with friends to take trips that they would like to take (Taylor, 1993).

A package tour is defined as a trip that is planned and paid for in advance at a single price. It generally covers both transportation and accommodation, and often includes side trips and meals (Morrison, 1989). Middleton (1991) defined the package tour as 'simply comprising any two or more elements of transport, accommodation, food, destination attractions, and other facilities and services' (p. 185). Consumers generally do not know the cost of individual line items because they have purchased a total package from a travel agent or a tour operator. The type of tourist who is attracted to buying a package tour is one who wants everything to be prepared and done in advance, and is happy to be relieved of all the responsibilities by other people such as travel agents and/or tour coordinators. Package tours are popular because they make travel easier and more convenient for people. At the same time package tours help the industry to increase business in off-peak periods as well as attracting new or specialized markets (Morrison, 1989).

Most people who opt for package tours are first-time travellers, older, single, lack language skills and are hesitant to travel on their own. Older people especially value the convenience of organized package tours when selecting their mode of travel choice. Single women in particular generally prefer to travel on a package tour because of safety and security reasons. Package tours also appeal to middle-class adults who are generally too busy to spend time organizing the trip and because of this prefer to leave this task in the hands of professionals. Furthermore, educated middle-class people often choose escorted package tours because they feel they will learn more from an expert guide about the history of art, architecture or wine growing than by going by themselves (Enoch, 1996). Therefore, the package tour provides many benefits for older people, and has been an important part of the tourism and travel industry for the last 30 years.

Benefits of Package Tours

Enoch (1996) stated that group package tours are an attractive option because of the following features:

• They are the most rational and effective means of accomplishing a travel goal as well as visiting the largest number of interesting sites on a restricted time schedule.
• They provide relatively safe travel to different countries with diverse cultures, unreliable transportation and sometimes doubtful standards of hygiene.
• They are usually cheaper as they enable the tour operator to buy hotel accommodation, meals and transportation at discount group rates.
• They provide companionship for many single and widowed older people who generally feel safer and more secure when they have company to share memorable experiences with.
• They provide groups of tourists with a set itinerary that is pre-designed to provide the best value for money and have the best sightseeing and visitation experiences within a limited time.
• They are predictable – once chosen, they generally proceed exactly according to a set itinerary. Conversely, it is a contractual obligation of the tour operator to ensure that the tourist receives everything that has been promised in the printed material that advertises the trip.

The National Tour Association (1989) identified three practical reasons why older Americans participate in package travel programmes:

1. Meeting other people with similar interests: because many older people live alone, travel provides them with the opportunity to make new friends and meet others with similar interests.
2. Trips are worry-free: because package tours are pre-planned in terms of travel, accommodation and side trips, they provide older people with a great sense of security. They do not have to carry large amounts of money around with them or be worried about tipping, etc. This reduces the normal stress that is associated with individual travel.
3. Cost-effectiveness: older adults benefit from group discounts that make the trip less expensive and they often receive extra side benefits because of the size of the group (Hudson and Rich, 1993, p. 39).

Discussion

Package tours are seen as a more attractive alternative for older travellers than undertaking independent travel, especially if they are single, widowed or divorced. This is because package tours are generally found to be cheaper, have a predetermined itinerary that enables a shorter time frame for travel, are generally perceived as safe and worry-free, as well as providing older adults with greater opportunities to meet and socialize with other like-minded people. Tour guides are extremely important to the success of tour packages as they provide an integrative and educational function, as well as a supportive purpose for overcoming language barriers and social isolation.

Group Package Tours and Asian Tourists

Researchers have concluded that travellers from Asian countries seem to be more attracted to package tours than travellers from Western countries. Several studies (Nozawa, 1992; Pizam *et al.*, 1997; Yamamoto and Gill, 1999; Wang *et al.*, 2000) concluded that travellers from the following Asian countries – Taiwan, Japan, Korea and China – are more likely to select package tours as their most popular mode of travel, especially for international trips.

Pizam *et al.* (1997) hypothesized that a person's nationality was related to a particular type of tourist behaviour. They used a sample of Dutch tour guides and asked them to identify their subjective impressions of tourists from Japan, France, Italy and America, so as to test whether there were significant differences between their perceptions about tourists from these four different countries. The sample consisted of 200 Dutch tour guides who were asked to complete a set of questionnaires about the characteristics of each nationality. Of the 200 guides, 63 returned the questionnaire, with a return rate of 31.5%.

Pizam *et al.* (1997) found that Dutch tour guides perceived that most Japanese tourists prefer to travel in groups, whereas the French prefer to travel independently. They attributed this to the fact that Japanese were raised in a 'collectivist' culture and because of this they prefer to travel with their own compatriots rather than to travel alone. Collectivism was also observed through the purchase of gifts for friends and relatives as a form of social obligation for those who were left at home. This represented atonement for the sin of abandoning members of the collective group and leaving them to go on a trip. Furthermore, sending letters and taking large numbers of photographs and videos was also a form of trip sharing for the collective group that had been left behind at home.

Japanese tourists were also perceived to have the highest preference for safe and passive-type leisure activities (shopping, sightseeing, commercial side tours, etc.), which significantly differed from the other three nationalities. Japanese and French tourists were perceived to be more interested in artefacts such as gifts and souvenirs, rather than meeting and sharing with other tourists. As a result, the Japanese were openly seen to avoid other tourists and mainly congregate with members of their own nationality (Pizam *et al.*, 1997).

These findings were confirmed by several other studies. Woodside and Jacobs (1985) developed a self-administered questionnaire to survey differences in perceptions of the benefits of package tours for Canadians, Americans and Japanese tourists when they visited Hawaii. The researchers found that Japanese visitors in particular reported that the main benefit of group travel was for family togetherness, while Canadians and Americans identified relaxation and cultural experiences as the most important benefits of group travel. In another study, Yuan and McDonald (1990) examined the differences in push and pull factors between Japanese, French, West German and British tourists when travelling overseas as part of a package tour. They found that for Japanese tourists, their budget was the most important pull factor, followed in descending order by the ease of travel, and having an interest in culture and history. These pull factors related specifically to the benefits of package tours.

Yamamoto and Gill (1999) used a 1989 Japanese tourist market survey and compared their results with one that was conducted in 1995. In this survey, over 1000 interviews were randomly conducted of adults who were aged 18 and older, and who had travelled overseas for 4 nights or longer during the last 3 years. This study found that when comparing time differences between the two surveys, group package tours were still the most dominant form of travel for the 1995 cohort group. The two most popular tourist destinations for Japanese group package tourists were Hawaii (81%) and Guam (89%). The main purpose of travel was for pleasure or to go on a honeymoon trip (nearly 75%). Not surprisingly, most package tourists (93%) used travel agents when booking their accommodation. Cost and value for money were found to be the most important considerations for all types of Japanese travellers who also expressed an increasing interest in nature-based eco-tourism.

Discussion

Asian travellers particularly from Japan, China, Korea and Taiwan show a strong preference to buy package tours and to purchase them mainly from travel agents. This was attributed in the research studies to the fact that Asian travellers are raised in a 'collectivist culture' that emphasizes the importance of travelling with people from the same nationality rather than travelling alone. The Japanese in particular are more interested in travelling together, taking photographs and videos, and buying gifts as souvenirs to take home to relatives left behind as a form of social obligation. Safety, cost and overcoming language barriers were also seen as potential benefits of package tours for the majority of Asian tourists, in comparison to more independent travellers.

Package Tours and Older Travellers

In one of the earlier studies, Sheldon and Mak (1987) developed a travel profile of package tourists by researching the types of travel that people used when visiting Hawaii. They found that people who purchased package tours were generally older, intent on visiting several destinations, preferred to travel with only a small number of people in their party, were intent on making a shorter visit, and were taking their first visit to Hawaii. They concluded that travellers were very responsive to the price savings from package tour travel.

Sheldon and Mak (1987) concluded that travellers tended to prefer package tours when they travelled to unfamiliar destinations, that they went to more than one destination and/or they wanted to spend a shorter amount of time on the trip. However, package tours were less attractive to larger party sizes, to people travelling with children because of the economic considerations, and repeat visitors because they had previously experienced the same or similar experiences. Conversely, travellers visiting friends or relatives, or desiring to participate in outdoor recreation activities during their trip were less interested in choosing package tours because of their need for greater flexibility in both the desired schedule and the activity component of the trip.

Quironga (1990) analysed the characteristics and peculiarities of tour groups by collecting data and personal observations from Latin American tourists on a guided coach tour of Europe. The sample size was 574 tourists who spoke mainly Spanish (13 different groups of coach travellers). The length of the coach trips varied from 18 to 32 days. Quiroga found that participation in guided tours increased up to a certain age and then began to decrease. In his sample, 62% of the tourists were older than 46, suggesting that people around 50 years and older were the most likely age group to take part in organized tours. The main reasons for participation in organized tours included 'getting the most out of the journey' (27.7%), 'personal safety' (19.9%) and 'not having to worry about things' (16.7%).

The most important reason for travelling in an organized tour was personal safety for people who were 65 years and older (29%). In contrast, younger students regarded personal safety as the least important factor (7.4%). Those who chose overcoming loneliness as their main travel motivation were mainly widowed people and people who were travelling alone. At the end of the trip, 87% of the tourists stated that they had made good friends within the group. Furthermore, the vast majority of organized tourists (97%) were of the opinion that the work of the tour guide was indispensable in enabling satisfactory group dynamics to occur (Quironga, 1990).

Javalgi *et al.* (1992) found in their study that many older people in the 55 and older age group preferred package tours that covered costs for both transportation and accommodation, and were also likely to incorporate travel by bus and/or plane. Javalgi *et al.* (1992) concluded that senior travellers generally preferred package tours at a much higher rate than younger travellers. They also found that although only less than one-quarter of the trips that were taken by seniors were package trips, seniors (55 years and older) still preferred them in comparison with younger people (under 55 years) (significant at $p < 0.001$). It was also evident from their study that older members (65 years and older) preferred package tours to seniors in the 55–64 age group. This was because retired older adults are on relatively fixed income and package tours offer the cheapest prices for travel. Furthermore, they were also more likely to use travel agents for making travel arrangements (significant at $p < 0.001$).

Hsieh *et al.* (1993) studied the Australian travel market in an attempt to identify which variables were important when distinguishing between the choice of package or non-package (i.e. independent) tours. They surveyed 1158 people from the five capital cities in Australia through personal in-home interviews between August and September 1988. Respondents were aged 18 and older and were selected on the basis of whether they had undertaken an overseas vacation in the last 3 years, or intended to take a trip in the next 2 years. Of the 1158 respondents surveyed, 563 (48.6%) stated that they preferred package tours while 595 (51.4%) preferred to be independent (or non-package travellers). The main differences between package and independent travellers were as follows:

1. Package tour travellers were found to be older (mean = 44.9 years) than independent travellers (mean = 42 years).
2. The proportion of single women travellers who selected package tours was slightly higher than for independent travellers.
3. Package travellers took shorter trips (mean = 37.3 nights) compared with independent travellers (mean = 65 nights).
4. People who travelled on package tours tended to travel with larger groups of people.
5. Respondents who used package tours travelled with an average of 2.3 children.
6. Most of the package travellers (81.7%) were more interested in touring/city/resort/cruise trips.
7. Package travellers tended to pursue the 'being and seeing', 'show and tell' and 'social escape' benefits while travelling overseas.

This study found that Australian travellers who preferred package tours were older, travelled in a larger party size and preferred touring around a city destination, staying in a resort or taking a cruise trip more than independent travellers. They also preferred the 'being and seeing' benefit. Furthermore, the age of the traveller did not seem to be the only factor that affected the choice of undertaking a package tour in comparison with the independent traveller. What was more important was the length of travel time as shorter-time trippers preferred package tours. This is because the tour option made the most economical use of time to see a greater number of attractions at specific destinations in a shorter time span, in comparison with the independent traveller.

Discussion

Studies have shown that older tourists are more likely to choose a package holiday than to travel independently, and that age was a significant variable for the selection of a package tour. The older sector of the population tend to choose this type of travel mainly for safety reasons, whereas younger people prefer to take organized tours to make friends. Older people feel protected on a group tour, and this prevents them from feeling lonely as well as reducing their sense of anxiety or fear when faced with a large amount of free time that is built into the itinerary. Therefore, older tourists tend to worry more about loneliness, especially if travelling alone, and as a result prefer to take optional trips to excursions to fill in their free time. Package tours organizers should avoid making older tourists walk long distances from their hotels, or force older tourists to use public transport because of a fear of getting lost, not being able to communicate and not being aware of local traditions. Organized tours seem to satisfy motives of a cultural nature, as well as providing opportunities for human contact through organized group activities.

Motivations for Older People to Undertake Package Tours

Touche Ross and Company (1975) undertook one of the first studies to explore the motivations behind why older people choose package tours. In their survey they asked older consumers their main reasons for choosing package tours. In their results, the researchers found that convenience was the most popular reason (26%), followed by cheaper prices (22%), unfamiliarity with the destination (13%) and to 'see more and do more' (12%). Therefore, convenience was the most frequently cited advantage of package tours that was regarded as most important for older travellers. This finding is not surprising as travel is often regarded as being quite strenuous, and older people in particular may find the physical requirements of independent travel (such as baggage handling and walking long distances at airports) quite demanding.

Milman (1998) concluded that the psychological well-being of a sample of senior escorted tour travellers (124 respondents) had improved as a result of undertaking a 7-day package tour of North America. In her study, older travellers had a mean age of 70 and the majority were not married (51.2%). Of those who were not married, 35.8% were widowed and 10.6% were single. Milman found that travellers were generally very satisfied, or satisfied, with the trip (93.3%). Their level of happiness was not significantly greater as a result of the package tour, but there was a positive association between their increased level of happiness and participation in a wide range of leisure activities on the trip. The most popular activities reported by the respondents were sightseeing, dining in restaurants, visiting historical places and shopping. Therefore, Milman concluded from her data, that older travellers who participated in a large number of trip-related leisure activities seemed to be much happier than travellers who were involved in only a few leisure activities.

Bai *et al.* (2001) conducted a large study that profiled a sample of seniors (55 years and older) who were travelling overseas to the USA using a tour package, and who were from three different countries: Japan, Germany and the UK. They used an in-flight survey on a sample of several international flights departing from airports in the USA in 1995. The sample utilized 1620 older pleasure travellers of which 1013 were Japanese, 274 were from the UK and 273 were from Germany. This study developed a separate profile for older people who preferred a package tour and were from the following three countries: Japan, the UK and Germany. Each case will be discussed separately.

Senior Japanese travellers who prefer package tours

The mean age of senior Japanese travellers was 62. Almost two-thirds of senior Japanese travellers (62.5%) preferred package tours in comparison with about half of the senior Germans (46.5%), while British senior travellers had the lowest rate of participation, with just over one-third (34.3%) preferring group package tours. This shows that older Japanese travellers preferred package tours, whereas more than a half of the British and German senior travellers who were surveyed preferred non-package (or independent) travel.

For Japanese senior travellers, more people were included in the travel party of the package tour (9.7 people compared with 7.1 on an independent trip). The Japanese also were found to take the shortest trips (5.1 nights compared with 7.8 for independent tourists). Furthermore, those who travelled with a spouse as part of a tour group preferred to take a package tour with the main purpose of shopping, to undertake commercially guided side trips and to enjoy sightseeing in the major cities.

Profile of a senior Japanese package tour participant

Preference	62.5%
Gender	Male 67.7%
Mean age	62 years
Travel party	9.7 people
Length of trip	5.1 nights
Travel companion	Spouse + tour group
Leisure activities	Shopping, dining in restaurants, sightseeing, commercial guided tours, visiting small towns and villages

(From Bai *et al.*, 2001, p. 158.)

Senior British travellers who prefer package tours

The average age of the senior British travellers who preferred package tours was 62.2 years. More men (64.1%) than women preferred package tours, while the average number of nights away from home was 13.3 compared with 18 for senior tourists who preferred independent travelling. Only 15.9% of the UK sample population were first-time travellers, which was the lowest percentage among the samples from the three countries. In regard to leisure activities, the UK package travellers preferred to dine in restaurants, shop, sightsee in the cities, visit small towns and villages, historical places and national parks.

Profile of a senior British package tour participant

Preference	34.3%
Gender	Male 64.1%
Mean age	62.2 years
Travel party	3.9
Length of trip	13.3 nights
Travel companion	Companions in tour group
Leisure activities	Dining in restaurants, shopping, sightseeing in cities, visiting small towns and villages

(From Bai *et al.*, 2001, p. 159.)

Senior German travellers who prefer package tours

The average age of the senior German traveller who preferred package tours was 60.8 years. More men (68.3%) than women preferred package tours, while the average size of the tour package group was 6.8 people compared with 2.4 for those who preferred to travel independently. The average number of nights away from home was 14.6 nights compared with 20.6 for senior tourists who preferred independent travel. In regard to leisure activities, the German package tour travellers wanted to shop, sightsee in major cities, dine in restaurants and visit national parks.

Profile of a senior German package tour participant

Preference	46.5%
Gender	Male 68.3%
Mean age	60.8 years
Travel party	6.8 people
Length of trip	14.6 nights
Travel companion	Companions in tour group
Leisure activities	Shopping, sightseeing in cities, dining in restaurants, visiting national parks

(From Bai *et al.*, 2001, p. 160.)

Discussion

Convenience and ease of travel were the major reasons stated by older people for preferring package tours to independent travel. Trip-related leisure activities were also found to be important when choosing the preferred type of package tour. When examining socio-demographic variables, gender and culture were seen as most important, with older men preferring package tours in comparison to older women. Older Japanese tourists had the strongest preference for package tourism in comparison to older German and British tourists. They also had the largest number of people in their tour party, and were away for the shortest amount of time in comparison to British and German travellers. This may be due to the collective attitude of the Japanese who prefer to travel with people from the same nationality and undertake shorter trips because of the social obligation to family and friends whom they have left behind.

Special Interest Tours

There is a growing market segment of relatively affluent, frequent travellers who want to participate in special interest tourism and are particularly interested in adventure travel packages (Sorensen, 1993). Instead of purchasing from packagers of escorted motorcoach tours or retail travel agents, they prefer to buy their tours directly from special interest tour packagers. One factor that makes this market segment particularly attractive is that they travel during the off-season. For example, many hobby groups such as stamp and doll collectors are willing to travel off-season because all their activities take place inside a hotel, and they do not really care about inclement weather. Conversely, hard adventure travellers who seek out physical activities with a high degree of physical risk generally travel only when the weather is suitable for this type of activity.

Special interest tour packagers differ from traditional tour packagers in that they:

- organize only a few small tour groups each year at specific locations;
- attract a market that is more motivated by the activities on the tour rather than by its price;
- include tour activities that are remote and inaccessible to people travelling on their own;
- include destinations that are off the 'beaten track' and not usually frequented by tour groups;
- advertise their packages in narrowly focused publications; and
- have a loyal market base characterized by 44% repeat business (Sorensen, 1993).

This market caters for a specialized group that prefers to go to new, exciting and interesting places. Therefore, it is important that special interest packagers continually attempt to diversify their destinations to meet the growing demand. For example, Globus and Cosmos of Littleton, Colorado, is the world's biggest escorted travel operator, and it has added eight tours since it started business such as river rafting in the Rockies and diving at Australia's Great Barrier Reef. They also added shorter tours of 2 weeks or less to accommodate the work schedules of the growing number of travellers who are not yet retired or are semi-retired. There are now at least a dozen adventure travel companies that market primarily to more than 50 travellers, with group package tours specializing in safaris, rafting trips, treks and sea kayaking. Mark Campbell, marketing director of Mountain Travel Sobek, stated: 'Our clients who are 60 years and over have been growing steadily. They have the money, the time, and the love of travel' (McDowell, 1999, p. 2).

Many older people prefer the safety and convenience of package tours in which meals, hotels, admissions and baggage transfers are included in the price, and where they can mix with people who have similar interests. Globus and Cosmos estimated that escorted tours represented about 4% of the more than $400 billion leisure travel market. Maupintour is another large tour operator that began in 1951 to cater for a small elite group who could afford to take longer escorted tours. Currently this tour operator has 150 tours in 50 countries and 35 states in the USA, and this includes eight first-time soft adventure tours that are primarily intended for travellers who are aged 45–60, but are also available to younger people. Five of the tours include horseback riding, hot-air ballooning, river and white-water rafting, hiking and canoeing (McDowell, 1999).

The hospitality industry needs to be able to quickly respond to these small companies that promote special interest tourism, and that will become the cutting edge of leisure travel buying in the future. Tour packagers report that 45% of their tour nights are spent in hotels as many seniors on hiking tours request a bed and a hot tub or shower after their outdoor experience. Furthermore, the adventure market is generally made up of business executives and professionals who are accustomed to staying in upscale hotels and resorts. Therefore, special interest package tours will help the hotelier to fill their rooms in the low and shoulder seasons as well as attracting more affluent tour groups through diversifying their market.

Recommendations for Tour Package Operators

Designing a package tour for senior travellers is complex and challenging, and the tour operator needs to be able to create a comprehensive itinerary that takes into consideration specific knowledge about the needs of older people (Gay, 1999). This should involve:

- health and diet: the travel agent needs to ask senior clients if they require a special diet or have a medical condition that requires prescription medication. This information should be relayed to the tour company to ensure that medical conditions are adhered to, and medication administered appropriately. Tour managers should be fully aware of any medical problems such as diabetes so they can respond appropriately should the need arise. In this situation, a liability waiver needs to be signed by the perspective tour participant.
- overnight stays: having more than 1-night stay at a particular destination is annoying to many older tourists as they loose time checking in and out of hotels, and they spend a lot of their time packing and unpacking their luggage. In addition, the lifting and handling of heavy luggage becomes an onerous task. Senior tourists should be aware that the lower-price tour itineraries include many 1-night stays and avoid this type of package tour if possible.

- hotels: seniors need private bathrooms and they are not always found in the lower-priced tours. They also prefer low-rise buildings, large well-lit rooms with private baths with tub-showers and grab bars. They should be located in the quieter sections of the hotel, and the management needs to be trained so that they are knowledgeable and caring for seniors.
- food and dining: seniors are often reticent to enter foreign restaurants where English is not spoken and the menu is in another language. Tour designers need to be aware of different needs of seniors and provide English translation sheets for foreign menu items if possible. Certain medical conditions such as diabetes, can affect their appetites and food intake, while few seniors can tolerate highly spiced foods.
- bus tours: tour designers need to schedule shorter and slower travelling periods for older people, and include regular toilet stops every 2 h. They should also insist that seniors remain seated while the bus is moving, as many have diminished eyesight, which can affect their balance. For others who have trouble hearing, this may distort the amplification of directions over a microphone. The tour guide needs to be aware that as many as half of the busload may not be able to hear instructions through the microphone. The use of smaller buses is much more suitable and generally reduces the majority of vision and hearing problems of older people (Gay, 1999).

Discussion

Special interest group packages are a new initiative to attract the more affluent baby boomer and senior market, and their increasing fascination for visiting new and exciting places that are often related to adventure tourism and hobby activities. This is especially attractive for the tourism and hospitality industry because these special interest packages occur in the off-season and generally require the booking of hotel rooms in the low and shoulder seasons as well as attracting a new market of affluent business executives and professionals who are mainly interested in adventure tourism activities. It is essential when dealing with older adults that group package operators consider the specific needs of older people. These include health needs and possible medical conditions, special diets required, staying overnight and problems with packing and unpacking, special facilities required at hotels for older people, problems with food and translation of menus, and special requirements for coach travel.

Conclusion

Package tours are an important part of the tourist industry and have been so since many years. Escorted or guided tours are particularly popular among older people from the Asian countries of Japan, China, Korea and Taiwan. Conversely, for many older people in Western societies the traditional tour package has become less popular at the expense of more independent travel. Independent travellers prefer the freedom to plan their own travel and to stay spontaneously for longer periods of time in countries and cultures that are of specific interest to them.

Research indicates that older adults who select package tours as their main mode of travel generally prefer the comfort and convenience, safety and security, as well as the camaraderie of meeting and developing new friendships with people from similar cultures and backgrounds. Group package tours take the hassles out of travel and are generally seen as good value for money. However, tour operators need to take greater efforts to cater for the individual needs of older passengers in their packages, so as to provide a balance between large amounts of physical activity and passive relaxing experiences. Recent trends suggest that baby boomers and senior travellers are generally becoming more sophisticated about their travel choices than previous generations, with a growing trend towards providing for more adventurous, active types of travel experiences for baby boomers and senior travellers.

As a result of this growing trend, special interest package tours are becoming increasingly popular as they are catering for the specific interests of baby boomers, such as their growing attraction to soft adventure, cultural and educational experiences, and/or fitness and health-related activities. Because many baby boomers do not like travelling in large groups, a growing trend is towards smaller escorted group programmes that specifically cater for their needs so as to attract this large market segment. Robert Whitley, president of the US Tour Operators Association, predicted that 'baby boomers are going to be tour operators' best customers ever' (Del Rosso, 2000, p. 14). Tour operators have stated that in the future tour itineraries are likely to become more leisurely, less regimented, while transport will be more flexible ranging from small motorcoach travel, high-speed trains, small cruise ships to even bicycles to travel from one point to another.

The traditional package tour in which tour participants are given no choice will be substituted to provide travellers with a wider choice of dining experiences, spending multiple nights at a given destination and using selected destinations as the base for different types of day excursions. The emphasis will be on the provision of a flexible timetable such as starting out in the morning with groups of older tourists, to split up at lunchtime into smaller groups or couples, and to travel at a more leisurely pace, while the original groups may meet up again in the evening for dinner. The emphasis will be on implementing a package tour that consists of unique activities that incorporate elements that people cannot organize on their own.

References

Bai, B., Jang, S.S., Cai, L. and O'Leary, J.T. (2001) Determinants of travel mode choice of senior travellers to the United States. *Journal of Hospitality and Leisure Marketing* 8, 147–168.

Cohen, E. (1972) Toward a sociology of international tourism. *Social Research* 39, 164–182.

Del Rosso, L. (2000) Experts forsee 'baby boom' in new century. *Travel Weekly* 21 September, 14.

Enoch, Y. (1996) Contents of tour packages: a cross-cultural comparison. *Annals of Tourism Research* 23, 599–616.

Gay, J. (1999) A guide to tour designing for seniors. *Tourism Recreation Research* 24, 90–92.

Holloway, J.C. (1981) The guided tour: a sociological approach. *Annals of Tourism Research* 6, 122–136.

Hsieh, S., O'Leary, J., Morrison, A. and Chang, P. (1993) Modelling the travel mode choice of Australian outbound travellers. *The Journal of Tourism Studies* 4, 51–61.

Hudson, S.D. and Rich, S.M. (1993) Group travel programs: a creative way to meet the leisure needs of older adults. *The Journal of Physical Education, Recreation and Dance* 64, 38–40.

Javalgi, R., Thomas, E. and Rao, S. (1992) Consumer behavior in the U.S. pleasure travel market: an analysis of senior and non-senior travellers. *Journal of Travel Research* 31, 14–19.

McDowell, E. (1999) Many older vacationers shun the bus tour for the chairlift. *The New York Times*, 20 February, C.1.

Middleton, V.T. (1991) Whither the package tour? *Tourism Management* 12, 185–192.

Milman, A. (1998) The impact of tourism and travel experience on senior's psychological well-being. *Journal of Travel Research* 37, 166–170.

Morrison, A.M. (1989) *Hospitality and Leisure Marketing*. Delmar, Albany, New York.

National Tour Association, Inc. (1989) *A Travel and Psychological Profile of the Mature Market*. NTA, Lexington, Kentucky.

Nozawa, H. (1992) A marketing analysis of Japanese outbound travel. *Tourism Management* 13, 226–234.

Pizam, A., Jansen-Verbeke, M. and Steele, L. (1997) Are all tourists alike, regardless of nationality? The perceptions of Dutch tour guides. *Journal of International Hospitality, Leisure and Tourism Management* 1, 19–39.

Quironga, I. (1990) Characteristics of package tours in Europe. *Annals of Tourism Research* 17, 185–207.

Schmidt, C.J. (1979) The guided tour: insulated adventure. *Urban Life* 7, 441–467.

Sheldon, P.J. and Mak, J. (1987) The demand for package tours: a mode choice model. *Journal of Travel Research* 25, 13–17.

Sorensen, L. (1993) The special-interest travel market. *Cornell Hotel and Restaurant Administration Quarterly* 34, 24–28.

Taylor, B. (1993) New service offers group travel options to singles. *Toledo Business Journal* 9, 8.

Touche Ross and Company (1975) *Tour Wholesale Industry Study*. Touche Ross, New York.

Wang, K.-C., Hsieh, A.-T. and Huan, T.-C. (2000) Critical services features in group package tour: an exploratory research. *Tourism Management* 21, 177–189.

Woodside, A.G. and Jacobs, L.W. (1985) Step two in benefit segmentation: learning the benefits realised by major travel markets. *Journal of Travel Research* 24(Summer), 7–13.

Yamamoto, D. and Gill, A. (1999) Emerging trends in the Japanese package tourism. *Journal of Travel Research* 38, 134–143.

Yuan, S. and McDonald, C. (1990) Motivational determinants of international pleasure time. *Journal of Travel Research* 24(Summer), 42–44.

Different Travel Markets: Adventure Tourism and the Baby Boomer Generation

8

The aims of this chapter are to:

- Provide an understanding of the demographic characteristics of baby boomers and investigate their emerging interest in more physically challenging and 'adrenalin-driven' soft adventure activities.
- Define and classify adventure tourism into soft and hard adventure, and ascertain what type of adventure is more suitable for baby boomers.
- Recognize the main motivations that contribute to baby boomers' participation in adventure tourism experiences.
- Suggest a different marketing approach to persuade baby boomers to participate in adventure tourism activities.

Introduction

According to the World Travel and Tourism Council, adventure tourism is one of the fastest-growing segments of the tourism market and has become so popular that about 100 million adults have chosen vacations in the past that could be classified as 'soft adventure' (Miller, 2003). Furthermore, the baby boomer cohort group (who were born between 1946 and 1964) have been identified as an emerging market for the increased consumption of adventure tourism activities (Muller and Cleaver, 2000; Muller and O'Cass, 2001). Schier noted in Tsui (2000) this shift in the lifestyle paradigm:

The previous sought-after dream identity for the affluent involved fine luxury cruises. Now, trends such as globalisation and environmentalism have fed into adventure travel. The new paradigm is the adventurer: a snowboarder in British Columbia or a surfer in Indonesia. The images of these heroes become the dream reality ... the media paradigm has shifted from valuing black cocktail dresses to valuing rock climbing equipment.

(p. 38)

Silver (1994) stated that seniors are flocking to adventure vacation, which is now regarded as one of the hottest niches in the travel business. He stated that at least one-third of the people who pay between $100 and $250 to 'rough it' on white-water rafts, snowmobiles, horse riding and trekking are in their 50s, 60s or 70s. Bradford Washburn, an eminent mountaineer and cartographer, explained this willingness to face adversity: 'If there is something that you think that you can do, or even dream that you can, begin it. Boldness has mystery and power and magic in it' (Washburn in Silver, 1994, p. 102).

This is because many baby boomers have indicated that they were becoming bored with merely being a 'mass tourist' and passively sightseeing, and were looking for more exciting, challenging and authentic experiences when they reached their travel destination. As Symonds (1998) explained, a new generation of retirees are 'hungry to go off the beaten path', and that the senior adventure travel business is now a $500 million segment, is growing at 30% per year, and is driven in part by 'more and more retirees with time, money, and a yen for the exotic' (p. 102).

Senior adventure travel is booming because retirees are generally healthier, wealthier and better educated than previous cohort groups of older people supporting their desire for more active, adventurous experiences (Muller and Cleaver, 2000). Many want to escape the stress and boredom of their everyday routine, to spend their vacation time on pleasure-filled trips with a range of exciting and new physical challenging activities, as well as expressing their need to meet people and build new friendships (Camden and McColl-Kennedy, 1991). Gene Wellman, a 71-year-old retired environmental consultant from Klamath Falls, Oregon, USA, typifies this type of traveller. 'Wellman has no desire to be herded on to sightseeing buses. So he and his wife Genevieve have joined a small group trip to French Polynesia and Peru' (Symonds, 1998, p. 102).

Why are baby boomers attracted to adventure tourist activities? Why do they choose a particular type of adventure activity over another? If this is a new and largely untapped market, what marketing approaches are best utilized to attract this older cohort of people? Few studies have really addressed the needs, motivations and expectations as dimensions of tourism behaviour within the concept of adventure tourism (Fluker and Turner, 2000). Hall and McArthur (1991) suggested that there is a need for researchers to investigate what the main motivations of baby boomers were to participate in adventure tourism activities.

The literature has shown that baby boomers and recent retirees have a greater desire for self-fulfilling activities than previous cohorts of older adults, and they actively want to participate in physically challenging leisure activities, rather than merely being a passive spectator on mass tourism trips. They have more time to travel and one of the first things that recent retirees state is that they want to take a trip, whether it is around Australia or overseas (Muller and Cleaver, 2000). Older people want to travel as indicated by the fact that 21% of all trips taken in the USA were by people who were aged 55 and older (Travel Industry Association of America, 1998). Their love for adventure tourism is reflected in the comments by 74-year-old Elaine Carr:

> Over the last 10 years, I have slept in a mountain hut while climbing 19,300 ft. Uhuru Peak on Mount Kilimanjaro and pitched a tent in a sandstorm in the Gobi desert. I have been to Mongolia, Madagascar and Peru and I am already planning this year's trips to the Andes and Ethiopia. When I first began travelling after my husband died in 1993, my friends could not understand why I did not choose more relaxing vacations in Hawaii or California. I told them that those were very nice places, but I can visit those places when I get older.
>
> (Bierman, 2005, p. 53)

Discussion

Baby boomers represent an important or potential target segment for tourist operators because of the sheer size of this cohort group. They are generally regarded as healthier, financially well off, better educated and more independent, and have a greater desire for self-fulfilling outdoor adventure activities than previous cohorts of older people. They also like to discover new and off-the-beaten-track destinations. They are fiercely independent in their travel behaviour although they often travel with tour operators who provide extra services to make them feel special. As a result, the one area that is attracting greater attention in the tourism and leisure literature is the need to cater for the very active, able, adventurous traveller. Many baby boomers and seniors are increasingly seeking out adventure tourism because of their desire for more meaningful and authentic experiences.

Adventure Tourism

Because tourists are increasingly looking for more meaningful and authentic experiences when they travel, they want to experience more than merely the sights; they want action, sensory stimulation, to be physically challenged and to be able to 'participate with their own skins' (Moeran, 1983, p. 17). As discussed previously, baby boomers are generally healthier, wealthier and have undertaken a higher rate of travel than previous cohort groups. As a result, they feel that they are at a stage where they have exhausted many of the traditional tourist destinations. In other words, they have been there; they have done it; and now they want to try something completely different by actually participating themselves.

The adventure tourism industry is a newly emerging and fast-growing sector of the tourism industry, and is already accounting for around 15% of all leisure travel, growing at a rate of around 8% per year (Hawkins, 1994; Loverseed, 1997; Fluker and Turner, 2000). In the USA, it was noted that 56% of baby boomers have taken an adventure travel holiday or trip in the last 5 years (Travel Industry Association of America, 1998). Similarly, about 45% of Canadians participated in various outdoor adventure activities in 2001, and this was ranked as the second most popular type of travel behaviour behind visiting friends and relatives (Canadian Tourism Commission, 2002).

These figures reveal the enormous growth and potential of the adventure travel market, with Australia now beginning to follow this notable upsurge in demand for adventure tourism (Moore and Carter, 1993). In fact, Muller *et al.* (1998) have forecast that Australian baby boomers will be attracted by the adventure potential of many overseas destinations, and as a result they have emphasized the potential of providing adventure tourism experiences that are more suitable for older, rather than younger, people. However, Brown warns that it may lead to 'more people who are competing for limited recreational resources and increasing conflict over environmental issues' (Brown, 1989, p. 37).

History of adventure tourism

Humans have travelled throughout history and for many people travel is intrinsically linked to adventure. Travel has traditionally involved hardship and was often seen as extremely arduous and expensive. Amodeo (2004) noted that for many, travel in the 19th century was inspired by 'an urge to transcend the familiar and the commonplace' (p. 83), while poet William Wordsworth 'not only saw nature as being imbued with great spirituality, but also chose to experience it on foot'. In *The Prelude*, written between 1799 and 1805, Wordsworth explained that 'physical exertion is a requirement for visionary experience' (in Amodeo, 2004, p. 84).

After the industrial revolution, new innovations such as railways and steamships opened up travel to remote locations for greater numbers of people, while at the same time removing much of the adventure from the travel experience. In the 1950s early adventure travel experiences began for the first time in the USA, with Army surplus DC-3s and jeeps opening up remote areas of the country. Recently, the scale and scope of tourism has expanded enormously, and the package tour holiday has made adventure travel as painless an experience as possible. Travellers now expect to participate in adventure experiences that involve little strenuous exercise, good food, hot showers and comfortable beds. Recently, older travellers have tired of this 'sanitized' version and this has led to a small, significant but growing demand among contemporary tourists for something that is considered different and more challenging. Travellers are now seeking authentic experiences that provide spontaneity and discovery, as well as demanding more personalized experiences that are unique and special.

Definition of adventure tourism

Swarbrooke *et al.* (2003) concluded that adventure is not defined according to specific activities that are undertaken, but more by the state of mind and approach of the participant. However, there is no doubt that adventure denotes action; it is not a passive experience and is generally found to be engaging and absorbing. Adventure also involves effort and commitment, and often mental and physical preparation or training is necessary.

An adventure is by its very definition a risky undertaking. Adventure travel has been defined as 'travel to places that require a bit of effort and commitment to get to . . . and is about the experience and the journey, rather than a list of places visited or the level of luxury' (Amodeo, 2004, p. 84). It has been seen as one of two things: physically demanding challenges frequently occurring in extreme environments; and culturally demanding visits to places incredibly different to the traveller's home (Pleasants in Amodeo, 2004, p. 84). Adventure travel should not be confused with extreme sports and is certainly not only for young people. Older travellers are now finding adventure travel more appealing, and are becoming more adventurous than previous cohort groups, wanting to experience something personally satisfying for themselves.

Muller and Cleaver (2000) defined adventure tourism as 'physically bracing, adrenalin-driven, somewhat risky, with moments of exhilaration punctuated by many opportunities to assess and reassess what has been done or accomplished' (p. 156). Examples of different types of adventure tourist activities are white-water rafting, horse riding, hiking, skiing, scuba-diving, mountain biking, backpacking and camping.

The Economic Intelligence Unit's Travel and Tourism Analyst (Market Segments, 1992) uses a different definition, which says that an adventure holiday is 'one that contains an element of personal challenge, through controlled risk, daring and/or excitement, often in an inaccessible (wilderness) environment' (p. 38). This suggests that an essential component of adventure tourism is travel to unusual, exotic and remote wilderness destinations (Millington *et al.*, 2001). Activity, experience, environment, motivation, risk and competence were identified as primary dimensions that might characterize the traveller's perception of adventure travel (Sung *et al.*, 1997).

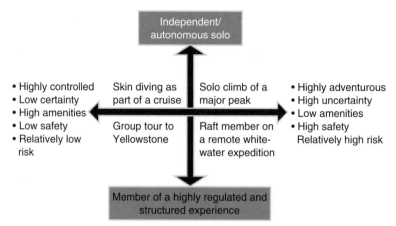

Fig. 8.1. The adventure tourism experience (from Ewert and Jamieson, 2003, p. 69).

Sung (2004) further synthesized these dimensions into three major attractions of adventure travel: activity, experience and environment. 'That is, an individual would be engaged in adventure travel for the purpose of gaining pleasure and personal meaning (experience) through participation in leisure pursuits in a specific setting (environment)' (Sung, 2004, p. 345).

Furthermore, the adventure experience can vary along a number of dimensions, including type of travel, group membership and the amount and spectrum of risk (Ewert and Jamieson, 2003) (see Fig. 8.1). The participant can engage in the adventure activity along several dimensions, such as the location (a remote wilderness trip travelling alone vs. a trip to Cancun as a member of a cruise ship), and this suggests that there are different levels and types of risk and danger that are expected and need to be seriously considered (Bentley and Page, 2001).

Soft and hard adventure

Several authors have distinguished between various types and levels of adventure activities and have categorized them as either 'soft adventure' or 'hard adventure', and these have been placed at opposite ends of the adventure continuum (see Fig. 8.2 and Table 8.1).

Hill (1995) referred to *soft adventure* as activities that are usually suitable for family involvement as well as providing an introduction to new and unique activities. This might include white-water rafting in oar-powered boats on Class 11 or Class 111 rivers, horseback riding on a guided breakfast ride, or hot-air ballooning with a commercial provider. Miller (2003) found several examples of soft adventure-type activities that older people are now participating in:

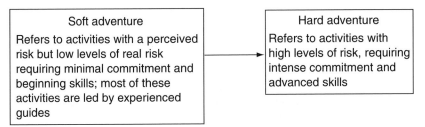

Fig. 8.2. Differences between soft and hard adventure (from Hill, 1995).

> Hiking the Scottish Highlands, biking across France, riding horseback across Mongolia, braving the rough Drake Passage to Antarctica, taking a walking safari in Zambia or canoe travel in Zimbabwe. Now they're even paddling the coastlines of the Fiji Islands, where once the main draw was watching the scenery from a beach chair while sipping a tropical drink.
>
> (p. S.2)

Hard adventure on the other hand requires advanced-level skills that are generally employed in dangerous situations. Travellers usually participate because of a deep interest and extensive experience in an activity that is usually outside the confines of a commercial provider. This may include climbing Yosemite's El Capitan, rafting through Cataract Canyon in a private group or hang gliding in the Telluride cirque (Hill, 1995). Experiences such as scaling Mount Everest, riding Moroccan camel trains and trekking through Mongolia demand fees ranging up to $25,000. Hard adventure travellers spend a median of $465 per trip, while soft adventure travellers spend a median of $325 per trip. The additional price of mountain gear elevates the expense, and the basic cost of outfitting a mountaineer is between $7000 and $8000 (Tsui, 2000).

Millington *et al.* (2001) more simply stated that the differentiation between hard and soft adventure was that hard adventure requires some previous experience and proficiency in the activity of the tourism experience, whereas soft adventure does not necessarily involve previous experience.

Table 8.1. Hard and soft adventure activities. (From Ewert and Jamieson, 2003, p. 69.)

Hard activities	Soft activities
Rock and mountain climbing	Camping
Snorkelling/scuba-diving	Biking
Caving	Flat-water canoeing
White-water boating	Photo safaris
Wilderness backpacking	Day hiking

A Travel Industry Association of America (1998) survey used adventure activities such as camping, hiking, cycling, animal-watching, canoeing, waterskiing and photo safari to define 'soft adventure'; while climbing, caving, backpacking in rugged terrain and kayaking were classified as 'hard adventure'.

However, this approach may be too simplistic and the placement of soft and hard adventure activities will vary along a continuum depending on other factors such as type of terrain, water levels and weather conditions encountered. For example, canoeing on a small lake with a gentle breeze is generally regarded as a soft adventure activity. However, if a sudden storm whips up the lake, the weather conditions may become very dangerous for canoeing and as a result this example needs to be re-classified as a 'hard adventure' activity.

Discussion

Adventure tourism is one of the fast-growing sectors of the tourist industry. This is because many travellers want action and excitement, to be physically challenged rather than being passive sightseers. Many seek unique and special experiences often in remote locations. This type of travel experience generally involves travelling in groups and experiencing different types of risks. Adventure tourism has been defined as physically challenging experiences that are engaging and absorbing and involve a level of commitment. They often occur in remote and exotic locations and involve different levels of risk, ranging from high level (hard adventure) to low level (soft adventure). These two categories are based on the risks involved, the skills or proficiencies required and the previous experience of the participants.

Adventure Tourism and Baby Boomers

Adventure opportunities are available for older people through travel in general, and the travel experience in itself is regarded as a learning adventure. Lipscombe (1995) stated that travelling is an important aspect of one's life adventure and exemplifies the search for meaning in later life. He felt that the taste for new adventures might be even more intense and addictive as we grow older. Older people are now craving new experiences with a substantial adventure component, and are requesting that they be part of the decision-making process. Older people are now demanding trips that 'involve physical challenge, if not actual danger, travel that involves an inner journey, intellectual challenge, as well as exploration of new places and cultures' (Friedan in Lipscombe, 1995, p. 44).

Muller and Cleaver (2000) concluded that baby boomers prefer soft adventure activities rather than hard adventure, because soft adventure activities are usually conducted under controlled conditions and led by trained guides who supply the educational component that older people prefer. One older woman recounted an adventure experience with the Colorado-based company Walking the World:

> I made arrangements through the company for a seven-day hiking tour of the Canadian Rockies, specifically Banff and Jasper national parks. I was in a group of six women and two men and two guides, a man and a woman. All of us were older than 60, nevertheless everyone was fit and had some hiking experience. Our guides were expert naturalists and planned daily walks that varied from four to six hours and took us to elevations of 2800 ft ... we all enjoyed the trip very much. I thought many times during the trip that travelling with my contemporaries increased my enjoyment. The vistas were the same but the pace was more leisurely. My group of 'elderlies' outwalked many younger people, and good spirits and fitness carried us further on the trail than some other groups ventured.
>
> (Harnik, 1998, p. 42)

Many of the adventure tourism providers scale back the physical demands of their trips for older people, such as reducing the number of miles travelled per day, lighter backpacks, optional rowing on a white-water trip, and providing a choice of vans or tents. Generally, tour companies warn clients that adventure travel can be taxing and even risky at times, and they need to prepare for strenuous hiking and rustic conditions on 5-day backpacking trips to Uganda, for example. As a rule, many of these trips offer training beforehand, especially for hiking and biking, as decent medical care may be many miles away. Some firms require older tourists to fill out a medical questionnaire before the trip, and may even request a physical examination if there are potential health problems (Silver, 1994). Therefore, travel companies need to be diligent and mindful about the physical capacity and health of their older clients before sending them off to rugged destinations. They also need to heed older people's preferences for slower pace tours, choosing their own food menus and avoiding too many early morning departures (Massow, 2000).

Researchers have calculated that in the USA alone over 207 million baby boomers have taken a soft adventure holiday or trip, whereas only 59 million people participated in hard adventure activities (Muller and Cleaver, 2000) (see Table 8.2).

Muller and O'Cass (2001) also noted gender differences: 'young at heart' older men were more likely to participate in white-water rafting, glacier hiking, rock climbing, caving and hot-air ballooning, whereas 'young at heart' older women preferred mountain hiking, rainwater treks, bird-watching and walking while on a travel holiday. A 'Marketing to Women' report (2000) suggested that these older women be termed the 'silent generation'.

The report described them as aged between 55 and 75, vital, affluent and willing to spend money. These women indicated that they preferred soft adventure travel such as going on safaris, hikes and trips to exotic locations. They stated that they preferred being in a safe environment with expert guides and in the company of their peers, especially with other women. However, there is always an exception, and recently an 80-year-old senior who travelled on a Grand Circle trip to New Zealand requested she try bungee jumping. Grand Circle is one of the leading companies specializing in mature tours and has recognized this new adventurous spirit of older people by taking over Cambridge Overseas Adventure Travel, an agency that specializes in worldwide adventures designed for travellers older than 50 (Morris, 1997, p. M1).

Another example is Elderhostel, which runs Bar H trail rides in Driggs, Idaho, USA. 'We have at least one or two trips every year for women over 50,' stated Edie Harrop, a Teton Valley rancher who has organized trail rides for women for more than 10 years.

'In the beginning, younger, adventurous women took the rides. Now we are seeing a lot of interest from mothers and the adult daughters and older women. We developed the market for "galloping grannies", which has created an opportunity for them.' They also organized a winter trip to Mexico that involved 3 days of 2-h rides near La Sierra Primavera and a 4- to 6-h ride on the fourth day. It combined adventure and luxurious accommodation: 'After the rides, women can relax in a very warm pool fed by hot springs, or swim in another pool that has

Table 8.2. Classification of adventure activities as either soft or hard adventures by baby boomers in the USA. (From Muller and Cleaver, 2000.)

Soft adventure activities	Demand (millions)	Hard adventure activities	Demand (millions)
Camping	64.7	White-water rafting/ kayaking	14.8
Hiking on gradually changing terrain	44.8	Snorkelling/ scuba-diving	12.4
Bicycle touring	27.2	Off-road biking/ mountain biking	10.8
Bird/animal-watching	24.3	Backpacking across rugged terrain	8.0
Horse riding	24.1	Rock/mountain climbing	7.4
Canoeing	22.5	Spelunking/ cave exploring	5.7
Total demand	207.6	Total demand	59.1

cooler water, or use smaller pools for soaking and relaxing, and there in this beautiful resort with a tropical feel, surrounded by lovely terrain' stated Harrop (Miller, 2003).

A further adventure travel company, Mountain Travel, organizes trips to the four corners of the world. They run a 2-week Antarctic cruise for approximately $6000. An 18-day voyage to the North Pole aboard a Russian icebreaker begins at $14,900, and almost everybody on the trip is a senior. They publicize the trips through a 130-page catalogue that includes Adventure Disc, a CD-ROM that shows pictures and sounds from previous trips. The company also has a listing on the internet and runs print advertisements in magazines such as *Sierra, Outside* and *Travel and Leisure.* Seniors are now seeking more inclusive travel with airfares, tours, food and even tips included. They are often drawn to more traditional travel excursions but with a more energetic approach. They want tours that get them out of the coach and doing things, rather than merely sightseeing from inside the motor coach (Zbar, 1994).

Discussion

Baby boomers in particular are often craving adventurous and authentic learning experiences. Most prefer soft adventure experiences under controlled conditions such as being less physically demanding, with trained guides employed to provide an educational component. Travel companies need to be aware of the preferences of older clients such as knowledge about each person's health needs, being less physically demanding, providing slower-paced tours, allowing choice in regard to food menus and providing plenty of social activities to encourage the group to mix and get to know each other. Gender differences are also evident, with men preferring more physically demanding activities such as white-water rafting, rock climbing and caving, while older women preferred less physically demanding but more educational activities such as bird-watching, horse riding and bush walking.

A Market Segmentation Approach for Older Adventure Travellers

Several studies have used psychographic research to segment the baby boomer market so as to ascertain whether adventure tourism is a popular tourist choice. Camden and McColl-Kennedy (1991) were one of the first researchers to study baby boomers who were aged 50 and older in Brisbane, Australia. They found that the biggest cluster identified in their study were those who engaged in pleasure and adventure when travelling. They termed this group 'experiential travellers' who preferred their trips to be filled with activities, as they indicated that they wanted to seek out new places, people and experiences.

Moschis (1996) segmented older Americans who were aged 55 and older into four main categories: healthy indulgers (18%), healthy hermits (36%), ailing outgoers (29%) and frail recluses (17%). Healthy indulgers seem to be the most likely group to choose adventure tourist activities – they have experienced the fewest number of negative life experiences such as widowhood and retirement, and do not suffer from chronic conditions. As a result, they are most likely to behave like younger consumers, with their main focus on enjoying life rather than trying to 'make it'. They were seen as the most likely group to afford expensive trips by air and cruise ship vacations.

Shoemaker (2000) used a cluster analysis to describe a market segment of older people he termed the 'active storyteller group' when he investigated the travel behaviour of older people in Pennsylvania, USA. This group was younger with a median age of 62, and were more likely to have recently retired. They wanted to escape everyday routine, and to have pleasure-filled trips with physical activities as well as to meet and build new friendships. Therefore, this market segmentation research used psychographic data to conclude that there is a specific segment of the boomer travel market that enjoys being active, seeks out pleasure and adventure, and wants to escape from a mundane lifestyle to find new and exciting friendships.

Sung (2004) used a stratified random sample of 1033 respondents from the mailing list of the Adventure Club of North America to define tourist types of travellers, and develop a traveller typology based on a segmentation approach of the adventure tourism market. An eight-page self-administered questionnaire about traveller and trip characteristics was used. The respondents were mainly younger, with 49% aged between 19 and 34, 67.6% were men, 54.5% were single, 44.2% worked in professional or managerial occupations, 92.4% were educated to a level greater than high school and 46.1% had an annual income of $50,000 or higher.

Classification of adventure traveller subgroups (Sung, 2004)

1. General enthusiasts (n = 243; 27.2%) appeared to be enthusiastic fans of adventure travel in general. They were mostly males (79.8%) with some college education, and they undertook at least one adventure trip per year (91.8%), mainly with friends (and their family 88.5%). They preferred hard challenge or rugged nature such as mountain climbing or sea kayaking rather than soft adventure activities.

2. Budget youngsters ($n = 193$; 21.6%) were mostly younger, aged between 19 and 34 (80.3%) and single (91.7%), with a relatively low income (61.7%). They were mainly highly self-orientated (68.4%) and made travel decisions and arranged trips by themselves. They preferred to take trips with friends (58.3%) and to take at least one adventure trip per year (94.3%), mainly to American destinations (57%).

3. Soft moderates ($n = 84$; 9.4%) were mostly middle-aged with the majority (56%) between 35 and 54 years, mainly women (54.8%), well-educated but disposable income was relatively low. They preferred soft nature-type adventure activities (66.7%) such as hiking, nature trips and camping mostly in American destinations (75%).

4. Upper high naturalists ($n = 128$; 14.3%) were mainly interested in soft adventure (46.6%), middle-aged (62.5% between 35 and 54 years) and married (71.1%). They preferred to seek novelty through visits to exotic destinations such as Europe or Africa (22.2%) or the Asia-Pacific region (31.6%). They generally stayed longer than 7 nights and spent more than the other groups (58.6% spent more than \$1000 per person per trip).

5. Family vacationers ($n = 119$; 13.3%) did not seem to be excited about taking an adventure trip, 83.2% were married, 80.7% were male, and many were engaged in professional or managerial occupations. They seemed to be mainly family-orientated when making travel decisions and taking trips, although most preferred travelling further than the soft moderates.

6. Active soloists ($n = 124$; 14.0%) were those for whom activity was generally important. They were highly motivated to participate in adventure travel, especially risk-taking activities such as hand gliding or windsurfing. They preferred to have travel arrangements made by adventure tourist establishments (57.6%) and sought novelty experiences at exotic locations such as in the Asia-Pacific region.

When examining this typology, the baby boomer group would seem to fit better into the 'soft moderate' or 'upper high naturalist' subgroups as they prefer soft adventure activities in exotic locations, are generally well-educated people with high incomes and who can afford the cost of travelling overseas.

Discussion

Psychographic studies have found that many baby boomers prefer to take trips that are filled with pleasure and excitement to escape their mundane lifestyle, and to meet new and exciting people in exotic locations. These types of people have been categorized as 'experiential travellers' or 'healthy indulgers', and are found to be well-educated older adults with high incomes who focus on living their lives to the fullest rather than concentrating on their career.

Older People's Motivations for Adventure Tourism

It has been generally accepted that *not* all baby boomers and older people want to do the same sorts of things, and they are seen as a heterogeneous group of people with different motivations, destination preferences, preferred modes of travel and personal values (Cleaver *et al.*, 1999). Some prefer to travel with their family in their own cars and caravans. A new trend that has been recently identified as 'grand travel' is one in which grandparents travel with their grandchildren. In fact, figures have been quoted that state that 20% of grandparents have been on a trip with their grandchildren in the previous year (American Demographics, 2001). Others are more adventurous travellers who travel with a companion or friends and explore new and different locations, while some prefer to totally enmesh themselves in a different culture, living in a new country for an extended period of time.

Why are older people generally attracted to adventure travel activities? The answer to this question is found in the baby boomers' lifestyle, as they place a great deal of importance on the value of fun and enjoyment in their lives, as well as achieving a sense of accomplishment, and wanting to become highly respected by others (Muller and O'Cass, 2001). Uncertainty and risk-taking also seem to be highly regarded as key elements of the adventure experience, as many older people want to experience the thrills and excitement of soft adventure activities (Morgan and Fluker, 2003). In this situation, clients also place a high priority on safety considerations (e.g. competence of guides, condition of rafts, past safety record with white-water rafting) in adventure experiences. Fluker and Turner (2000) discuss the role of activity risk as one of the main motivations for people undertaking white-water rafting. With too little risk, the customer finds the experience dull and boring, while with too much risk, the operator may be faced with a crisis situation (Morgan, 2000). Weiler and Hall (1992) described the motivations for adventure tourism as improved physical well-being, social contact, risk-seeking and self-discovery resulting from the experiences.

Milman (1998) emphasized the importance of leisure activities rather than the total travel experience for the older tourist. In her research study, she explored the impact of travel and tourism experiences on the traveller's psychological well-being or level of happiness. She concluded from her results that travel by itself was not a significant change agent for the level of tourist happiness. Other intervening variables such as the activity level on the trip were more highly regarded. Milman (1998) concluded that leisure-related activities were seen to be more important than the actual trip itself, and contributed towards establishing a positive change in the senior travellers' psychological well-being. This finding can be applied to adventure tourism, where the actual feelings associated with adventure activities such as when experiencing white-water rafting, kayaking and rock climbing are the main motivations for baby boomers undertaking the trip.

The novelty aspect is very important for some people, as they want to try out a new soft adventure activity that provides a different experience. Others want greater change, variety and challenge so as to escape their monotonous lives. They are often bored with their daily routine at home and want to escape and be exposed to risk-taking situations that increase their arousal level to optimum levels. After satisfactorily completing a challenging activity, you often hear people exclaim excitedly: 'I did it and it felt fantastic.' These psychological feelings are rarely experienced in other mundane aspects of a person's life such as in the workplace or in the home, and as a result people are much more likely to experience feelings that have been described as 'flow' (Csikszentmihalyi, 1975, 1990) or 'optimal arousal' (Ellis, 1973), which have been extensively discussed in the leisure studies literature. Based on Ellis's theory of optimal arousal, all people are continually seeking out new and challenging experiences to maintain or increase their arousal levels, and one way this can be achieved is through the adventure experience. Zuckerman (1990) used another term – 'sensation seeking' – to describe this drive for optimal arousal experiences, which he defined as 'the need for varied, novel and complex sensations and experience and the willingness to take physical and social risks for the sake of such experience' (p. 313). These feelings are regarded as very unique to the moment, and to achieve something like abseiling down a cliff for the first time can be such an exhilarating and memorable experience for all types of people, especially older adults.

Muller and O'Cass (2001) hypothesized that the concept of 'subjective age' is a major reason why baby boomers undertake adventurous travel. Older people generally feel that they are much younger than they actually are, and their travel preferences are often similar to those of younger people. Muller and O'Cass (2001) noted from previous studies that many older people who feel more self-confident, outgoing, socially venturesome, physically active and influential in dealing with others, possess younger subjective ages than their less confident, risk-adversive peers. This was found to be the case in a study of an extreme activity called 'jet boating' (people travelling in a specifically designed boat at high speeds through a narrow canyon in Queenstown, New Zealand) that was increasingly attracting older people as potential customers (Cater, 2000). Cater found that large numbers of older people whom he interviewed were attracted to this activity because they remarked that it made them feel young again. He concluded that this was related to the need for older people to rejuvenate their bodies through participation in soft adventure or hard adventure activities, and they believed that through the consumption of this experience they could buy (or bring back) their youth and stay 'forever young'.

Cater (2000) also noted that the jet boating company excluded older people who suffered long-term medical conditions, which restricted them from participating in this hard adventure tourist activity. He concluded that many older people were often forced into a situation where they had to supply medical

certificates to satisfy both the operator and the insurer about their state of health
before participating in adventure tourism activities. This was an example of age-
ism and discouraged older people from participating in specific adventure activities that enforced restrictions based on their chronological age.

Discussion

Older adults travel for a variety of different motivations. Generally they
want to experience the thrills and excitement of soft adventure activities.
Novelty and arousal are also important as many want to undertake risk-
taking experiences as an escape from a boring and monotonous lifestyle.
Many also want to feel younger again so as to rejuvenate themselves in an
attempt to buy back their youth.

Marketing the Adventure Tourism Experience to Baby Boomers

The boundary between leisure and tourism research is becoming increasingly
blurred and more fluid because of the growing realization that leisure and
adventure activities are an integral part of the tourist experience (Milman,
1998). Milman concluded that leisure and adventure experiences helped to
contribute to the traveller's psychological well-being and level of happiness.
While the visitor to a resort is traditionally classified as a tourist, most of the
activities that tourists pursue while at a tourist destination are leisure-related.
Coke and Perkins (1998) reinforced this when they stated that adventure tourism is fundamentally about active leisure participation and that the emphasis of marketing campaigns and slogans should be placed on new metaphors
based on 'doing', 'touching' and 'seeing', rather than merely 'seeing'.

   In the past, leisure researchers have made better use, and showed greater
understanding, of social psychological theory to describe the actual feelings
that participant's experience through their participation in adventure activities. The use of such words as enjoyment, fun, excitement, optimal arousal,
sensation seeking, flow and intrinsic motivation need to be emphasized by
marketeers to describe the leisure experience that is associated with adventure
tourism. In other words, the emphasis should be on the actual feelings and
emotions that people experience while participating in adventure tourism.

Discussion

Adventure activities are an integral part of the tourism experience. As a
result, any marketing campaign that targets baby boomers needs to focus
on the thrills, sensations, feelings and emotions associated with the actual

experience. This can be achieved by showing older adults the experience of soft adventure with an emphasis on the enjoyment, fun and excitement associated with the experience, rather than the dangers and risks involved in adventure activities.

Conclusion

Although there is general acceptance that the baby boomer travel market is a heterogeneous group of submarkets, there is an increased awareness that the adventure tourism market will grow more quickly than other segments of the market over the next few years. Independent adventure travel is becoming popular, especially if it is marketed with an educational or activity-based theme. Whether it is a wine tour to France or a hiking trip to the Scottish Highlands, the focus will increasingly be on interacting with local residents and gaining an in-depth knowledge of the local area.

Over the next 10 years, adventure travel will grow steadily, and with more and more specialist holidays available, it will soon become possible to choose the specific adventure activities that you desire. Multi-activity trips are likely to become more popular, combining outdoor activities such as trekking, rafting and diving as well as an added cultural component. Visits can also be arranged for sightseeing and to places of cultural or historical interest, either beforehand or after the main adventure activity part of the programme.

At present, the industry is focused on the young, wealthy and able-bodied adventure tourist; however, this is beginning to change as marketeers become increasingly aware of the more active and adventurous older baby boomer market. Adventure tourism is poised to become a larger part of the leisure market. Those older than 50 are more adventurous than their parents, and are driven to discover new destinations and to try new and exciting leisure activities. Many yearn to escape to a foreign country and be surrounded by a different culture for an extended period of time.

Therefore, based on an examination of the current research literature, future marketing campaigns need to place greater emphasis on the authentic statements used by older people that enable them to describe their 'real' experience, such as a sense of adventure, escapism and the challenge of actual involvement. Terms such as enjoyment, flow, optimum arousal, as well as meeting new friends should be emphasized so as to encourage feelings associated with a sense of freedom, fun and escape from a mundane and sometimes boring lifestyle at work and perhaps an unhappy family life. In addition, marketing strategies that promote images of older people engaged in soft and hard adventure activities so that they can feel younger and healthier by literally 'buying back their youth' should also be encouraged in the media.

References

American Demographics (2001) *The New Family Vacation*. Primedia, 1 August, 42–47.

Amodeo, C. (2004) Putting the adventure back into travel. *Geographical* 76, 83–92.

Bentley, T.A. and Page, S.J. (2001) Scoping the extent of adventure tourism accidents. *Annals of Tourism Research* 28, 705–726.

Bierman, F. (2005) For some, adventuring never gets old. *New York Times* 27 February, 5.3.

Brown, I. (1989) Managing for adventure recreations. *Australian Parks and Recreation* 25(4), 37–39.

Camden, D. and McColl-Kennedy, J. (1991) Travel patterns of the over 50's: practical implications. In: *Papers on the over 50's in the 90's: Factors for Successful Marketing of Products and Services*. Esomar, Amsterdam, The Netherlands.

Canadian Tourism Commission (2002) Canadian tourism facts and figures 2001. Available at: http://ftp.canadatourism.com/ctsuproads/en_publication/tourism2002.pdf

Cater, C. (2000) Can I play too? Inclusion and exclusion in adventure tourism. *The North West Geographer* 3, 50–60.

Cleaver, M., Muller, T., Ruys, H. and Wei, S. (1999) Tourism product development for the senior market based on travel-motive research. *Tourism Recreation Research* 24, 5–12.

Coke, P. and Perkins, H.C. (1998) Cracking the canyon with the awesome foursome: representations of adventure tours in New Zealand. *Society and Space* 16, 185–218.

Csikszentmihalyi, M. (1975) *Beyond Boredom and Human Behavior*. Jossey-Bass, San Francisco, California.

Csikszentmihalyi, M. (1990) *Flow: The Psychology of Optimal Experience.* Harper Perenial, New York.

Ellis, M.J. (1973) *Why People Play.* Prentice-Hall, Englewood Cliffs, New Jersey.

Ewert, A. and Jamieson, L. (2003) Current status and future directions in the adventure tourism industry. In: Wilks, J. and Page, S. (eds) *Managing Tourist Health and Safety in the New Millennium.* Pergamon, Boston, Massachusetts, pp. 67–83.

Fluker, M.R. and Turner, L.W. (2000) Needs, motivations and expectations of a commercial whitewater rafting experience. *Journal of Travel Research* 38(4), 380–389.

Hall, C.M. and McArthur, S. (1991) Commercial white water rafting in Australia: motivations and expectations of the participant and the relevance of group size for the rafting experience. *Leisure Options: Australian Journal of Leisure and Recreation* 1, 25–31.

Harnik, E. (1998) Seniors seek adventure hiking Canadian Rockies. *Insight on the News* 14(18), 41.

Hawkins, D.E. (1994) Ecotourism: opportunities for developing countries. In: Theobold, W.F. (ed.) *Global Tourism: The Next Decade.* Butterworth-Heineman, London.

Hill, B.J. (1995) A guide to adventure travel. *Parks and Recreation* 30(9), 56–65.

Lipscombe, N. (1995) Appropriate adventure: participation for the aged. *Australian Parks and Leisure* 31, 41–45.

Loverseed, H. (1997) The post-war generation and the North American travel industry. *Travel and Tourism Analyst* 3, 44–59.

Marketing to Women (2000) Silent generation women are active, affluent and often overlooked by marketeers. *Marketing to Women: Addressing Women and Women's Sensibilities* 12(13 December), 1–3.

Massow, R. (2000) Senior sojourns. *Travel Agent* 299(12), 1–2.

Miller, A.J. (2003) Travel: older vacationers pursue exciting itineraries, hiking, biking, riding, visiting unusual places become options so many. *The Atlantic Journal – Constitution.* Atlanta, Georgia, 24 September, p. S.2.

Millington, K., Locke, T. and Locke, A. (2001) Occasional studies: adventure travel. *Travel and Tourist Analyst* 4, 65–97.

Milman, A. (1998) The impact of tourism and travel experience on senior travellers psychological well-being. *Journal of Tourism Research* 37, 166–170.

Moeran, B. (1983) The language of Japanese tourism. *Annals of Tourism Research* 10, 93–108.

Moore, S. and Carter, B. (1993) Ecotourism in the 21st century. *Tourism Management* 14, 123–130.

Morgan, D.J. (2000) Adventure tourism activities in New Zealand: perceptions and management of client risk. *Tourism Recreation Research* 25, 79–89.

Morgan, D.J. and Fluker, M. (2003) Risk management for Australian commercial adventure tourism operations. *Journal of Hospitality and Tourism Management* 10, 46–59.

Morris, J. (1997) Seniors on the go. *Boston Globe.* Boston, Massachusetts, 3 August, p. M.1.

Moschis, G.P. (1996) Life stages of the mature market. *American Demographics* 18, 44–48.

Muller, T. and Cleaver, M. (2000) Targeting the CANZUS baby boomer explorer and adventure segments. *Journal of Vacation Marketing* 6, 154–169.

Muller, T. and O'Cass A. (2001) Targeting the young at heart: seeing senior vacationers the way they see themselves. *Journal of Vacation Marketing* 7, 285–301.

Muller, T., Chalip, L., Faulkner, W. and Green, C. (1998) Tourism product development for the ageing baby boomer segment. *Cooperative Research Centre for Sustainable Tourism (Griffith University) and Queensland Tourist and Travel Corporation, Joint Research Grant.* Gold Coast, Queensland.

Shoemaker, S. (2000) Segmenting the mature market: 10 years later. *Journal of Travel Research* 39, 11–26.

Silver, M. (1994) A trek on the wild side. *US News and World Report* 116(23), 102–103.

Sung, H.H. (2004) Classification of adventure travellers: behaviour, decision-making, and target markets. *Journal of Travel Research* 42, 343–356.

Sung, H.H., Morrison, A.M. and O'Leary, J.T. (1997) Definition of adventure travel: conceptual framework for empirical applications from the provider's perspective. *Asia Pacific Journal of Tourism Research* 1, 46–67.

Swarbrooke, J., Beard, C., Leckie, S. and Pomfret, G. (2003) *Adventure Tourism: The New Frontier.* Butterworth-Heinemann, Oxford, UK.

Symonds, W.C. (1998) Far from the tour bus crowd: track gorillas in Uganda, explore a rainforest, or pedal across France. *Business Week 3587* (New York) 20 July, 102.

Travel Industry Association of America (1998) *The Adventure Travel Report, 1997.* TIA, Washington, DC.

Tsui, B. (2000) Marketing adventures: exotic, far away travel destinations lure customers as advertisers trek along with campaigns, strategies. *Advertising Age* 71(25 September), 38.

Weiler, B. and Hall, C. (1992) Special Interest Tourism. Bellhaven, London.

Zbar, J.D. (1994) More than a cool bus ride needed to sway seniors. *Advertising Age* 27 June, 34, 37.

Zuckerman, M. (1990) The psychophysiology of sensation seeking. *Journal of Personality* 58, 313–345.

Different Travel Markets: Educational Tourism and Older Adults

9

The aims of this chapter are to:

- Discuss the growing demand for leisure learning by older adults, particularly among the baby boomer generation.
- Explore the growing trend to combine travel and learning for older adults.
- Appreciate the history and development of the Elderhostel network as an educational travel programme for older adults.
- Examine the links between educational programmes and commercial tourism packages.

Introduction

Older adults generally value lifelong learning and continually seek out educational opportunities as a way of adjusting to the challenges of moving into the third stage of life (Adair and Mowsesian, 1993). Lifelong learning interests do not fade away because individuals retire. On the contrary, their need for educational programmes and services often increases as they have more time to study and explore topics of interest (Pearce, 1991). Furthermore, opportunities for senior adults to participate in formal and informal educational programmes have improved dramatically over the last 30 years. In the USA, this has been attributed to the increased demand from servicemen and women who returned after the Second World War to attend

©I. Patterson 2006. *Growing Older: Tourism and Leisure Behaviour of Older Adults* (I. Patterson)

college, and who were supported under the auspices of the GI Bill. For many of the families that followed them, post-retirement has become a time for continued education, personal growth and active living. Because the older adult population is now rapidly increasing, there is a need to understand more deeply their learning needs and its relationship to tourism and travel.

Lifelong Learning

Lifelong learning encompasses all the learning a person does from birth to death – as we age we often learn simply for the pleasure of learning, as a form of leisure. Lifelong learning is associated with adult education as there has been a steady increase in the number of people taking courses for purely personal or recreational reasons (Cross, 1992). Cross (1992) analysed trends relating to the participation patterns of adult education and found that there was 'a category that includes education for participation in community activities, for personal and family interests and for social and recreational interests' (p. 94). Miller (1997) quoted figures that stated that approximately 86% of the nearly 5 million adult education students aged 65 and older in 1997 undertook classes purely for personal and social reasons.

Can older adults continue to learn cognitively and attitudinally as they age and still retain what they have learnt? Woods and Daniel (1998) conducted research to determine the answer to this question. They used a 40-min presentation on tourism (lecture and film on the beauty of the Mississippi River) to determine if this approach was an effective means of facilitating favourable attitude changes and information recall in older adults. The participants were 213 older adults who attended American Association of Retired Persons (AARP) meetings, as well as a church-based group. Of these, 119 were randomly assigned to the experimental group and 94 to the control group. Participants then completed a survey on the Mississippi tourist awareness programme, which concentrated on cognitive (knowledge) recall and measured respondents' attitudes towards tourism.

The results found that older adults can learn from information presented in an incidental fashion (i.e. information they are not actively seeking but presented while engaged in another activity such as a social gathering). However, as expected, the retention of this information tended to decline after a 1-month lapse. Nevertheless, the experimental group achieved higher scores than the control group on the two outcome variables, indicating that older adults can learn and retain at least some of the information presented. However, another finding was that attitude scores changed significantly less than knowledge scores over a longer period. This can be explained by the fact that the attitudes developed by older adults may be formed over many years and are difficult to change. In summary, older adults can learn information from one exposure, and retain information in areas that they found were particularly meaningful to them (Woods and Daniel, 1998).

Profile of an older learner

The profile of an older learner indicates that he or she does not want to do any homework, have grades or have any hassles, and is often more interested in learning about what will enhance the quality of his or her life and provide a leisure experience, rather than studying to obtain formal educational qualifications (Cross, 1992). 'They are in search for opportunities to increase their knowledge, nurture their creativity, and engage in lively discussion and debate among a group of their peers' (DeGirolamo, 2003, p. 60). Older learners expect to be involved in their learning rather than take a more traditional passive role, which is a characteristic of pedagogical studies (Manheimer, 1998). Thus, older students are more likely to participate purely for the joy of learning and personal contact with their peers. Edith Seiden described older students whom she had taught in her Shakespeare class over the previous 5 years: 'The members are here for no other reason than the joy of it, and they take studying very seriously' (Miller, 1997, p. 22).

Many older people have enjoyed a lifetime of learning and will continue to do so in their retirement years (Arsenault and Anderson, 1998). For example, Hedy Werner (in DeGirolamo, 2003) was a library branch manager before she retired, and stated:

> Upon retirement I found I needed something that would put me in touch again with the whole world of knowledge and information, and would allow me to interact with people having similar goals . . . retirees bring a myriad of skills, a ton of knowledge and a past history of hard work and willingness to learn into their new life.
>
> (pp. 60–61)

Future programmes need to focus on ways that connect older adults with special causes that promote the common good, such as the plight of children in poverty (Manheimer, 1998; Levinson, 2003). Because of this, older volunteers are assisting in schools through reading tutorial programmes, as storytellers to help children at primary or elementary schools, as career counsellors and tutors in high schools, and in co-learning classes at undergraduate university level to take advantage of multigenerational perspectives (Manheimer, 1998). Older and younger volunteers also work together in community activities in local neighbourhood health services. Furthermore, grandparents are increasingly assuming greater responsibility for childcare in working families as well as for single parents.

Many older people are seriously concerned about the meaningful and satisfying use of leisure time after a lifetime of work. Cohen (2000) argued that every older person is capable of discovering his or her own creativity, whether it is a hobby such as arts and crafts, taking an educational course or simply volunteering. Cohen asserted that a person's creative spirit needs to find expression despite facing such obstacles as poor health or disability that tend to increase with age. He insisted that the emphasis should not be on the quantity of time that is left for older people, but on the desire for quality use of this time. Thus, instead of lamenting that you are 'over the hill', the universal challenge for creative expression in life is that there is 'another peak to climb' (Csikszentmihalyi, 1996).

One way that older people have been able to rejuvenate this creative expression in their lives is by joining specialist educational organizations whose primary mission is to promote education for seniors. Because of this specialized need, Institutes for Learning in Retirement (ILRs) have been established in the USA as well as Canadian colleges and universities, while SeniorNet was established as a National Association catering for mature aged computer users.

Institutes for Learning in Retirement

During the 1960s and early 1970s there was a growing interest in the educational needs of older people. For example, in 1971 the White House Conference on Aging awarded a 2-year grant to the American Association of Community and Junior Colleges to explore ways that community colleges might highlight the needs of older people and to contribute to their quality of life. Another expressed outcome was to make education readily available to older people at little or no cost, and to help seniors to successfully cope with the problematic aspects of retirement and growing older.

ILRs were originally formed in 1962 by a group of schoolteachers in New York who were dissatisfied and unchallenged by the available educational opportunities for seniors. In 1977, Harvard and Duke Universities launched member-led ILRs that were based on a model of peer learning which began at the New School for Social Research in New York in 1962. These programmes consisted of small groups of well-educated retirees who took control and managed their own continuing education and acted as their own experts (Manheimer, 1998).

The mission and goals of ILRs are to serve the educational needs of older adults at a community level, and they differentiated themselves from other organizations by stating that they were a community of older learners who were self-funded, democratically governed by their members and who relied almost exclusively on volunteers to teach their classes. In most cases, ILRs were placed in continuing education departments of higher education institutions as examples of the institution's provision to fulfil their mandate to serve adults of all ages. Most ILRs were obliged to cover their own operating costs either by collecting fees or through the use of volunteer instructors. During the last 40 years, more than 148 ILRs have been established throughout North America serving more than 25,000 participants (Verschueren, 1995).

One of the oldest and most extensive ILR programmes is the Duke Institute for Learning in Retirement (DILR) in Durham, North Carolina, which has a current membership of 1200 older people and offers more than 70 classes each semester. The list includes courses such as book discussions, bridge, chamber music, line dancing, photography, recorder music, computer issues and more. At Duke, DILR member Pete Selleck, who describes himself as a retired army officer and who enjoyed a second career as a manager for an engineering firm, stated:

> I take numerous courses and teach several others throughout the year
> in subjects that interest me, such as the history of canals, energy issues,
> World War I, and the historical novels of Patrick O'Brien. I have served
> on curriculum committees, as well as having been President of DILR
> for one year. Currently I am involved with the DILR data base and
> registration system, which I developed and now maintain.
>
> (DeGirolamo, 2003, p. 62)

Martin and Preston (1994) saw the emergence of a new type of older adult that will become commonplace in the 21st century. They described this older person as healthy and active, better educated and more financially secure than previous cohorts of older people. As a result, larger numbers of older people are now seeking out educational programmes and services specifically designed to meet their learning needs.

Educational opportunities for rural seniors

In the past, many of the leisure and educational needs of rural older adults have been ignored because of the high costs and distances involved in providing educational programmes and activities to a widely dispersed population of older adults. This is slowly changing as many community colleges in rural areas such as the Aims Community College Senior Education Program (SEP) in Colorado provide opportunities for lifelong learning, creative expression, group discussion and sociability for older adults at 19 different sites and in 14 rural communities (Blanding *et al.*, 1993). SEP is an outreach leisure/educational programme offering courses in exercise, health, fine arts, history, literature, computer science, writing, geography, as well as other educational and recreational courses. A guide for teaching seniors was developed because of the need to educate instructors about the specific needs of rural seniors (i.e. lower income levels, lower educational levels, etc.) in comparison to their urban counterparts. Instructors also receive in-service training to keep them up to date with current trends and issues regarding rural seniors. The courses are offered at different sites at a variety of community facilities such as schools, community colleges and recreation centres, with the use of a well-developed cable broadcast system that allows seniors to use videotapes when adverse weather conditions prevent travel to the class site.

Discussion

Adult learning is growing in popularity with older people, many of whom are constantly seeking out new and varied educational experiences as they move into their retirement years. These educational experiences are mainly for leisure and social purposes rather than the quest for more formal qualifications. As a result, a number of Institutes of Learning have sprung up in the USA to provide increased learning opportunities for older adults in rural and urban areas, and are now offering a wide range of leisure-related courses to cater for the increased learning demands of older adults.

Educational Tourism

Many seniors want to incorporate travel with their learning needs. This has been termed educational tourism or 'edu-tourism' and is defined as 'a program in which participants travel to a location as a group with the primary purpose of engaging in a learning experience directly related to the location' (Bodger, 1998, p. 3). The emphasis is on actually experiencing or seeing the subject matter in its natural context or original location. The advantages of educational travel are that it provides:

- an immediate and personal experience of an event, place or issue that cannot be duplicated;
- opportunities to explore specific interests with other participants and the leader in a way that is often impossible in traditional educational environments;
- opportunities to combine leisure with learning experiences that are directed and meaningful; and
- daily exposure to a different set of cultural values that often leads to a change in the tourist's attitudes and values (adapted from Bodger, 1998).

Therefore, educational travel programmes fall naturally within a continuum of lifelong learning, and as a result are often featured in the publicity provided by many continuing education providers. Universities, for example, often provide non-vocational adult education programmes during their lecture-free times.

Educational tourists

Educational tourists are defined as people who take part in study tours or who attend workshops to learn new skills or improve existing ones while on vacation (Gibson, 1998). Kersetter (1993) set out to find out more about the attitudes, interests and opinions of college-educated older people toward pleasure travel. She used a random systematic sample of 412 respondents (250 males and 162 females) from a membership list of the alumni association of a large north-eastern university in the USA. The list was restricted to alumni who had graduated between 1945 and 1954 and as a result were aged between 55 and 64, and who indicated that they had travelled for pleasure or enjoyment during the previous year. Respondents completed a questionnaire that included 32 statements which assessed the travel-specific attitudes, interests and opinions that had been specifically drawn from the tourism literature.

This study found that college-educated older adults who travelled internationally had greater agreement with the notion that travel was intrinsically appealing. This suggested to the researcher that mature travellers were more interested in enriching their lives with 'experiences' than through hands-off entertainment (Kersetter, 1993). As a consequence, Kersetter suggested that marketeers should make greater efforts to understand older adults' attitudes, interests and opinions towards pleasure travel. Marketing campaigns needed to focus on the experiential nature of the travel product, and target older adults' need for greater emphasis on the educational travel experience (e.g. self-exploration or enhanced knowledge of other cultures and people), and for the travel industry to develop unique products that older adult travellers will seek out and purchase.

Gibson (1994) surveyed 1277 New England residents about their preferred type of tourism. She found that 20% of males and 25.8% of females preferred educationally focused vacations. Gibson found that educational travel was mainly preferred by ageing baby boomers who were 65 and older, and was more popular among older women than men. Her thesis concluded that older women in their 50s were more likely to participate in educational tourism. These women were mainly college-educated and believed that as they aged they needed to explore further avenues for self-expression, creativity and growth in their lives. For older men, the opposite pattern was common as they reported less interest in educational tourism than women. The men who were surveyed were more affected by their post-retirement transitions, with many experiencing negative feelings of uselessness and loss of identity brought on by retirement and/or entry into late adulthood. Those who were attracted to educational tourism were on average in their 60s, college-educated and relatively affluent.

Pennington-Gray and Lane (2001) surveyed the travel preferences of Canadians who were aged between 55 and 64. When their survey was completed, they found five distinct clusters of people of which the second highest scores were found in a cluster they labelled 'educational and cultural travellers'. This cluster scored high on the following items: 'opportunities to increase one's knowledge', 'variety of things to see and do' and 'historical places and buildings to visit'. Pennington-Gray and Lane (2001) concluded: 'This suggests that the preference for learning while travelling is a large component of the older generation's travel preferences' (p. 89). In a further study by the Travel Industry Association of America (2001) of people aged 55 and older, the report identified that visiting historical places and museums (15%), attending cultural events and festivals (12%) and gambling (11%) were among the top ten activities. This supported their findings that learning was important for older adults, especially in regard to learning about their own country's culture through heritage tourism experiences.

In another study on educational tourism by Gibson (2002), she conducted semi-structured interviews with six men and five women aged between 65 and 90 in the USA. She found that since retirement more than half of the respondents undertook extended trips and regarded travel as a significant part of their lives. They considered getting to know more about other cultures and taking time to research future trips as important to them, especially if they were interested in taking an Elderhostel-sponsored trip (van Harssel, 1994; Thomas and Butts, 1998). Achkoyan and Mallon (1997) also concluded that intellectual curiosity and spirituality are primary motivations that encourage older adults to travel.

Discussion

Educational tourism involves travel as part of the learning experience and caters for older people's preference to experience the subject matter in its natural context and/or its original location. Educational tourism is more popular with ageing people who have recently retired, particularly older, college-educated women. Men (20% or 1:5) generally reported less interest in educational tourism than women (25% or 1:4). This is because older adults now have the time to travel to different countries and are attracted by opportunities to visit and learn about different cultures from a first-hand experience. To older travellers, educational travel is intrinsically appealing, suggesting that they are more interested in enriching their lives with experiences rather than being entertained. Women in particular are looking for the opportunity to explore further avenues for self-expression, creativity and growth in their lives. However, older men indicated that they were less interested in educational tourism because many were still dealing with the post-retirement transition and negative feelings associated with uselessness and loss of identity. The older men who were attracted to educational tourism were in their 60s, college-educated and relatively affluent. Further detailed research found that older adults preferred to visit historical places and buildings, museums, cultural events and festivals, and casinos for gambling. The main motivations to travel were for intellectual curiosity and to gain greater knowledge about other cultures and historical events.

Elderhostel Programmes

The tourism and leisure education industry is made up of different types of organizations and institutions that provide opportunities to learn and to travel. Since the 1970s, international organizations such as Elderhostel and the University of the Third Age in Europe and Australia, and the ILRs in North America have been established to meet the educational needs of older adults. Elderhostel in particular has been recognized as the first educational travel programme that was specifically designed for older people. The mission statement of the Elderhostel programme declared:

> Elderhostel is an educational program for older adults who want to continue to expand their horizons and to develop new interests and enthusiasm. We're for older citizens on the move not just in terms of travel, but in terms of intellectual activity as well. Our commitment is to the belief that retirement does not represent an end to significant activity for older adults but a new beginning filled with opportunities and challenges.
>
> (Mills, 1993, p. 5)

The Elderhostel concept was originally developed by Martin P. Knowlton and David Bianco in 1975 at the University of New Hampshire and was incorporated as a non-profit organization in 1977. The inspiration to design a travel study programme for older adults came after a 4-year walking holiday in Europe by Knowlton. As he travelled through France, Germany and Scandinavia living in youth hostels, Knowlton was 'impressed by the way in which the availability of a network of modest accommodations encouraged and nurtured an adventuresome spirit in European youth' (Goggin, 1999, p. 86). He was also impressed by the Scandinavian folk school model that encouraged older adults to pass down their culture and traditions such as folk arts, music and dance to younger generations. On his return to the USA he created a model programme with his friend Bianco that combined the best traditions of education and hostelling for older adults.

Elderhostel specifically caters for the leisure education needs of adults who are 55 and older. In 2002, the average age of Elderhostel travellers increased to 72 years, which was older than 68 years that had been reported just 4 years previously (Ruffenach, 2004). Its popularity has soared from 220 enrolments in 1975 to over 309,000 people who undertook Elderhostel trips in 1999. The programme has grown to include over 2300 campuses and institutions in the USA and Canada, and over 70 countries worldwide. The programmes specifically cater for people older than 55 in all states of America, and are typically of 5 or 6 days, while internationally they may be for 2–3 weeks long. The daily routine generally involves three 1.5-h classes taught by local faculty in addition to learning taking place through field trips, excursions and extracurricular social activities. Generally, participants in the American programmes must arrange their own transportation to the programme site. Participants often stay in campus accommodation and eat in dining halls just like undergraduate students, but they do not have the worries associated with homework, exams or grades (Miller, 1997).

Unlike other study tours, Elderhostel's international programmes are planned and conducted by educators and travel coordinators in the host country. Participants are met, transported, housed and educated by representatives from the country they have arrived to study in. This provides added appeal to the programmes, as they allow special opportunities for older students that are not usually available to the general public. New programme development generally occurs in countries where Elderhostel does not have programmes or where there is a lack of a certain type of programme that Elderhostel believes would have a wide appeal (Goggin, 1999).

Thus, Elderhostel provides the opportunity to study a wide range of subjects ranging from culture and history to anthropology, the arts and both the physical and social sciences. It also offers opportunities for educational travel in addition to the leisure education, which is seen as an essential component of Elderhostel programmes (Szucs *et al.*, 2001) (see Fig. 9.1).

Motives for attending Elderhostel programmes

The Elderhostel movement has been described as a unique programme although it has received little serious attention by researchers in the past.

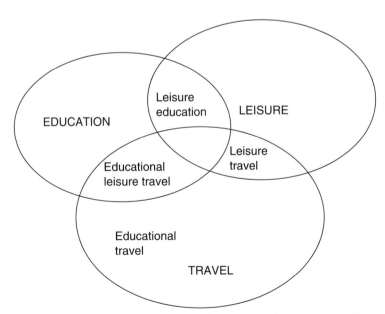

Fig. 9.1. Educational leisure travel (from Arsenault and Anderson, 1998, p. 29).

However, several academic studies have been conducted over the last 10 years. Elderhostel participants have been characterized as older, wealthier, better educated and more self-actualized than a typical sightseeing tourist (Mills, 1993). Long (1995) supported this finding when he investigated the main outcomes of Elderhostel participation and found that participants were much more motivated to travel by the 'seeking' dimension than by the 'escape' dimension.

Thomas and Butts (1998) investigated the leisure motives and satisfiers of a group of international Elderhostel travellers. The subjects for their study were a group of Elderhostel participants on a trip to Budapest, Hungary. A total of 39 participants volunteered to participate ranging in age from 58 to 80, with a mean age of 68. A leisure motivation scale (Beard and Ragheb, 1983) was used to gather information regarding older adults' leisure motives and satisfactions. The researchers found that 'intellectual stimulation' was the highest rating dimension for both the motivation and satisfaction categories. However, in contrast to studies of pleasure-seeking travellers, Elderhostelers reported that 'social interaction' or 'escape' motives were not strong motivators for leisure behaviour. The researchers explained that the main reason for this finding was related to the independent nature of this particular population who were characterized as being generally more self-actualized than the general population. As one Elderhosteler stated: 'I didn't come here to develop friendships, I came here to learn about the culture' (Thomas and Butts, 1998, p. 36).

However, 'social interaction' was rated more highly as a satisfaction motive even though it was not regarded as a strong motivating influence for participation. This finding suggested that social interaction might not be a major reason for Elderhostelers' participation, yet it enhanced their experiences when travel began. That is, they enjoyed the interaction and camaraderie of others while pursuing other higher priority needs for their main growth experiences. The 'escape' dimension was also not viewed as a high level motivator for participation by the Elderhostelers. This was attributed to the fact that Elderhostelers did not have the same occupational demands as younger pleasure travellers, and as a result preferred to seek stimulation rather than avoiding it (Thomas and Butts, 1998).

Arsenault *et al.* (1998) examined the main factors that influenced Elderhostel participants' decisions to attend courses, and the reasons why they selected specific programmes. This study collected data from 154 Elderhostel participants with a mean age of 68 who had enrolled in one of ten programmes in a number of Canadian provinces during May and June of 1996. The data were collected through focus group discussions and in-depth interviews and evaluated by eight senior Elderhostel Canada staff members and two expert advisers. This study asked participants to identify the factors that influenced their decision to attend Elderhostel and then asked how these factors were sequenced.

After considerable reflection and transcript reviews, 14 separate factors were identified and defined by the researchers. These were location, travel, programme, course content, accommodations, cost, dates, negotiation with a travel partner, social, sites, organization, personal requirements, escape and information. One participant stated:

> Location is number one, I want to be away from a large city and I like the scenery, not that this necessarily means the mountains. As far as the subject matter is concerned I prefer courses with outdoor activities and nature studies. As far as accommodations are concerned I appreciate the comfortable facilities which are offered in this hotel, but I have been to other Elderhostels in primitive conditions, and as a matter of fact, it was the Elderhostel I enjoy the most, not because of the accommodations.
>
> (Arsenault *et al.*, 1998, p. 105)

When sequencing the decision-making factors, it was a common practice that participants merely prioritized them into a list such as location, course content and accommodations. Another gentleman explained the process:

> We'd been receiving Elderhostel catalogues for some time and never took it upon ourselves to make a decision. Finally, last year we made a decision and I think the reason we went there was that we could drive and it tied in with visiting folks we used to know. This year's location was really based more on timing, we had a timeframe that would tie in with our vacation. Time frames first, and an activity that was not cerebral, but physical. After a lifetime of working I needed something outside.
>
> (Arsenault *et al.*, 1998, p. 108)

After analysing the data, a participant typology of six Elderhostel participants emerged that best described how participants chose their programmes. The six different types of people were: activity-oriented, geographical guru, experimenter, adventurer, content-committed and opportunist:

1. Activity-oriented: selects an Elderhostel site based on the fact that there is an activity component included. This type of person wants to spend time outdoors, explore the natural environment and be actively engaged in their learning. This may take the form of a genealogical library search, a field trip or a nature hike, or be sports-orientated such as golf, hiking or tennis.
2. Geographical guru: selects a site based on the fact that he or she wants to visit the area or region so as to see, explore and learn about this area. As one person said: 'I'll take a lot of programs I don't like because I want the location. Even if they are studying basket weaving, if I want the area I'll go because I know I will learn something.'
3. Experimenter: is a novice participant who wants to explore the different possibilities that Elderhostel has to offer. The first experience is close to

home to keep the initial financial investment low and permit a quick retreat if he or she does not enjoy himself or herself. The experimenter also worries about the academic level of the learning experience. This fear of the classroom directs many experimenters towards sites where he or she either has a prerequisite knowledge of the subject matter or can engage in some form of physical activity.

4. Adventurer: is willing to go anywhere and try anything; he or she is looking for new experiences in learning and socializing and will even sacrifice accommodations just to have a new experience. As one experienced hostelier affirmed: 'I'm the kind of person who likes to try something different. I can't say exactly which program I am choosing, but it's something that I have never done before and might find interesting.'

5. Content-committed person: is willing to travel anywhere to find the site where the programme supports his or her learning interest. This person is interested in quality instruction at university level and meeting people who share his or her passion for the subject area.

6. Opportunist: is not interested in the programme and uses Elderhostel as a means for a cheap holiday, a better breakfast or as a means to some other end. The following comments were made by one participant: 'Oh yes, you can spot a fraud a mile away, Elderhostelers don't want these types of people filling up the places. We were at one site where this person used Elderhostel as a cheap room and board for a house-hunting trip and showed up only for meals. This is not a good plan' (Arsenault *et al.*, 1998, pp. 110–112).

Szucs *et al.* (2001) compared 223 international with 223 domestic Elderhostel participants, to ascertain whether there were differences in specific motives for participation in international and domestic Elderhostel programmes. The researchers used logistic regression analysis and found that there were five major differences between international and domestic educational travellers. The following reasons were given for participation in the international Elderhostel programmes:

1. An appreciation of the history and culture of the sites that were visited.
2. The safety that Elderhostel programmes offered.
3. The desire to travel and the excitement of visiting new places.
4. The desire to socialize with local people at the sites.
5. Ancestry and the desire to visit an area where family previously lived.

The following reasons were given for participation in the domestic Elderhostel programmes:

1. The topic of the course.
2. The opportunity to escape from personal problems.
3. The dates of the programme.
4. The influence of acquaintances to participate.
5. The standard of the available accommodation.

The future of Elderhostel

The future of Elderhostel is bright and the projections are for continued growth. With demographic trends showing an increase in the older population, the organization's greatest challenge will be to provide enough programmes to meet the increased demand. In addition, as part of its strategic planning process, Elderhostel has attempted to research and study the learning and travel patterns of American adults 55 years and older, and plans to take creative approaches to reach new audiences.

Innovations in programme location have already begun and Elderhostel programmes are in some cases moving from college campuses to include a variety of different educational and outdoor centres and parks. New partnerships have also been forged between Elderhostel and museums and other specialized institutions. 'Moving' courses where participants, for example, trace a pioneer trail, learning geography and period history along the way, are being implemented. In terms of programming content, theme programmes in which three courses relate to one broad subject such as fine arts, music and creative writing are also becoming popular.

Elderhostel is planning to offer programmes under a separate programme name to appeal to baby boomers in their 50s, who are approaching retirement or pursuing options for enrichment and educational travel. Educational programmes that include highly active, experiential learning opportunities are likely to be selected for a new set of offerings. Plans are also underway to extend the Elderhostel experience to older adults in other European countries, as participants in Elderhostel programmes at present are solely from North America. An expansion to other parts of the world will follow as the organization begins to serve a global market (Goggin, 1999). However, Elderhostel holds fast to what works, the original programme design – one weekend, three courses, no tests and a mix of extracurricular activities (Mills, 1993).

Discussion

Elderhostel was the first educational travel programme that was specifically designed for people aged 55 and older. The programme has grown from 220 enrolments in 1975 to over 309,000 in 1999, with 2300 campuses and institutions involved in the USA and Canada, as well as over 70 countries worldwide. Generally, participants live in campus accommodation and eat in dining rooms although they do not have to do homework, sit for exams or compete for grades. Generally, international programmes may run for up to 2–3 weeks with classes of three 1.5-h sessions, as well as field trip excursions and social activities. Participants are more motivated to travel because of the 'seeking' and 'intellectual stimulation' rather than the 'escape' motive, which was not found to be a strong motivator for leisure or tourism behaviour of older adults undertaking Elderhostel trips. The location of the educational trip was also a key factor in its appeal for potential participants. Once they had selected a particular trip destination, participants were keen to seek out and explore the natural environment and surroundings, as well as being actively engaged in their learning. For domestic participants, the course topic was the main motivating factor. Future programmes are planning to include a variety of other educational institutions such as museums, outdoor centres and parks. 'Moving' courses in which participants use a number of different disciplines to trace a particular historical period of time are also likely to be introduced to provide experiential learning opportunities.

Commercial Educational Tourist Opportunities

Educational programming is regarded as a fast-growing area, and is seen as a natural progression for resort activity departments to move from purely fun activities to those with educational components. Holdnak and Holland (1996) suggested that older participants wanted to take something home at the end of the vacation such as a lost or forgotten hobby, rather than merely participating in a range of activities. As a result, many travel agencies are specializing in group tours to educational destinations. For example, Siesta Tours in Florida provides guided tours to the historic centre of Mexico. 'Their clients are totally immersed in the history and culture of the region rather than just left sitting on the beach sipping margaritas' (Holdnak and Holland, 1996, p. 75).

A travel group in Boston has recently introduced a new programme titled 'Road Scholar' (Ruffenach, 2004). This programme is intended to provide an alternative to the Elderhostel style of travel. It is pitched at younger–older adults and differs from traditional Elderhostel excursions in the following ways: groups are smaller (generally limited to 23 participants compared with 39 for Elderhostel), there is more free time (1 free day for every 7 days of travel, as well as time every afternoon) and fewer meals built into the schedule. The emphasis is more on experiential learning through discussions with local residents out in the field, rather than traditional lectures in classroom settings. For example, Road Scholar offers a 13-day trip titled 'Exploring Scotland's Highlands and Wild Islands' to immerse visitors in the natural history and folklore of the region. While this excursion has a formal structure in which 1 day will be spent on the Isle of Skye, participants will be given a choice of options during most travel days. For example, during the day on Skye, participants can either examine the ruins of Armadale Castle or study the habitats of otters and basking seals. James Moses, a director, explained: 'The flexibility is going to be the biggest difference, and most of the program takes place out of the field. You really come away from it having experienced a part of the world that you could never experience on your own' (in Ruffenach, 2004, p. R6).

The Disney Institute in Orlando, Florida, USA, was opened in 1996 and offers more than 80 hands-on learning programmes that range from culinary arts to topiary gardening, rock climbing and story telling. However, it does not come cheaply, with a visit to the Disney Institute starting at $729 for a minimum 3-day stay. Disney's goal is to encourage every guest who leaves to have more than just pleasant memories of pleasant experiences – they want to facilitate new knowledge, skills and a sense of 'expanded horizons'. It also provides an artists-in-residence programme and guest speaker forums (Holdnak and Holland, 1996).

Conclusion

The educational travel market is still quite small. However, academics are forecasting that as the population ages and baby boomers start to reach retirement age, the demand for educational programmes and services will dramatically increase during the next 20 years. Already, lifelong learning has been recognized as an important educational need in Western countries, resulting in a number of Institutes of Learning being established in North America, the UK and Australia that cater specifically for adults who are 55 years and older.

Furthermore, the current baby boomer cohort group will take their educational values with them into retirement and be eager to combine them with overseas and domestic travel. This has created exciting opportunities for the combination of overseas travel with cheaper accommodation at many different university campuses. Educational tourism provides older adults with the stimulation of gaining intellectually challenging experiences as well as learning through hands-on experiences about different cultures and ancient civilizations.

The success of the educational travel market will depend on providers creating the right image and making it clear to consumers that they offer 'added value'. This added value is related to offering something that is truly novel and different, such as the possibility of an in-depth study of a topic of personal interest with like-minded people under expert guidance and tuition. Road Scholar is one such commercial operator that is challenging traditional Elderhostel programmes and pitching its excursions at the younger-older market. Although it is generally more expensive, the tour groups are smaller, offer more flexibility and greater experiential learning than Elderhostel trips. The successful educational providers of the future will be those who can create an image, offer value for money, provide exciting destinations and packages, and whose reputation for the provision of quality educational packages is high.

References

Achkoyan, M. and Mallon, P. (1997) American retired people: a promising market. Marketing touristique et tranches d'age. *Cahiers-Espaces* 54, 40–44.

Adair, S.R. and Mowsesian, R. (1993) The meanings and motivations of learning during the retirement transition. *Educational Gerontology* 19, 317–330.

Arsenault, N. and Anderson, G. (1998) New learning horizons for older adults. *The Journal of Physical Education, Recreation and Dance* 69(3), 27–31.

Arsenault, N., Anderson, G. and Swedburg, R. (1998) Understanding older adults in education: decision-making and Elderhostel. *Educational Gerontology* 24, 101–114.

Beard, J.G. and Ragheb, M.G. (1983) Measuring leisure motivation. *Journal of Leisure Research* 3, 219–228.

Blanding, C.W., Turner, J. and Gerbrandt, M. (1993) Creating leisure opportunities for rural seniors. *Journal of Physical Education, Recreation and Dance* 64, 24–26.

Bodger, D. (1998) Leisure, learning and travel. *The Journal of Physical Education, Recreation and Dance* 69(4), 2–5.

Cohen, G.D. (2000) *The Creative Age: Awakening Human Potential in the Second Half of Life.* HarperCollins, New York.

Cross, K.P. (1992) *Adults as Learners: Increasing Participation and Facilitating Learning.* Jossey-Bass, San Francisco.

Csikszentmihalyi, M. (1996) Creativity: flow and the psychology of discovery and invention. In: *Creative Ageing*, Chap. 9. HarperCollins, New York.

DeGirolamo, J. (2003) Retirees: the 'new kids' on campus. *USA Today Magazine* 132(July), 60–62.

Gibson, H. (1994) Some predictors of tourist role performance for men and women over the adult life course. Unpublished doctoral dissertation, University of Connecticut, Storrs, Connecticut.

Gibson, H. (1998) The educational tourist. *The Journal of Physical Education, Recreation and Dance* 69(4), 6–9.

Gibson, H. (2002) Bus travellers: leisure-travel patterns and meanings in later life. *World Leisure* 2, 11–20.

Goggin, J.M. (1999) Elderhostel meets the silent revolution. *Tourism Recreation Research* 24, 86–89.

Holdnak, A. and Holland, S.M. (1996) EDU tourism: vacationing to learn. *Parks and Recreation* 31, 72–75.

Kersetter, D.L. (1993) The college educated older adult traveller. *Visions in Leisure and Business* 11, 26–35.

Levinson, R.W. (2003) Aging and time-binding in the 21st century. *ETC: A Review of General Semantics* 60, 46–52.

Long, H. (1995) Outcomes of Elderhostel participation. *Educational Gerontology* 21, 113–127.

Manheimer, R.J. (1998) The promise and politics of adult education. *Research on Aging* 20, 391–415.

Martin, L.G. and Preston, S.H. (1994) *Demography of Aging*. National Academy Press, Washington, DC.

Miller, B. (1997) The quest for lifelong learning. *American Demographics* 19, 20–22.

Mills, E. (1993) *The Story of Elderhostel*. University Press of New England, Hanover, New Hampshire.

Pearce, S.D. (1991) Towards understanding the free participation of older adults in continuing education. *Educational Gerontology* 17, 451–464.

Pennington-Gray, L. and Lane, C.W. (2001) Profiling the silent generation. *Journal of Hospitality and Leisure Marketing* 9, 73–95.

Ruffenach, G. (2004) Road scholars: a new travel program try to take some of the elder out of Elderhostel. *Wall Street Journal* (New York) 23 February, R6.

Szucs, F.K., Daniels, M.J. and McGuire, F.A. (2001) Motivations of Elderhostel participants in selected United States and European educational travel programs. *Journal of Hospitality and Leisure Marketing* 9, 21–34.

Thomas, D. and Butts, F. (1998) Assessing leisure motivators and satisfaction of international Elderhostel participants. *Journal of Travel and Tourism Marketing* 7, 31–38.

Travel Industry Association of America (2001) *Newsline: February 2001*. Travel Industry Association of America, Washington, DC.

Van Harssel, J. (1994) The senior travel market: distinct, diverse, demanding. In: Theobold, W. (ed.) *Global Tourism in the Next Decade*. Butterworth-Heinemann, Oxford, pp. 363–377.

Verschueren, J. (1995, August) Study before you go? The promise and the pitfalls? Paper presented at the Educational Tourism and the Needs of Older Adults Conference, Montreal, Quebec.

Woods, L.L. and Daniel, L.G. (1998) Effects of a tourism awareness program on the attitudes and knowledge of older adults. *Educational Gerontology* 24, 69–78.

Tourism and Leisure Needs of Older Adults in Retirement Communities

10

The aims of this chapter are to:

- Discuss the growing trend towards active living that may affect older people's accommodation needs.
- Identify the main factors that influence older people's decisions to migrate to another location.
- Examine the process of relocation for retirees who move to other countries or interstate based on their previous tourist experiences.
- Describe the trend towards active living in age-integrated retirement communities.

Introduction

Ageing has often been viewed as a 'problem' in the social gerontology literature as it has been defined in terms of loss, especially related to physical and social competencies (McHugh, 2000). Kaufman (1986) discussed the ongoing battle between the media stereotypes of old age and what she referred to as the 'ageless self' or a positive view of ageing that encompasses such notions as continuity, coherence and integrity. Kaufman advocated the need for older people to continually battle the negative stereotypes of ageing, such as those that have emphasized loss and decline by speaking out and modelling positive aspects of the ageing process. This is because many older people are able to make a distinction between their outward appearance and their internal sense of self. Ida, a 92-year-old, told Kaufman (1986):

> There is this feeling of being out of one's skin. The feeling that you are not in your own body....I always think of myself as younger, though not at any specific age, just at some time in the past. Whenever I am walking downtown, and I see myself in a shop window, I'm shocked by how old it is. I never think of myself that way.
>
> (pp. 9–10)

This view of the 'ageless self' fits snugly into consumer and popular culture images of what has been termed 'ageing well'. This perspective has begun to gain acceptance through the growing realization that older people are generally fitter, healthier, wealthier and more independent than previous cohorts of older people. Gone are outdated beliefs that *all* older people are in poor health, feeble-minded, confined to nursing homes, a burden on their children, unhappy, bored and lonely. It is true that some older people are ill and disabled and live out their lives in nursing homes; however, frail aged people are generally in a minority and most are healthy and live well into their 80s and 90s before they may have to be institutionalized (Cockerham, 1991).

Older people are now showing a greater preference for active living and leading more meaningful lives than previous cohort groups. Active living helps older people to retain a positive outlook on life and this is achieved by feeling fitter and healthier, which has been linked to a balanced diet, regular exercise, adequate time for relaxation and sleep, avoidance of tobacco, moderate use of alcohol, mental stimulation and regular social contact, as well as access to preventative and high-quality medical services (Satariano, 1997).

As older people move into retirement, many are free from work commitments and may decide to move elsewhere to enjoy warmer weather or be closer to their children or grandchildren. Others may be faced with constant ill health and/or disability and are forced to make decisions about what type of housing is more appropriate for their medical condition and the type of care that might be required.

Types of Accommodation Available for Older People

In response to changes in their situation or in their level of confidence due to disability or frailty, older adults generally have to make adjustments to their living arrangements. They may have to:

- change their community and move elsewhere (residential mobility);
- change their household composition (living arrangements); and
- change their housing type (institutionalization).

Other possible changes that may need to be considered relate to a decreased level of competence and mobility that may involve modifying one's home; requiring increased assistance from family members or friends; participation in support programmes such as transportation, housekeeping and care support services that enable older people to live independently in their own homes as long as possible (Speare *et al.*, 1991).

Research has concluded that there are three interconnected reasons why older people change their housing location: self-selection, selective recruitment and network recruitment (Longino, 1992):

1. Self-selection occurs when people weigh up their quality of life in their current home against that of a potential destination. Retirees are no longer constrained by their job or school considerations for their children, and can now concentrate on what gives them the best quality of life. Retirees generally want easy access to important essential services such as living near a pharmacy or a hospital. Migrants are also concerned about the levels of crime and congestion in the big cities, and as a result people who have recently retired often prefer the lifestyle of small towns in rural areas.
2. Selective recruitment is another name for marketing. Developers target older people who are nearing retirement age and mail them brochures that extol the pleasures of living at a picturesque mountain location, or promoting the enjoyment from beautiful beaches and a view of the ocean.
3. Network recruitment is where residents make their community known to their family and friends. Older people are more likely to move if they know someone else in the area who can provide them with initial support, encouragement and friendship.

Malroutu and Brandt (1997) identified the main factors that affect retiree preferences for age-integrated or age-segregated neighbourhoods. They were also interested in looking at whether the identified factors had changed after 10 years of retirement in their present communities. The researchers used a mail survey of 947 pre-retirees between the ages of 40 and 64 in four states of the USA (Idaho, Michigan, Oregon and Utah). The mean age was 51 with the majority of respondents being male (82.2%), married (81.8%) and in good (45%) or excellent health (47.2%).

The researchers established that most respondents felt that their spouses or partners had a strong effect on their retirement decision, whereas only 15% felt that the influence of their children in their retirement decision was important. Two-thirds of the respondents (66.4%) preferred to retire in their present community, with 34% strongly preferring, and 32.4% somewhat preferring, their own communities. Only 17% stated that they were very likely to move away from their present community and this was dependent on whether their spouse's health was excellent.

Overall, only some women and unmarried respondents preferred to live in age-segregated neighbourhoods after 10 years of retirement. This was attributed to the fact that unmarried women generally experience greater financial stress during retirement and are more likely to prefer living in age-segregated or institutionalized settings (Chappell, 1991). Respondents who have lived in their communities for a number of years indicated that they were unlikely to move away, especially if they have appropriately sized homes that are suitable for retirement living.

In Australia, Manicaros and Stimson (1999) concluded that the majority of older people retire and live in their present home because of feelings of 'rootedness' (McDonald, 1986). Home ownership is also an important consideration as the home represents a combination of personal and financial security, family memories and a sense of place and well-being. By remaining in their present home, older people are able to maintain their network of family and friends as well as having access to health services and shopping facilities that are familiar and readily available.

There are a small but significant number of retirees who migrate longer distances from the colder southern states of Australia to the warmer coastal Sunbelt areas. They are attracted to retirement-orientated amenities such as the golf courses or beaches, better housing accommodation, warmer climates, lower housing rents and larger concentrations of older people (Stimson *et al.*, 1996). However, generally when older people decide to relocate, they move only relatively short distances and mainly in response to changing life circumstances. Burgess and Skeltys (1992) found that the highest rates of mobility were for older people who were separated or divorced (around 40%). Approximately 25% of couples move deliberately to a smaller dwelling while only 4% move because of health reasons. However, lone-person households stated that health and illness were the primary motivations for moving as they were forced to because of their lack of family care and support.

Age-integrated Community Housing

Overseas holiday and retirement migration patterns

Southern Europe has become a popular holiday and retirement market for retirees, particularly from the UK. This is because the warm climate is valued as it facilitates an outdoor lifestyle, while the relatively low cost of living and housing is attractive for potential holidaymakers and migrants. Retirement migration has been viewed as a two-step process rather than a single event that is related to the actual decision to move: a decision to migrate followed by the selection of the specific destination (Wiseman, 1980).

Tourism was found to be a critical factor in the selection of a specific destination to live in, with few migrants moving to places they had not previously visited as tourists on a regular basis (Longino, 1992). Williams *et al.* (2000) found that nearly three-quarters of their sample had previous holiday connections with a destination, and this was especially pronounced in Algarve and Costa del Sol. Second-home ownership was also another important tourism link with retirement migration, and this has often provided a 'stepping stone' from holiday visits to seasonal visits and finally to permanent migration. Williams *et al.* (2000) confirmed the importance of prior second-home ownership, especially in Algarve (49.8%) and Tuscany (47.2%). The researchers concluded that tourism contributes to shaping retirement migration as it helps to provide in-depth knowledge about potential places to live in.

Casado-Diaz (1999) examined the international retirement migration (IRM) patterns of people from northern Europe to Spain. Specifically, a case study was presented of Torrevieja, a small coastal town on the Costa Blanca with a total population of 35,000 people. Casado-Diaz (1999) found that the British expatriate community was the largest in this town, numbering 3600 people, with 72% of them aged 55 and older, who had lived there for at least 6 months of every year. A questionnaire was distributed to 300 people (of which 213 were returned) from British, German and Nordic origin who had retired and were aged 50 and older. A further 20 in-depth interviews were undertaken with retired British immigrants and several key informants. Overall, 56% of the respondents were found to be aged between 50 and 64.

Various pull factors were cited by the respondents when asked about their reasons for moving to Spain. The highest stated reason was for the climate (90%), followed by the lower cost of living (56%), the slower pace of life (53%), health (53%) and accessibility to the UK (49%). The majority of retirees (88%) were very satisfied with their move to Spain and many regretted not having moved to Spain at an earlier stage in their life. Furthermore, approximately 80% stated that they had no intention of ever returning to the UK. According to information recorded in the in-depth interviews, there was little contact between the British retirees and Spanish people. This was mainly attributed to language barriers, with only 6% of respondents stating that they spoke Spanish fluently. Most social activities for older people were organized by the numerous associations existing throughout the Costa Blanca area that were advertised regularly in the non-Spanish papers. Problems were expressed about the poor health care service in comparison with the UK, as Spanish health services (particularly specialist care) were not available in the rural areas and in small towns.

Interstate migration patterns

Older people who live in the USA and move interstate after retiring are rare, with 84% of adults aged 55 and older stating that they would prefer to stay in their current homes and never move (American Association of Retired Persons Survey in Knack, 1996). However, for those who do move interstate, census data on interstate migration by Americans over the age of 62 have indicated that there are common patterns of migration that many retirees follow. Sunbelt states remained the most popular destinations from 1960 to 1990, particularly Florida, Arizona, Texas and California. In fact, half of the older interstate migrants moved to just eight states in the USA between 1985 and 1990. Florida received 24% of all older interstate migrants while California, Arizona and Texas were next with a combined total of 16%. Florida has now 3.8 million residents older than 60 years, representing the highest percentage of any state. It has been estimated that the older residents spend $135 billion in Florida every year, paying out about $4 billion in taxes, as well as contributing $3.5 billion in donations (Goldblatt and Knack, 2004).

Naisbett researcher John Elkins has been quoted as stating that Florida was the most important state in the USA when pinpointing emerging lifestyle trends for older populations. Elkins reported on the growing market emphasis on health, fitness and medical care as well as the older market's penchant for eating out, which boded well for the future growth of restaurants and bars. He noted that 'growing discretionary income among Florida's retirees who have generally paid off their mortgages, no longer support their children, and who benefit from pensions, Social Security payments and interest income, have helped to create a stable retailing environment in the State' (Fannin, 1985, p. 73). Other retirees prefer the coast and living near to large bodies of water in a more moderate climate mainly for recreational purposes (e.g. the East Coast from New Jersey to Florida, or the West Coast around Oregon). Mountains, hills and forests were also quite popular among retirees (e.g. the Blue Ridge of western North Carolina, the Adirondacks of New York and the Ozark Plateau of Missouri) (Watkins, 1994).

Economic considerations were also critical in the decision to migrate to another state or country. After retirement, reliance on a relatively fixed income that is provided by superannuation, pensions or investments often results in an emphasis on cost reduction. Therefore, a comparison should be made of comparative housing prices, cost of living and the tax structures of potential destinations. Additional factors such as social, cultural and infrastructure attractions are also crucial considerations that help to maintain a basic quality of life. Physical attractions were of a lower priority as they were not strongly associated with basic needs such as personal survival and emotional well-being (Watkins, 1994).

Government programmes to attract seniors to relocate to age-integrated community housing

Urban planners are becoming increasingly aware of the importance of creating environments that promote and encourage physical activity participation (Goldblatt and Knack, 2004). For example, Destination Florida has implemented a statewide project entitled 'Communities for a Lifetime'. This initiative has asked communities to assess their retiree friendliness in seven main areas: physical spaces, transportation, land use, community development, health, education, and cultural and social activities. In return, the state has offered technical and financial assistance to help individual communities to address problem areas such as installing audible traffic signals at busy intersections, developing a programme to repair footpaths and to convert buildings into adult day care centres. The report also stressed that the retirement patterns of baby boomers are likely to be different from those of their parents. In particular, younger retirees are more likely to plan to continue working at least on a part-time basis and seek out locations that still offer a range of employment opportunities.

As a result, government agencies have developed marketing campaigns to encourage the relocation of retirees, and to 'embrace them as vibrant and energetic citizens of a truly intergenerational community' (Goldblatt and Knack, 2004, p. 32). The advantages of this are many: they are healthy and active, have more disposable income and are less demanding on municipal services than younger families or the very old. Retirees can also transfer large sums of capital in the form of savings and investments, which increases the lending power of local banks. Because they are no longer responsible for supporting their children, many have paid off their mortgages and as a result can contribute high levels of spending to support local enterprises in the community. There was also clear evidence that retirees contribute significantly as volunteers in local hospitals, community service organizations and educational institutions (Watkins, 1994).

In the South, the 10-year-old hometown Mississippi retirement programme has encouraged 3500 senior households to live in 20 officially designated 'certified retirement cities'. The criteria for selection as a designated retirement city include affordability, low taxes, low crime rate, good medical care, recreation, and educational and cultural opportunities (Goldblatt and Knack, 2004). In another case study, it was found that business suffered in Blacksburg Virginia, a large college town, when students left for their summer vacation. With this in mind, the Economic Development Section of the local county decided to focus on attracting retirees, and plans were developed to adopt a more flexible zoning code to attract developers of retirement housing. They were aware of a 1993 American Association of Retired Persons Survey (in Knack, 1996) that found that 62% of respondents preferred living in a small town or rural setting, within a 15-min walk of a grocery store and a doctor's office. As a result, they have attempted to build retirement housing where possible in close proximity to basic food and health services.

In San Francisco, the non-profit Bridge Housing Corporation has been building and managing senior housing complexes in the Bay Area for many years. Recently, it has announced the introduction of a new project where 30% of its units are reserved for tenants whose income is lower, between $10,000 and $25,000 a year. They are aware of, and have advocated for, a variety of housing types for seniors based on different income levels. They want to encourage larger numbers of older people to walk rather than using their car, and have proposed to give rent rebates to people who do not require a car parking space (Knack, 1996).

Another emerging trend is to build retirement communities on, or adjacent to, university campuses where residents have full access to university facilities. Besides the educational and cultural stimulation of free or discounted tuition, another appealing aspect of campus life is that seniors can freely mingle with younger university students (Goral, 2003). Indiana University has been a leader with its Meadow Wood Retirement Community, which was built in the 1980s, and since then at least a dozen or more universities such as Penn State, Duke, Notre Dame, Stanford and the University of Arizona have followed Indiana's example. Pennsylvania State University and the University of Florida have issued IDs to older residents that provide them with the same rights and privileges as faculty staff, including access to campus recreation, dining facilities and discounts at the university's golf course and tennis courts. At Penn State University they have even set aside 200 football tickets for their senior members. For these privileges, many communities require entrance fees of at least $100,000 as well as monthly maintenance charges (*Business Week*, 2004).

Discussion

Generally, older people prefer to live in their present home after retiring, especially if they have previously lived there for a number of years and have a suitably sized home for retirement. Only a small percentage prefer to move away, based on the attraction of many overseas countries or interstate locations that have warmer climates, lower cost of living and/or a slower pace of life. For many older people who live in the UK, the southern European countries of Spain, France and Italy are seen as popular retiree migration destinations. For these retirees, most have previously visited these European destinations while on holiday, and some may have bought a second holiday home as a 'stepping stone' to permanent migration.

Many other retirees prefer to move interstate within their home country such as in the USA where Sunbelt states such as Florida, Arizona, Texas and California have proved to be the most popular. Others prefer to live near the coast or enjoy the mountains, hills and forests. State governments are developing marketing campaigns to promote friendly retirement communities and actively seek out healthy and active seniors because of their attractiveness in terms of greater disposable income, and who have been found to be less demanding on municipal services than younger families. As a result, retirement communities that are targeting seniors at all income levels have started to spring up. With an emerging trend towards lifelong learning, many older people prefer to live adjacent to, or within, university campuses and enjoy the same rights and privileges as younger students to lifelong learning.

Age-segregated Retirement Communities

It has been forecast that baby boomers who are now entering the retirement phase of their lives, will place increasing pressure on active age-segregated senior communities. In the USA, for instance, it has been estimated that this demand will be phenomenal as 80 million or more people will be entering retirement over the next 15 years (Barista, 2001).

Apart from this increased demand, the changing needs of baby boomers are also creating changes in residential housing. Some of these issues centre on the social implications of what to do with older people as they age, when their health starts to decline and dependency needs begin to increase.

Furthermore, many baby boomers are likely to require different styles of retirement living than their parents. This is because baby boomers are not as careful about their saving patterns and have a greater disposable income than their parents. Because of this, they are demanding larger and more luxurious housing and better health facilities than previous generations. Minnigan in Barista (2001) stated:

> Because the baby boomers are much more savvy than their parents, developers will be even more competitive with the facilities and services they offer. They are looking to create an environment that is lifestyle and community driven, not the 'old folks home'.
>
> (p. 42)

Future housing trends suggest that baby boomers will also require a home office, space for exercise equipment, and upgraded wiring for computers and the internet. It is likely that the emphasis will be placed on mixing luxury and accessibility to create spaces that are senior-friendly, but without the institutional feeling that active seniors dislike (Barista, 2001).

Active living in age-segregated retirement communities

Retirement communities are specially designed for older people who are generally in good health and able to live independently (Grant, 2003; Graham and Tuffin, 2004). Residents mainly own their own unit or home and are responsible for their own household chores. The literature indicates that companionship, safety and freedom from household maintenance are the main reasons why people move into retirement villages (Gardner, 1994; Buys, 2000).

Furthermore, retirement villages usually offer a range of social and leisure activities such as opportunities for playing cards, exercise classes and indoor bowls. Retirement villages tend to promote their health and fitness facilities and services as a major focus, with many offering biking and walking trails, swimming pools, and gymnasiums with exercise rooms becoming popular draw cards for older adults. One such example is 'Williamstown Landing', a 450-resident retirement centre located on 123 acres near Williamsburg, Virginia, USA. Apart from 4 miles of inter-connected trails and footpaths through the six communities that consti-tute Williamsburg Landing, they have also built an 8000 sq.ft. spa and swimming pool.

Pollard *et al.* (2000) assessed the current level of participation in physi-cal activities among older people who were living in five retirement commu-nities in the south-western region of the USA. The study sample consisted of 259 people aged between 62 and 96, with a mean age of 79. The sample consisted of more females (n = 209) than males (n = 50). Data were col-lected door to door using a 'Fitness for the Future' (FFF) survey that con-sisted of 58 items with a numeric rating scale used to measure strength, muscular endurance and flexibility. The FFF survey included 22 physical activity correlates, with three conceptual domains being identified: bio-medical, demographic and psychosocial.

This study found that the level of physical activity among older adults who were living in retirement communities was low. In fact, 76 subjects (29%) scored zero on all four measures because they did not participate in any physi-cal activities at all. In regard to energy expenditure that indicates overall activ-ity level, approximately 85% were at a low level, 12% at a moderate level and only 3% were at a high level. Overall, only 15% of older adults in the sample conformed to the required standards that were advocated by the US Public Health Service (1990) in regard to participation in activities that enhance and maintain muscular strength, muscular endurance and flexibility.

In this study, belief in their ability to exercise (similar to self-efficacy) and a positive attitude were seen as essential factors among those older adults who participated in physical activities at the required levels. The authors concluded that if older people were to increase their physical activity levels, they needed to believe that it was appropriate for them to exercise. Body image and appear-ance issues such as being overweight, wearing athletic clothes or a swimming costume, and wrinkled skin were found to discourage physical activity partici-pation. Another possible strategy to help improve physical activity levels was to include supervised home-based physical activity programmes that involved additional face-to-face, individualized instruction sessions followed up by regu-lar staff-initiated phone contact. In this way, older adults are able to improve both their fitness and their image without being viewed by others in an exter-nal exercise environment (Pollard *et al.*, 2000).

However, recent figures indicate that the prevalence of inactivity is still high among adults aged 65 and older. Among those who participate in physical activity, adherence rates show that only 30% of older men and 15% of older women actually participated in regular sustained activity (US Department of Health and Human Services, 1996). Persuading older people to become physically active is a difficult task. Many believe them-selves to be too old or frail for physical activity, while others have a pre-ponderance of health problems that creates barriers to their involvement in physical activity (Schutzer and Graves, 2004). Poor health and injuries were the major barriers to exercise participation stated by respondents in an investigation of inactive, elderly Australians aged between 60 and 78 (Booth *et al.*, 2000). Booth *et al.* also found that older people who were not living in close geographic proximity to a recreation facility, park, golf course or swimming pool were found to be significantly more inactive.

Discussion

Age-segregated retirement communities are becoming more popular as an increasing number of older people are living longer, are in good health and are able to live independently. The main reasons why people move into retirement villages are for companionship, safety and freedom from household maintenance. Because many seniors are very health-conscious, retirement communities promote health and fitness as a major focus, and provide facilities such as walking trails, gymnasiums, swimming pools and spas. Swimming and aqua aerobics have accepted therapeutic benefits for older people, particularly for those who have arthritis and osteoporosis. However, although excellent facilities are now available, levels of fitness and energy expenditure are still low for the majority of older people who are aged between 60 and 90. Only 30% of older men and 15% of older women participate in regular sustained physical activity. One strategy to improve fitness levels is to offer individualized fitness trainers to work with older people in their own home, as well as regular follow-up phone contact.

Sun City as an example of a successful age-segregated retirement community

Sun City Retirement Community is an outstanding example of a very successful age-segregated retirement community that began from nothing in the desert of Arizona in 1959. Dell Webb Development Company (DEVCO), the giant in retirement community development, was responsible for the construction of Sun City as a suburban housing development. In the beginning, telephone research was conducted with 1200 seniors living in Arizona to ascertain their main reasons for retiring to this state. Seniors responded that the weather, quality of life and presence of friends and family topped the list of reasons for choosing Arizona as a retirement destination.

The grand opening of Sun City occurred over the weekend of the 1960 New Year and an estimated 100,000 people attended the 3-day event. DEVCO ran an extensive advertising campaign in many local and national newspapers as well as magazines to encourage readers to plan for their retirement by sightseeing and vacationing in what they proudly boasted was the world's most famous resort retirement community. DEVCO successfully created a marketing campaign that advocated a lifestyle that promoted a complete separation of work and leisure, but also recast leisure as a purposeful recreational activity through the building of housing with an emphasis on community living. They redefined retirement as 'active living' for America's senior citizens, and listed endless recreational facilities and activities to match every retiree's desire (Luken and Vaughn, 2003).

On 8 May 1960 a DEVCO advertisement about Sun City stated that it added 'life to years':

> This remarkable community has completely changed the meaning of retirement . . . to ACTIVE LIVING. Sun City has been designed and equipped to give you the most out of every treasured minute of those golden years of freedom. There is something doing . . . and something to do at all hours of the day plus the company of those who share your interest and your love of an active life. What's your favourite sport, your favourite creative outlet, your favourite social activity? It's waiting for you in Sun City.
>   (Luken and Vaughn, 2003, p. 150)

The leisure activities that were illustrated included croquet, ceramics, golf, gardening and swimming. The text completely redefined retirement as active living or a time of life that is valuable: 'golden' and 'treasured' for people to enjoy 'freedom' from paid employment, and for those who are willing and able to commit themselves to a life filled with low-impact sports as well as artistic and other leisure activities. In other words, DEVCO constructed a particular type of senior citizen who was portrayed as an able-bodied, heterosexual, white, middle-income Christian with no children. The theme was 'residents work actually to retire' by taking up golf, bridge and vacationing.

Retirees quickly made Sun City the fastest-growing city in Arizona. DEVCO helped to reinvent retirement when they created a city of gaily painted houses with low-maintenance lawns. Golf courses sprang up everywhere and hobby clubs were created, such as for square dancing and lawn bowls. Residents boasted that 'if you can't find something to do in Sun City, you're probably already dead' (Shapiro, 1999, p. 78).

Gerontologists have been quick to criticize Sun City as a ghetto for the elderly, 'a place for tanned and grey-haired pensioners to wind down their final days in mind numbing rounds of golf, shuffleboard, and idle cocktail party chatter' (Shapiro, 1999, p. 78). Laws (1995) also critiqued Sun City as a dreary world devoid of youth and spontaneity, and as a plastic landscape, excessively tidy, trim and monotonous. She referred to 'landscapes of consumption . . . marked by compulsorily tidy lawns and populated by tanned golfers . . . who audaciously separate themselves from other generations'. Kastenbaum (1993) argued that seniors in adult retirement communities like Sun City have a 'fortress mentality' and a deep-seated belief that the world is not a safe place. He introduced the term 'encrustation' to mark the passage from innocence to experience, so as elders seek to protect themselves and their way of life from societal change and the 'dissolving acid of post modern time' (p. 181) when he stated:

> The adult retirement community with its manicured streets and pulsing schedules represents a haven, an alternative universe of co-creation that can succeed only if a great many people keep pedalling.
>
> (Kastenbaum, 1993, p. 181)

However, despite these criticisms, Sun City has prospered and grown to become America's largest retirement community with 46,000 residents.

DEVCO now owns eight Sun City retirement communities, including Sun City West, which is next door to the original; other locations include Tucson in Arizona, Hilton Head in South Carolina and Roseville in California. DEVCO always conducts research before selecting a new site for one of its Sun City communities. However, DEVCO uses the same development model that includes golf courses, and recreation centres going up before the first houses are sold. The name has changed from retirement communities to 'active adult communities'. A white, concrete block wall surrounds the entire area, with entry limited to east–west and north–south arterial roads. Golf carts are the preferred transportation mode of choice for people, and they are everywhere, at the recreation centre and at the golf courses around the lake. In an increasingly affluent community of 38,000 people, the median annual household income is $25,000, or $7500 more than the national median for this age group. Housing values have remained high and taxes are relatively low. With no children in Sun City there are no schools to pay for (Shetter, 1996).

Sun City is getting older and younger at the same time. Current residents are living longer, while a new generation of retirees are arriving who are still reasonably young and in good health. The only thing that keeps retirement communities from ageing is a continuous flow of youthful retirees moving in. Among this new wave of retirees are 55-year-old Leonard Vincent and his wife Judy, 53. Vincent knows that his friends back in Indiana do not understand why he gave up a successful dentistry practice to move to Sun City: 'I get asked all the time, what do you do all day? I answer golf, hiking, or new sports like rock climbing.' Judy signed up for college courses in the autumn, and Leonard found a place to do charity dentistry. This suggests that there has been a trend away from the traditional leisure-orientated model of retirement towards a lifestyle that combines volunteering and community service with continuing education.

People who moved when they retired stated that they wanted to change their lives. Carol O'Brien affirmed this: 'People talk about retirement as being put out to pasture, but it's really an opportunity to do new things (Longino, 1992, p. 29). Sharon Dunn is 51 years old and retired early from her job as the facilities maintenance manager at Los Alamos National Laboratory in New Mexico. She moved to Sun City Grand in Arizona where she intended to look for another job. However, she states: 'Now I haven't the time because my calendar just fills up. There's golf two or three times a week, bicycling, and hiking nearby mountain trials. I was terrified of retiring, as my life was my job; I worked 10 to 12 hours a day. I had no idea how much I disliked it. Now it's like being a kid again' (Smart and Pethokoulis, 2001, p. 57).

A total of 222,000 people aged 60 and older packed their bags between 1985 and 1990 to leave New York, where most retirees came from, and relocated to warmer climates. Sun City in Arizona still continues to be a popular destination for active, older people. Although Sun City is starting to show signs of ageing, younger retirees are buying houses there or inheriting them, as residents who arrived in the 1960s and 1970s have died. For younger baby boomers, work will play a much larger role in their lives than previous cohort groups. Many want to continue working after they retire, especially in a part-time capacity. As a result, the newer homes being built at Sun City have a home office to allow room for a computer and modem. Baby boomer women are also accustomed to paid work outside the home and more are financially secure at retirement, especially those who are widowed or divorced (Mergenhagen, 1996).

This flow has rejuvenated the community and keeps it attractive as a retirement destination. Once people have retired to an area, services and amenities are built to accommodate them, and as a result the area becomes more attractive and further people move in. Sun City is still attractive to many older people. Larry Fitch, who lived at Seneca Lake midway between Syracuse and Rochester for 36 years, stated: 'We have wonderful friends here, this is our home but the taxes and the winters are hard to take. We want a moderately priced low maintenance house or condominium, and it just doesn't seem to exist here' (Longino, 1998, p. 30). The Fitches stressed that they are looking for a well-rounded community with outdoor recreation, lower taxes and mild winters, which are selling points, but this is not enough: 'Florida is too hot and too flat, we might visit it for a month but we want to live in a real town' (Longino, 1998, p. 30).

Discussion

Sun City in Arizona is an example of a flourishing age-segregated retirement community that has been successfully marketed since 1960 as a 'leisure haven' for active, retired older people. Although Sun City has been criticized by several gerontologists as a world 'lacking in youth', a 'plastic landscape of manicured and tidy lawns' and 'populated by tanned golfers', it has grown to become the largest retirement community in North America with 46,000 residents in eight different communities. Although Sun City is starting to age, a continuous flow of youthful retirees are still moving in who are wealthy and in good health. Many are still working on a part-time basis and require a home office with computer and internet facilities. This has rejuvenated the community and has kept it attractive as a popular retirement destination.

Continuing Care Retirement Communities

As people age and approach their later years, they generally become more fragile and disabled, and as a result decisions have to be made about whether they need to be placed in segregated accommodation with associated services. They may still be capable of living in an independent living unit or they may need other more supportive forms of residential care such as 24-h skilled nursing care (Newcomer *et al.*, 1986).

One of the more popular options for seniors is to live in Continuing Care Retirement Communities (CCRCs). These communities combine independent living apartments with services that are mainly limited to housing and meals, provide assisted living facilities for residents who need some help with daily activities like bathing and dressing, and offer skilled nursing beds and special care facilities for seniors with medical conditions such as Alzheimer's disease (Siwolop, 1999). Furthermore, optional services such as social events, therapeutic recreation and sports activities, social services and health clubs are also available on site. Other specialist services such as medical doctors, physiotherapy, occupational therapy, dental care and opticians may also be included. All these facilities are located in one major complex that provides lifetime care so that residents are not forced to move away when their physical and/or mental health deteriorates (Young and Brewer, 2001).

In 1995 there were over 900 CCRCs in the USA, and the number was expected to increase to 1500 within the next 5 years. The typical CCRC has approximately 200 independent living units, 100 assisted living and 100 24-h skilled nursing beds. A CCRC offers residents freedom from daily living tasks and household responsibilities (Brewer *et al.*, 1995). Brewer *et al.* (1995) conducted a study of seniors residing in CCRCs in Pennsylvania, USA, to gather information about their vacation and travel patterns and preferences. The sample contained 1543 residents with 919 responses from ten randomly selected CCRC facilities, resulting in a response rate of 60%. The demographic profile showed that 66.4% of the respondents were between 76 and 85 years, mainly female (67.1%), with only 35% being married at the time of the survey.

The results of their study concluded that older seniors still love to travel. Travel was identified as a favourite way to spend leisure time (35%), second only to reading (43%). Some preferred to travel with family members (28%) or with their spouse (46%), while others preferred to travel in tour groups (9%) or with friends (10%). Seniors travel for longer periods and often, with more than half the sample (51.1%) taking vacations ranging from 8 to 21 days, while more than one-quarter (26.7%) took vacations of 22 days or more. Approximately 41% of the CCRC residents reported having made travel plans for the coming year, with 23.5% indicating they wanted to travel to warm climate destinations, 17.1% to local and neighbouring communities, 12.2% to Europe and 8.5% wanted to visit family and friends.

Other findings showed that seniors liked to visit new places and experience new things, with 30.8% reporting that they always went on vacation to a different place and 52.2% stating that they generally vacationed at a different place each year. Nearly one-quarter of seniors (23.3%) still consider themselves to be adventurous and like to explore new cultures and geographic areas as part of their travel plans. Seniors are also very health-conscious and place importance on their daily physical exercise, a balanced diet and eating regularly every day (78.7%).

Discussion

CCRCs have become a popular option for older people who are becoming frail and disabled, and are beginning to lose independence and control over their lives. These communities provide a range of independent learning units, assisted living and 24-h skilled nursing beds. They also provide additional services such as leisure and social activities, while specialist services such as physiotherapy and occupational therapy may also be included. Although many members are over 75, they still love to travel for relaxation and adventure, while family visits are also very important. Many preferred to visit new places and experience new things, while just under one-quarter considered themselves to be adventurous and wanted to explore new cultures and geographic areas as part of their travel. Seniors are also very health-conscious in terms of their diet and desire to participate in regular physical activity.

Conclusion

Older adults are changing the negative stereotypes that had previously existed about 'old age' that emphasized aspects such as loss, decline and loneliness. They are now speaking out and modelling positive views, advocating that older people are generally fitter, healthier, more independent and lead more meaningful lives than previous cohorts of older people. Baby boomers in particular are retaining a positive attitude towards life through more active participation in physical activities, eating nutritional food as well as the maintenance of strong social networks with family and friends. An active lifestyle has been shown to be important for older adults so as to maintain physical functioning, mobility, social contacts and emotional well-being.

Active living is also becoming a major focus for older people who are moving into age-segregated retirement communities such as Sun City in Arizona. Many retirement centres are offering leisure facilities such as trails for walking, swimming pools, spas and indoor gymnasiums. Sun City created the slogan 'active living or the time of your life' in their publicity campaigns to promote a full leisure lifestyle. This included low-impact sports such as golf and swimming, as well as hobby clubs and artistic groups that have been established for leisure activities such as square dancing, line drawing and lawn bowls. Although an active lifestyle has been promoted, research has found that the physical activity levels of older adults who are living in retirement communities are generally low. Only 15% of older adults conformed to the required guidelines that were advocated by the US Public Health Service for measures of strength, endurance and flexibility.

CCRCs have also become popular in recent years as they provide a continuum of care ranging from independent living units to 24-h skilled nursing beds for people who are frail and disabled. Many of the more active and independent older people in community care still love to travel, especially with their spouse or family, for longer periods of time ranging from 8 to 21 days, to be adventurous, exploring new cultures and visiting exciting places.

References

Barista, D. (2001) Designing for the big boom: active senior retirement communities incorporate luxury and a healthy lifestyle to attract the next generation of retirees. *Building Design and Construction* 42, 40–42.

Booth, M.L., Owen, N. and Bauman, A. (2000) Social-cognitive and perceived environment influences associated with physical activity and older Australians. *Preventive Medicine* 31, 15–22.

Brewer, K.P., Poffley, J.K. and Pederson, E.B. (1995) Travel interests among special seniors: continuing care retirement community residents. *Journal of Travel and Tourism Marketing* 4, 93–98.

Burgess, R. and Skeltys, N. (1992) *Housing and Location Choice Survey: An Overview of Findings*. National Housing Strategy, Canberra, Australia.

Business Week (2004) Big seniors on campus: colleges are appealing to retirees by offering housing complete with academic perks. *Business Week* 3893 (26 July), 99, McGraw-Hill.

Buys, L. (2000) Care and support assistance provided in retirement villages: expectations vs. reality. *Australasian Journal on Ageing* 22, 136–139.

Casado-Diaz, M.A. (1999) British retirees living on the Costa Blanca: from tourists to residents. Paper presented at the Royal Geographical Society Institute of British Geographer's Conference, Leicester, 4–7 January 1999.

Chappell, N.L. (1991) Living arrangements and sources of care giving. *Journal of Gerontology* 46, S1–S8.

Cockerham, W.C. (1991) *This Aging Society*. Prentice-Hall, Englewood Cliffs, New Jersey.

Fannin, R. (1985) The greening of the maturity market. *Marketing and Media Decisions* 20, 72–81.

Gardner, I.L. (1994) Why people move to retirement villages: home owners and non-home owners? *Australasian Journal on Ageing* 13, 36–40.

Goldblatt, L. and Knack, R. (2004) Recruiting retirees: what state and local governments are doing to attract and retain ageing baby boomers. *Planning* 70, 30–32.

Goral, T. (2003) Grandma's cramming: campus retirement communities let seniors act like freshman again. *University Business* 6, 2, 11.

Graham, V. and Tuffin, K. (2004) Retirement villages: companionship, privacy and security. *Australasian Journal on Ageing* 23, 184–188.

Grant, B. (2003) Retirement villages: an alternative place to live. *Australasian Journal on Ageing* 22, 136–139.

Kastenbaum, R. (1993) Encrusted elders: Arizona and the political spirit of postmodern ageing. In: Cole, T.R., Achenbaum, W.A., Jacobi, P.L. and Kastenbaum, R. (eds) *Voices and Visions of Aging: Towards a Critical Gerontology*. Springer, New York, pp. 160–183.

Kaufman, S.R. (1986) *The Aging Self: Sources of Meaning in Later Life*. University of Wisconsin Press, Madison, Wisconsin.

Knack, R.E. (1996) Grey is good: increasing senior populations in public communities. *Planning* 62, 20–24.

Laws, G. (1995) Embodiment and emplacement: identities, representation and landscape in Sun City retirement communities. *International Journal of Aging and Human Development* 40, 253–280.

Longino, C.F. (1992) The forest and the trees: micro-level considerations in the study of geographic mobility in old age. In: Rogers, A. (ed.) *Elderly Migration and Population Redistribution*. Belhaven, London, pp. 23–34.

Longino, C.F. (1998) From sunbelt to sunspots. *American Demographics* 16, 22–29.

Luken, P.C. and Vaughn, S. (2003) Active living: transforming the organization of retirement and housing in the US. *Journal of Sociology and Social Welfare* 30, 145–170.

Malroutu, Y.L. and Brandt, J.A. (1997) Factors influencing community preferences for retirement. *Family and Consumer Sciences Research Report* 25, 298–315.

Manicaros, M. and Stimson, R. (1999) *Living in a Retirement Village: Attitudes, Choices and Outcomes.* The Australian Housing and Urban Research Institute, Brisbane, Queensland.

McDonald, J. (1986) Retirement villages: segregated communities. *Australian Journal on Ageing* 5, 40–46.

McHugh, K.E. (2000) The 'ageless self'? Emplacement of identities in Sunbelt retirement communities. *Journal of Aging Studies* 14, 103–115.

Mergenhagen, P. (1996) Sun City gets boomerized. *American Demographics* 18, 16–19.

Newcomer, R.J., Lawton, M.P. and Byerts, T.O. (1986) *Housing in an Aging Society: Issues, Alternatives and Policy.* Van Nostrand Reinhold, New York.

Pollard, J.M., Taylor, W.C. and Smith, D.P. (2000) Patterns and correlates of physical activity among older adults residing independently in retirement communities. *Activities, Adaptation and Aging* 24, 1–17.

Satariano, W.A. (1997) Editorial: the disabilities of aging: looking to the physical environment. *American Journal of Public Health* 87, 331–332.

Schutzer, K.A. and Graves, B.S. (2004) Barriers and motivations to exercise in older adults. *Preventive Medicine* 39, 1056–1061.

Shapiro, J.P. (1999) No sunset for Sun City. *US News and World Report* 126(25), 78–81.

Shetter, K. (1996) Sun City holds on. *Planning* 62, 16–19.

Siwolop, S. (1999) The many lifestyles of senior housing. *New York Times* 16 May, p. 1, section 11.

Smart, T. and Pethokoulis, J.M. (2001) Not acting their age: baby boomers doing retirement their own way. *US News and World Report* 130(4 June), 55–58.

Speare, A., Avery, R. and Lawton, L. (1991) Disability, residential mobility, and changes in living arrangements. *Journal of Gerontology* 46, S133–S142.

Stimson, R., Minnery, J., Kabamba, A. and Moon, B. (1996) *Sunbelt Migration Decisions: A Study of the Gold Coast.* Bureau of Immigration, Multicultural and Population Research, Canberra, Australia.

US Department of Health and Human Services (1996) Physical activity and health: a report of the Surgeon General. National Center for Chronic Disease Prevention and Health Promotion, Washington, DC.

US Public Health Service (1990) Healthy people 2000: full report and commentary. DHHS, Publication No. PHS 91-50212. US Government Printing Office, Washington, DC.

Watkins, J.F. (1994) Retirees as a new growth industry? Assessing the demographic and social impact. *Review of Business* 15, 9–14.

Williams, A.M., King, R., Warnes, A. and Patterson, G. (2000) Tourism and international retirement migration: new forms of an old relationship in southern Europe. *Tourism Geographies* 2, 28–49.

Wiseman, R.F. (1980) Why older people move: theoretical issues. *Research on Aging* 2, 141–154.

Young, C.A. and Brewer, K.P. (2001) Marketing continuing care retirement communities: a model of residents' perceptions of quality. *Journal of Hospitality and Leisure Marketing* 9, 133–151.

11 Conclusions and Recommendations

The aims of this chapter are to:

- Summarize the major findings of the research conducted on the tourism and leisure behaviour of older adults.
- Offer suggestions for future research for academics and make recommendations for government policymakers.
- Discuss the implications of this research for the tourism and leisure industry.

The Dimensions of the Older Market

Older travellers represent a growing market segment and an increasing challenge for the tourism industry. The World Tourism Organization (2001) has calculated that people aged 60 and older undertook over 593 million international trips in 1999. By 2050 this figure is projected to be greater than 2 billion. This is because older adults are now placing leisure-related travel as a higher priority in their retirement years than previous generations. Most are healthier and more independent, better educated and with an abundance of free time. At the same time, many are experiencing a reduction in social and family obligations compared with younger people. In the USA, tourism was ranked as one of the top leisure activities for those older than 50, while travelling abroad was ranked the highest out of 17 possible choices of trips (American Association of Retired Persons and the Roper Organisation, 1992). Travel to Europe by senior tourists also increased by 10% between 1988 and 1991 and was expected to reach 255 million trips in 2001. Seniors made 142 million domestic trips and 41 million international trips, a total of over 180 million trips in 1992 which was an increase of 80% on 1990 (Clech, 1993).

Future Growth of Older Travel

Travel among the senior and baby boomer cohort groups is rapidly increasing and is beginning to dominate the tourism and travel market in the 21st century. This is because these older cohort groups have a relatively large share of most of the country's discretionary incomes, and the older than 65 age group is the second richest cohort group in the USA. Apart from being more affluent, they are also more physically and psychologically active. Seniors generally think and act as though they are younger and enjoy relatively youthful activities while on holiday.

Researchers have used the term 'subjective age' (Neugarten, 1968; Markides and Boldt, 1983) to describe the main difference between people's perceived age and their actual chronological age. People perceive themselves to be younger than their chronological age and middle-aged adults place their self-perceived ages as 5–15 years younger, while more than half of adults older than 60 felt 16–17 years younger (Underhill and Calwell, 1983). Because of this, older males generally prefer to spend their vacation time with younger people participating in more youthful, physical activities and sports (Cleaver and Muller, 2002).

Furthermore, older adults generally prefer to take longer holiday trips and stay away from home for longer periods of time than younger age groups, because many are retired and have more free time at their disposal (Eby and Molnar, 1999). This is the main reason why senior travellers are the main consumers of luxury travel, coach tours and ocean cruises (Smith and Jenner, 1997). Because of this trend, older people are now placing greater demands on the travel industry to provide a wider variety of destination options so as to cater for their special needs. Furthermore, holiday tours are becoming more specialized and older people are now looking for a broader range of educational and cultural experiences.

Why Are Older Travellers a Primary Target?

Retirement and more free time

By 2005, it has been forecast that in the USA 30% of men and 46% of women in the 55–64 age group will have taken early retirement. Retirement has had a crucial effect on the senior market as it provides freedom from paid work and allows more time to enjoy a personal lifestyle that is often filled with hobbies, leisure activities and voluntary work. Retirement also allows more free time to be available to travel as many retirees are 'empty nesters' due to their children growing up and leaving home, and as a result have more disposable income than at any other time in their lives. However, for many retired people who may have the money to travel, their plans may change because of the need to care for a loved one who has suddenly become ill or disabled. Many expressed a particular sense of loss in regard to their leisure travel, while others identified resentment and anger as a result of their caregiving responsibilities (Gladwell and Bedini, 2004).

Wealth and increasing prosperity

Generally, older people build up a relatively large amount of discretionary money through superannuation and pension payouts, and as a result want to spend some of it on travel. Several studies in the USA and Canada have indicated that people older than 50 control between 75% and 80% of their country's wealth in stocks, bonds, bank accounts and real estate. As a result, people in this age group are the heaviest consumers of expensive lifestyle products, including overseas travel, luxury condominiums and cars, and recreational vehicles (RVs) (Chisholm, 1989).

Furthermore, older people have greater amounts of discretionary income because many have paid off their homes and built up their savings because their children are generally no longer dependent on them. In Australia, nearly 80% of seniors 60 years and older own their homes. Because Australian baby boomers are more likely to have higher incomes than the average, they are overrepresented in the highest household income quintile. Additionally, 63% of married baby boomers are dual-income couples, which increases the amount of discretionary income that can be spent on travel (Golik, 1999).

Health and fitness

Baby boomers in particular are increasingly enjoying more active lifestyles, perceive themselves to be younger than they actually are, and do not want to be identified as older people or to mix with people of their own age. In the UK, for example, participation studies have shown that those in the 45–59 age group still participate in active leisure pursuits such as swimming and walking, going to concerts and theatre visits, as well as leading the trend in regard to eating out in restaurants (Henley Centre, 1992). Because many older people feel much younger in their outlook, similar areas of behaviour and attitudes are overlapping between younger and older adults. For example, leisure activities such as going to the movies, participating in do-it-yourself activities, eating out and watching DVDs are now blurring across different age groups. Because many baby boomers are increasingly healthy and affluent, they are travelling more, are more discerning and demanding, and are continually looking for special interest travel as well as new and innovative experiences.

The desire to buy an experience

Many older people want to feel young again, or at least to relive some of the more pleasant experiences that characterized their youth. They want to reminisce about their past life, particularly about when they were younger and more active. This can help older people to mentally adjust to the feelings associated with the process of becoming older, and help them to accept the fact that ageing can be a positive experience with the right mental attitude.

Because of this, travel is a high priority among all age groups up to around 75 years. One of the main reasons for this is the intangible quality of travel and the fact that seniors often prefer to buy experiences rather than material possessions. They feel that travel will help to enrich their lives and make them feel young again. For example, the extreme adventure activity of jet boating in New Zealand is increasingly attracting older people as potential customers (Cater, 2000). Cater found that large numbers of older people were attracted to this activity because it enabled them to feel young again. He concluded that this was related to the need for older people to rejuvenate their bodies through participation in adventure-type activities, and that they could buy (or bring back) their youth which helped them to feel 'forever young'.

Seniors also prefer real life experiences in which they can learn and broaden their minds. Many have attained higher levels of formal education than previous cohort groups, and now have the time to travel to different countries to visit and learn about different cultures from a variety of first-hand experiences. They are now more interested in enriching their lives through gaining knowledge rather than being entertained so as to satisfy their needs for self-expression, creativity and internal growth.

The loneliness factor

One of the main attractions of travel is to overcome loneliness, particularly for older people who are single, divorced or widowed. Loneliness is often created by retirement and the loss of daily contact with work friends. This is why many travel companies emphasize in their marketing campaigns the importance of companionship during the travel experience. The single largest component of the senior market is women, particularly single and widowed, many of them seeking companionship, romance and the possibility of a new partner when they travel. Thus, ocean cruising has become a popular form of leisure travel as shipboard life is regarded as a popular way of meeting single people, especially for the large numbers of widowed women in society.

Off-season travel

Seniors can make substantial savings by travelling in the off-peak times when booking their travel. Generally they do not have paid work or family commitments to worry about as younger people do, many of whom are usually forced to travel during school holidays because of their children. Because of this, many retired older people are free to travel during the off-peak season and receive substantial discounts on travel and accommodation during these periods. Travel companies readily provide special deals for seniors who are older. Thrifty Car Rentals offers a 10% discount to anyone older than 55, while airlines offer coupon programmes similar to frequent flyer programmes. Travellers are now able to purchase books of coupons valid for travel anywhere in a certain region at a much cheaper rate.

There are many advantages of travelling in the off or shoulder season, such as lower tour prices, smaller groups, fewer tourists, children have returned to school, lower restaurant and shopping costs, and quieter and less crowded hotels. Many older tourists prefer to seek out tours that are designed and operated specifically for the senior market, especially to warmer climates. They are commonly referred to as 'snowbirds' in the USA or 'grey nomads' in Australia because they have the freedom to travel to warmer climates for an extended period of time.

Snowbirds are older people who travel 'or flock' from colder, winter climates in Canada to warmer or Sunbelt destinations in the USA such as Florida, Arizona, Texas and California, as well as to Mexico and the Caribbean. Presently, sales of RVs and caravans are booming in the USA and Australia. In Australia, caravan sales increased by 17% in 2002, with 80% of these sales to older age groups (Brannelly, 2003). In the USA, over one-quarter of RV owners stay in commercial campgrounds for longer than 25 days, and many use their RVs for months at a time (National Parks Service, 1986). For people who stay for longer periods of time in the off season, temporary communities are established with other people who come together because of their shared interests in group-orientated leisure activities (Mings and McHugh, 1995).

Recommendations

Segment the market

The tourism industry should not consider older adults as one single distinct group, but see them as a heterogeneous group of people that includes many distinct market segments. The broad range of people that are classified as older adults actually includes ages ranging from approximately 50 to 100 or older. Every cohort group (50–60 years; 60–70 years; 70–80 years, etc.) has lived through a particular time in history that distinguishes them from other cohort groups because they possess their own distinct characteristics, needs and interests.

However, chronological age is one of the most widely used measures that is still used in market segmentation studies. Recent approaches to segmentation analysis include psychographic segmentation variables other than age that are based on other aspects of older people's lifestyles that particularly relates to travel characteristics such as the amount of money spent, retirement status and preferences for different leisure activities. For example, Shoemaker (1989) conducted the first segmentation study on senior travel and found that there were three distinct groups, which he classified as 'family travellers', 'active resters' and the 'older set'. He replicated the study in 2000 and once again found similar results. He concluded that his studies had shown that it is possible to clearly differentiate between different segments of older travellers based on a wide range of psychographic variables that remained fairly stable over time. Further studies have supported these findings and concluded that there is great heterogeneity within the older travel market. Older people travel for a variety of motivations: to experience new things and different cultures, to learn, to visit friends and relatives, to meet new people, to participate in active and adventure-related leisure activities, to rest and relax, and sometimes for nostalgic reasons.

Age

Recent research has indicated that marketing to the chronological or actual age of a person rather than to his/her cognitive age may be a dangerous precedent. People generally age at different rates, and do not always look or act their age. Several researchers (Wylie, 1974; Markides and Boldt, 1983) confirmed that people continually assess their subjective age as different from their chronological age. Seniors typically feel a decade younger (average of 10.2 years) than their actual age, and as a result often prefer to spend their holiday activities with younger people (Cleaver and Muller, 2002). This gap seems to become larger as a person ages. For example, travellers from the USA who were 80 and older still felt they had a subjective age of around 65 (Smith and Jenner, 1997). Furthermore, older people as a group are quite heterogeneous because many of their socio-demographic characteristics such as life stage, disposable income, family composition, working status and health varies, and is much less predictable than for younger age groups.

Income

There is a growing market of wealthy seniors who are able to afford a higher quality of travel. Package tours are very popular because many middle- and upper-class people are often too busy to spend time organizing their trip plans themselves, and as a result prefer to leave this task in the hands of professionals such as travel agents. The overall price of the trip is important for this market segment; however, value for money is still the most important criterion for selecting a particular travel destination and package.

Special interest tourism has become more popular in recent years, but trips are very expensive because of the tour companies' desire to cater for the older adults' need to travel to remote areas of the world, sometimes with limited access by air. This is because guided tours such as soft adventure activities that include wildlife safaris, white-water rafting, mountain treks and sea kayaking are generally more expensive to organize. These increased costs have been attributed to the specialized nature of the trip and their related insurance costs, increased travel fares to remote locations, and the need to employ more highly skilled and qualified guides.

Gender

Women generally outnumber men in their later years, and if they are well educated and have a higher income, they are more likely to want to travel overseas than any other age group. For many older women, their strong need to socialize and communicate with other people has resulted in preferences such as attending cultural and heritage activities as well as festivals. Many single, widowed or divorced older women often prefer to join a group package tour because it provides them with greater opportunities for social interaction as well as increased safety and protection from terrorism. Men on the other hand prefer activities that are outdoors and emphasize their health and fitness through sporting activities such as golfing, fishing and hiking.

Single older women are a large segment of the senior market, and many men and women prefer to travel after retirement as it provides them with a retirement transition activity, which is a psychological barrier between the end of paid work and the beginning of unpaid leisure activities. However, overall, older women do not like to travel as much as older men, although this is slowly changing, with more women preferring shorter trips possibly because they do not want to be away from their family and pets for longer periods of time. The travel industry needs to discover new ways to reduce the barriers that make the older, single woman reluctant to travel.

Physical fitness

With improving health levels, a greater number of older adults are now enjoying a more active lifestyle, have a better knowledge about the health risks associated with a sedentary lifestyle and have greater access to higher levels of health care. Because of the trend towards healthy and active living, record numbers of older people are now regularly participating in physical activities such as walking and gardening, eating more nutritious and low-fat foods as well as remaining socially active (Kendig *et al.*, 1996). Because many seniors are now more health-conscious, retirement communities are promoting health and fitness through their emphasis on swimming pools, spas, gymnasiums and walking trails. Swimming and aqua aerobic classes have become popular because of their well-known therapeutic benefits, particularly for older people who have arthritis and osteoporosis. Retirement communities such as Sun City in Arizona have emerged from nothing but desert in 1959 to a large community of 46,000 seniors. The success of Sun City has encouraged DEVCO, the developer, to expand their concept to provide residents with the choice of living in eight different retirement communities in Arizona, South Carolina and California. The emphasis of their advertising campaigns has been to promote active adult communities and is pitched at encouraging older people to enjoy the freedom of a range of leisure activities such as croquet, ceramics, golf, gardening and swimming that highlight a 'golden' or 'treasured' time of life.

Recent retirees have also expressed a greater desire than previous cohort groups to participate in physically challenging leisure activities, rather than merely being passive spectators on an organized package tour. This is providing greater challenges for the tourism industry, as preferences for gentle exercise programmes and relaxing beach vacations are now being replaced by a greater desire for soft adventure tourist activities that are often located in remote and exotic locations. These trips generally demand higher levels of fitness than for previous generations, as well as promoting social interaction and companionship, especially for older people who are lonely and single.

Attitudes

Several studies have shown that chronological age, particularly 50 years, is regarded as a boundary marker that differentiates between younger and older people and their travel behaviour. Penalta and Uysal (1992) have suggested that people who are under 50 are more likely to participate in active, sport-orientated activities while on holiday. On the other hand, people older than 50 prefer pleasure trips for rest and relaxation, and to visit historical and cultural sites, as well as their friends and relatives. Older travellers are generally more responsive to advertising promotions and package tours, spend more time planning trips, travel greater distances and stay away from home for a longer period, and spend significantly more money on their trip than people who are under 50. Therefore, the market is clearly divided between seniors who wish to be treated as a special category of people who spend their holidays with people of their own age and seniors who wish to participate with younger people because they do not want to 'feel old'.

As greater numbers of baby boomers move into the older age group, many are influenced by their 'subjective age' or their self-perceived or cognitive age that relates to how they are actually feeling, irrespective of their chronological age. Cleaver and Muller (2002) found that the difference between people's subjective age and their chronological age was 10.2 years and this increased as people aged. People who are 60 generally feel much younger, around the 50-year mark; however, by the time they reach 80 the difference may be up to 15 years.

These 'young at heart boomers' prefer to enjoy their holidays with younger people and still be involved in active and more adventurous leisure activities. Recent research has found this to be the case, and that the 45–59 age group participate more in active leisure pursuits. It has also been found that many older people are becoming younger in outlook, with similar types of behaviour overlapping between the younger and older age groups. As a result, leisure activities such as going to the movies, undertaking do-it-yourself renovation activities, eating out and watching DVDs at home were found to be blurred across a range of different age groups (Henley Centre, 1992).

Leisure activities

As people age, they accumulate a core of leisure activities that tends to remain fairly stable during their older years. These activities are commonly centred around the family and generally take place in and around the home. They include shopping, gardening, walking, watching television, socializing with friends and family, and reading (Kelly and Kelly, 1994).

In a longitudinal study, Strain *et al.* (2002) found that more than two-thirds of older people (67%) who were tracked over an 8-year period continued to travel for pleasure. Wei and Millman (2002) concluded that tourists' psychological well-being was positively related to the variety of leisure activities in which they engaged while on a vacation trip. The most popular activities that travellers participated in while on tour were city sightseeing (89.3%), visiting historical places (88.1%), dining in restaurants (85.7%) and shopping (77.4%). Leisure activities encourage tourists to engage in conversations that help to facilitate social interaction, and this was found to be one of the strongest factors that helped to contribute to leisure satisfaction

(Thomas and Butts, 1998). Shopping has also been identified as a favourite travel activity and is acknowledged as a primary means of generating tourism revenue as well as contributing to economic development. Littrell *et al.* (2004) found that for senior travellers with an average age of 65, shopping was regarded as an important activity that was integrated with other travel interests such as visiting museums, attending the theatre and eating out at local restaurants.

The interests of seniors are highly diverse and many require different types of travel packages and programmes. There is a growing market segment of relatively wealthy, frequent travellers who want to participate in special interest tourism and are particularly interested in adventure travel packages that take them to new, exciting and interesting places (Sorensen, 1993). In particular, special interest groups are promising niche markets that require specialized tours to serve their needs. There are now at least a dozen adventure travel companies that market primarily to the older than 50 traveller with a range of group package tours specializing in safaris, rafting trips, treks and sea kayaking.

Many older people prefer the safety and convenience of package tours in which meals, hotels, admissions and baggage transfers are included in the price, and where they can mix with people who have similar interests. The hospitality industry has been able to quickly respond to the small companies that promote special interest tourism, and that will become the cutting edge of leisure travel buying in the future. As a result, special interest package tours will help the hoteliers to fill their rooms in the low and shoulder seasons as well as attracting more affluent tour groups through diversifying their market.

Reaching the Older Market

The travel industry itself

The older travel market is a primary growing market and its needs are beginning to be considered as important by tourism operators. This is mainly because of its sheer size, diverse lifestyle patterns and consumption habits, which are very different from previous generations of older people. The average age of retirement is falling and many people in this age group are now 'empty nesters' whose children have left home. They are healthy, highly educated and financially secure, and as a result want to increasingly enjoy special interest travel that caters for new and innovative hands-on experiences. This is true of older women, especially those who are widowed and single, who will become a large and increasing segment of the older adult market.

Issues that need to be considered when catering for the older traveller

The travel industry must place greater emphasis on quality and customer satisfaction. Older people are more discerning and place greater emphasis on quality, courteousness and good service, yet they are keen to obtain value for money.

Tour operators need to review their marketing messages so as to better represent seniors in their promotional imagery. One of the problems in the past has been to project the right image and the appropriate message to older people, as seen in the analysis of tourism brochures in the UK.

Operators need to review the vacation products directed towards seniors. Older people are now more adventurous, and are seeking out cultural and heritage sites from an educational perspective. As a result, there is a growing trend towards more independent, long-haul and activity-filled holidays that may eventually replace traditional tour packages and beach holidays with their emphasis on rest and relaxation.

Marketing to older adults

Marketeers need to use the expertise of seniors for their products. Older people are usually good judges of what they want and value services if they are what they need. Above all, marketeers must recognize and acknowledge the heterogeneity of the market, and the individuality of all older people, so as to avoid patronizing stereotypes in the tourist promotion literature.

References

American Association of Retired Persons and the Roper Organization (1992) *Mature America in the 1990s.* Maturity Magazine Group, New York.

Brannelly, L. (2003) Grey nomads keep caravan industry rolling along. *Australasian Business Intelligence* 13 July, 1008.

Cater, C. (2000) Can I play too? Inclusion and exclusion in adventure tourism. *The North West Geographer* 3, 50–60.

Chisholm, P. (1989) Postponed pleasures: the over fifties are spending freely on fun, and now the marketplace is beginning to take notice. *Maclean's* 102(9 January), 24–25.

Cleaver, M. and Muller, T.E. (2002) The socially aware baby boomer: gaining a lifestyle based understanding of the new wave of ecotourists. *Journal of Sustainable Tourism* 10, 173–190.

Clech, C. (1993) The European senior travel market: a golden opportunity from the travel and tourism industry. In: Brent, R.J.R. and Hawkins, D.E. (eds) *World Travel and Tourism Review*, Vol. 3. CAB International, Wallingford, UK, pp. 135–138.

Eby, D.W. and Molnar, L.J. (1999) *Guidelines for Developing Information Systems for the Driving Tourist.* The University of Michigan Intelligent Transportation System Research Center for Excellence, Ann Arbor, Michigan.

Gladwell, N.J. and Bedini, L.A. (2004) In search of lost leisure: the impact of care giving on leisure travel. *Tourism Management* 25, 685–693.

Golik, B. (1999) *Not over the Hill, Just Enjoying the View: A Close-up Look at the Seniors Market for Tourism in Australia.* Department of Families, Youth and Community Care, Brisbane, Queensland.

Henley Centre (1992) Demographic background. *Leisure Futures* 3, 16–20.

Kelly, J.R. and Kelly, J.R. (1994) Multiple dimensions of meaning in the domains of work, family and leisure. *Journal of Leisure Research* 26, 250–274.

Kendig, H., Helme, R., Teshuva, K., Osbourne, D., Flicker, L. and Browning, C. (1996) *Health Status of Older People Project: Preliminary Findings from a Survey of the Health and Lifestyle of Older Australians.* Victorian Health Promotion Foundation, Melbourne.

Littrell, M.A., Paige, R.C. and Song, K. (2004) Senior travellers: tourism activities and shopping behaviours. *Journal of Vacation Marketing* 10, 348–361.

Markides, K.S. and Boldt, J.S. (1983) A structural modelling approach to the measurement and meaning of cognitive age. *Journal of Consumer Research* 19, 292–301.

Mings, R.C. and McHugh, K.E. (1995) Wintering in the American Sunbelt: linking place and behaviour. *Journal of Tourism Studies* 6, 56–62.

Neugarten, B.L. (1968) The awareness of middle age. In: Neugarten, B.L. (ed.) *Middle Age and Ageing.* University of Chicago Press, Chicago, Illinois, pp. 93–98.

Page, K. (1987) The future of cruise shipping. *Tourism Management* June, 166–168.

Penalta, L.A. and Uysal, M. (1992) Aging and the future travel market. *Parks and Recreation* 27, 96–99.

Smith, C. and Jenner, P. (1997) The seniors travel market. *Travel and Tourism Analyst* 5, 43–62.

Strain, L.A., Grabusic, C.C., Searle, M.S. and Dunn, N.J. (2002) Continuing and ceasing leisure activities in later life: a longitudinal study. *The Gerontologist* 42, 217–223.

Thomas, D. and Butts, F. (1998) Assessing leisure motivators and satisfaction of international Elderhostel participants. *Journal of Travel and Tourism Marketing* 7, 31–38.

Underhill, L. and Calwell, F. (1983) 'What age do you feel?' Age perception study. *Journal of Consumer Affairs* 22, 137–157.

Wei, S. and Millman, A. (2002) The impact of participation in activities while on vacation on seniors' psychological well-being: a path model analysis. *Journal of Hospitality and Tourism Research* 26, 175–185.

World Tourism Organization (2001) *Tourism 2020 Vision: Global Forecasts and Profiles of Market Segments*, 7. World Tourism Organization, Madrid, Spain.

Wylie, R.C. (1974) *The Self Concept.* University of Nebraska Press, Lincoln, Nebraska.

Zbar, J.D. (1994) More than a cool bus ride needed to sway seniors. *Advertising Age* 27 June, 34, 37.

Index